U0830211

外贸函电与单证历练教程

WAIMAO HANDIAN YU DANZHENG LILIAN JIAOCHENG

● 黄永全 编著

華南理工大學出版社
SOUTH CHINA UNIVERSITY OF TECHNOLOGY PRESS
·广州·

内容简介

本书共分3个学习情景，以3种典型的业务案例，结合国际贸易实务的各个环节，通过对业务知识的简明介绍，引入相关函电的写作与单证的缮制，使学习者能够将国际贸易实务的知识和相关专业英语融会贯通，从而熟练掌握和运用不同业务背景下的函电写作和单证制作。书中通过实例业务的工作流程介绍外贸函电的特点、格式、结构和各种必备单证的要点、格式、结构，每个模块都辅以注释及正式或非正式文体的函电写作技巧，同时还配有练习题，具有渐进性、系统性和实用性。

本书的主要读者对象为高职高专商务英语专业、国际商务专业、国际贸易专业的学习者或英语专业二、三年级的学习者，也可用作外企白领阶层的自学用书。

图书在版编目（CIP）数据

外贸函电与单证历练教程/黄永全编著. —广州：华南理工大学出版社，2011.8（2025.1重印）

ISBN 978-7-5623-3506-1

Ⅰ.①外… Ⅱ.①黄… Ⅲ.①对外贸易－英语－电报信函－写作－高等学校教材②对外贸易－原始凭证－高等学校－教材 Ⅳ.①H315 ②F740.44

中国版本图书馆CIP数据核字（2011）第162870号

总 发 行：华南理工大学出版社（广州五山华南理工大学17号楼，邮编510640）

营销部电话：020－87113487 87110964 87111048（传真）

E-mail：**scutc13@scut.edu.cn http://www.scutpress.com.cn**

责任编辑：庄 严

印 刷 者：广州小明数码印刷有限公司

开 本：787mm×1092mm 1/16 **印张**：12.5 **字数**：296千

版 次：2011年8月第1版 2025年1月第7次印刷

印 数：6 001～6 500册

定 价：25.00元

版权所有 盗版必究

前　　言

《外贸函电与单证历练教程》是商务英语专业及国际商务专业的核心课程之一，是一门将英语与外贸业务相结合的课程，它介绍外贸出口业务英语函件和英语电子邮件的写作以及出口贸易的单证制作，旨在培养提高学习者英语水平，同时使其熟练掌握外贸实务的常用术语、表达技巧和必要单证，提高和强化外贸业务处理能力，为国家培养胜任外贸工作的高水平应用型人才。本书主要特点是：

一、教材内容先是以教师为主导向学生解读外贸案例中的英语函电特点和商务单证要点，后是以学生为主体操练外贸业务员（跟单员或单证员）所经历的函电写作和单据制作。函电既包括传统信函中正统式的写法，又包括现代邮件中简约式的写法。单证中基本涵盖外贸出口业务常用单据和信用证。

二、案例中的函电以一来一回的方式出现，使学习者容易跟随业务进展。

三、教材内容精选出口贸易活动的典型工作案例，组成三大模块，形成以下三个学习情景：①T/T + FOB 出口业务下的函电写作与单证制作；②L/C + CIF 出口业务下的函电写作与单证制作；③D/P 与 L/C 相结合 + CIF 出口业务下的函电写作与单证制作。

四、教材中学习情景的设计反映以工作过程为导向的高职教学理念，并以时间的推移作为业务进展程度的标志，让学习者容易参与学习。

五、三个情景的学习由浅入深，由简单到复杂，由了解到探究；有发散又有归纳，有叠加又有扩展，有巩固又有提高。三大模块内容基本涵盖外贸函电与单证工作的主要环节，同时，每一环节后都配有一项与其内容相近或技巧相同的练习，每一学习情景后也配有与其情景相仿的综合实训，让学习者在充分模仿操练中提高函电写作和单据制作的能力。

此外，本书还从英语修辞的角度介绍达至正式函电体裁和非正式函电体裁的要领。

本教程所需学时共为 72 学时：学习情景 1 需 20 学时，学习情景 2 需 34 学时，学习情景 3 需 18 学时。

我们为选择本书作教材的教师提供了电子文本和参考答案。由于编写时间和水平有限，书中不妥之处在所难免，敬请同仁和广大读者不吝赐教，批评指正。

编　者

于江门职业技术学院

2011 年 6 月 8 日

前　言

[illegible]

[illegible]

[illegible]（1）PLC＋FDB [illegible]；（2）[illegible]；（3）PLC 与 PLC [illegible]

[illegible]

[illegible]

本教材[illegible]20[illegible]

[illegible]

编　者

[illegible]

2011年6月

CONTENTS

(* Spotlight of the Module)

Module 1

Business Correspondence and Documents under T/T + FOB

Learning Objectives

Following are the goals for this module. Read them and consider your personal goals.

1. To know the transaction flow under T/T + FOB.
2. To learn the basic format and the elements of business correspondence.
3. To practice and master writing business correspondence in a formal style.
4. To learn making commercial invoice, packing list, Certificate of Origin, Commodity Inspection Application and Customs Declaration Form.

Case Study of Transaction under T/T + FOB

A business of embroidered slippers and cotton shoes under T/T + FOB had been concluded between Fujian Shoes Import & Export Corporation, located at 45 Baoding Street, Fuzhou, Fujian, P. R. China and Macdonald & Evans Co., Ltd., situated at 58 Lawton Street, New York, U. S. A. Eight different letters had been exchanged between them as they went through the several stages of establishing business relations, enquiry and offer, counter-offer and counter counter-offer, placing orders and sending S/C before the deal was finally done successfully. These letters are successively displayed for study in full format, followed by notes and exercises in this respect. Then documents concerning the transaction are showcased in full layout, also followed by notes and exercises in this respect.

In international trade, T/T + FOB is one of the most common ways of transaction. T/T refers to telegraphic transfer, which is one of the basic payment methods, besides L/C, D/P or D/A. Telegraphic Transfer or Telex Transfer is an electronic means of transferring funds overseas. It is the importer that purchases the goods who is responsible for sending payment to the exporter. The importer may take the initiative to remit or post money upon request from the exporter. A transfer charge is collected while sending money.

FOB refers to free on board, which is one of the thirteen trade terms commonly used in cross-country transactions. FOB is an abbreviation for Free On Board. The term FOB (often seen as f. o. b.) is commonly used when shipping goods, to indicate who pays loading and transportation costs, and/or the point at which the responsibility of the goods transfers from shipper to buyer. FOB shipping is the term used when the ownership/liability of goods passes from the seller to the buyer at the time the goods cross the shipping point to be delivered. When used in trade terms, the word "free" means the seller has an obligation to deliver goods to a named place for transfer to a carrier.

I. Establishing Business Relations of Both Sides*

Macdonald & Evans Co., Ltd. ①

58 Lawton Street, New York, U. S. A.
Tel: 1-10-5624××××
Fax: 1-10-5624××××
E-mail: ××××@msn.com ①

August 20, 20×× ②

Fujian Shoes Import & Export Corporation
45 Baoding Street, Fuzhou, Fujian, China ③

Attention: Mr. Wugang, Sales Department ④

Dear Sirs, ⑤

⑥
We have obtained your name and address from Fort & Co., Ltd, and we are writing *in the hope that* you would be willing to *establish business relations with* us.
We have been *leading importers* of casual shoes for many years. At present, we are interested in *extending our range* and would *appreciate* your catalogues and quotation.
If your prices are *competitive* we would like to *place a trial order with* you.
We *look forward to* your early reply. ⑦

Yours faithfully, ⑧

Macdonald & Evans Co., Ltd.

Michael Evans ⑨

Michael Evans
Manager ⑩

Fujian Shoes Import & Export Corporation

45 Baoding Street, Fuzhou, Fujian, P. R. China

August 25, 20 × ×

Macdonald & Evans Co., Ltd.
58 Lawton Street, New York, U. S. A.

Dear Mr Evans:

Thank you for your letter of the 20th August. We *are desirous to* enter into business relations with your company.

Our shoe industry *concentrates on* designing and producing various traditional and *vogue* men and women's shoes. We have developed and marketed a series of products such as slippers, indoor slippers, cotton slippers, embroidered slippers of new style, child's shoes and cotton shoes. We can *satisfy different market needs* both at home and abroad.

In compliance with your request, we are sending you, *under separate cover*, our *latest catalogue and pricelist covering* our *export range* available at present.

Should you be interested in any *items*, please let us know. We are looking forward to your *specific enquiries.*

Yours sincerely,
Fujian Shoes Import & Export Corporation

Wugang

Wugang
Manager of the Exporting Department

Notes

① **Letterhead** 信头、写信人信息 usually the writer's name, address, telephone number, fax number and email address

② **Date line** 日期 which shows when the letter is written

③ **Inside name and address** 收信人姓名、地址 usually the name, address, telephone number, fax number, and email address of the receiver

④ **Attention or subject line** 转交或事由 usually highlighting the person-in-charge to receive the letter, the main idea of the letter or the involving matter of the letter

⑤ **Salutation** 称呼 usually "Dear Sirs", "Dear Madams", "Dear Sirs and Madams", "To Whom It may Concern" followed by a comma

⑥ **Message of the letter** 正文 usually consisting of three main parts, the first of which is the source of information about the receiver, a connective between the past event and the present event, or an acknowledgement or summary of a letter, to which this letter is responding

⑦ **Closing sentence** 结束句 the last part of the message, usually the expectation for early reply or favorable news

⑧ **Complementary close** 结尾客套话 usually "Yours faithfully", "Faithfully yours", "Yours sincerely", "Sincerely yours", "Yours truly", "Truly yours", etc.

⑨ **Signature** 签名 usually the hand-writing name written below the name of the company with the printed name alongside

⑩ **Title** 职务 usually the position of the writer in the company

⑪ ***We have obtained sth. from sb.*** 承蒙某某人介绍，我方获悉……

Phrases of similar meaning:

On the recommendation of sb., we...

We are indebted for sth. to sb.

Through the courtesy of sb., we...

Your name and address have been passed on to us by sb.

⑫ ***in the hope that*** 希望 We hope that...

⑬ ***look forward to*** 期盼

Expressions of similar meaning:

We are looking forward to sth.

We are expecting sth.

We are anticipating sth.

We are awaiting sth.

⑭ ***leading importers*** 大型出口企业，出口企业中的领头羊

⑮ ***extending our range*** 扩大经营范围 enlarging our business scope

⑯ ***appreciate*** 十分感激 be grateful, show thanks for sth.

Sentence patterns of similar meaning:

We shall be thankful if you could do sth.
We shall be obliged if you could do sth.
We shall appreciate it if you could do sth.
It would be highly appreciated if you could do sth.

⑰ ***competitive*** 有竞争力的 Here it means reasonable price, low price.
⑱ ***place a trial order with* you** 向你方试订
⑲ ***establish business relations with* us** 建立业务关系 build up business connections
⑳ ***are desirous to*** 热切希望 We wish very much to
㉑ ***concentrates on*** 专注于 focus on
㉒ ***vogue*** 时尚的 fashionable
㉓ ***specific enquiries*** 具体询盘 An indication of interest by a potential customer or client. A request in which one customer asks another to make an offer on a commodity concerning the detailed terms of price, payment, shipment, etc.
㉔ ***In compliance with*** 应……要求，与……一致 in agreement with
㉕ ***under separate cover*** 另封邮寄 by separate mail, in another letter
㉖ ***latest catalogue and pricelist*** 最新的产品目录和价目单
㉗ ***covering*** 关于、涵盖 about, including
㉘ ***export range*** 出口商品范围
㉙ ***item*** 某个商品 specific commodity
㉚ ***satisfy different market needs*** 满足市场的需求 meet the needs of various customers

Exercises

Fill in the following chart by analyzing the given letter.

Dear Sirs,

We have your name and address from the Commercial Counselor's office of the Chinese Embassy in Ghana.

We wish to inform you that we specialize in both industrial products and chemicals, and shall be pleased to enter into trade relations with you.

In order to develop the market in Africa, we have specially designed a new series of products according to our market survey. We are confident that our brands, with their wide range of products, will reflect your customers' demand.

To give you a general idea of our products, we enclose a complete set of leaflets showing various products being handled by our corporation with detailed specifications and means of packing. Quotations and samples will be sent upon receipt of your specific enquiries.

We look forward to your early reply.

Yours faithfully,

Letter of Establishing Business Relations		
Writer: （写信人）	□Seller （卖方）	□Buyer （买方）
Receiver: （收件人）	□Seller （卖方）	□Buyer （买方）
Source of information （信息来源）		
Purpose: （写信目的）		
Introduction: （公司介绍）		
Reputation of brand: （品牌声誉）		
Strategy to develop: （市场开拓策略）		
Things to enclose: （随附资料）		
Possible response of the receiver: （收信人处理意见）		

58 Lawton Street, New York, U. S. A.
Tel: 1 – 10 – 5624 × × × ×
Fax: 1 – 10 – 5624 × × × ×
E-mail: × × × × @ msn. com

Macdonald & Evans Co. , Ltd.

August 30, 20 × ×

Fujian Shoes Import & Export Corporation
45 Baoding Street, Fuzhou, Fujian, China

Attention: Mr. Wugang, Sales Department

Dear Mr. Wu,

Thank you for your letter *dated* August 25. We are pleased to know that you are producing different kinds of slippers and shoes.

We are interested in your various casual shoes *recommended* in your letter, particularly embroidered slippers and cotton shoes. Will you kindly send us a copy of your *illustrated* catalogue and some samples with further information? We shall be *obliged* if you could also *quote* your lowest prices *FOB Fuzhou*, stating earliest date of *shipment*.

Casual shoes of high quality are popular. We believe there is *a promising market* in our area for *moderately priced* goods of the types mentioned. If your price is competitive, we will consider *placing an order* for 5, 000 pairs with you.

We are looking forward to your *urgent reply*.

Yours faithfully,
Macdonald & Evans Co. , Ltd.

Michael Evans

Michael Evans
Manager

II. Enquiry and Offer*

Fujian Shoes Import & Export Corporation

45 Baoding Street, Fuzhou, Fujian, P. R. China

August 31, 20 × ×

Macdonald & Evans Co., Ltd.
58 Lawton Street, New York, U. S. A.

Dear Mr. Evans,

Thank you for your letter of the 30th August.
The *enclosed* illustrated catalogue and samples will give you details of the two sorts of shoes in which you are especially interested. The *illustrations* will also *give you information about* other casual shoes we are exporting. *As to* our terms and conditions, please see page 8 of the catalogue. Under cover, we are sending you our offer on FOB Fuzhou, for shipment in October. Usually we require *T/T* for payment, 30% in advance and the rest 70% before shipment.
Embroidered slippers and cotton shoes are our products of latest style. Because of their excellent quality and low prices, you *can be sure* that our products will help you *expand* your market.
We are looking forward to your *trial* order.

Yours sincerely,
Fujian Shoes Import & Export Corporation

Wugang

Wugang
Manager of the Exporting Department

Notes

① ***Dated*** *adj.* 注明日期的 marked with a date

a letter dated August 25 8月25日的信件（=a letter of August 25）

② ***recommend*** *v.* 推荐，建议 to suggest, to advocate

e. g. 承蒙史密斯先生推荐，得知你方从事鞋的业务已有多年。

You have been recommended by Mr. Smith that you are in the line of shoes for many years.

③ ***illustrated*** *adj.* 带有插图的 with explanatory or decorative features

e. g. 随函附上有彩图的样本书。

Enclosed is our sample book illustrated with colorful drawings.

④ ***obliged*** *adj.* 感激的 grateful, thankful, appreciative

e. g. 如蒙你方给我方报最优惠价格，我方将不胜感激。

We shall be obliged if you could quote us your favorable price.

⑤ ***quote*** *v.* 报价 to give quotation, to state a price for goods

⑥ ***FOB Fuzhou*** 福州港船上交货价 free on board Fuzhou

In maritime international commerce, an agreement between a seller and a buyer indicating that the seller has fulfilled his/her obligation to deliver a good when he/she has transferred it to the ship on which it will be transported. All cost and risk transfers to the buyer when the good crosses the ship's rail. The buyer designates the ship onto which the seller must deliver the good.

Compare: FOB … named port of shipment 装运港船上交货（……指定装运港）

CFR … named port of destination 成本加运费（……指定目的港）

CIF … named port of destination 成本、保险费加运费（……指定目的港）

⑦ ***shipment*** *n.* 装运，货物装船 the act of sending off goods by a large vessel, dispatch of goods

e. g. 期待你方早日装运。

We are anticipating your early shipment.

⑧ **a *promising market*** 销路良好 a market that is likely to develop in a desirable manner, a hopeful and encouraging market

⑨ ***moderately priced*** 中等价位的 of medium-ranged price

⑩ ***placing an order*** 下订单，订购 submitting an order with sb. for sth.

⑪ ***urgent reply*** 急复 compelling immediate response, immediate action that takes precedence over others

be in urgent need of 急需

e. g. 我方的一个客户急需一批高质量的大米和大豆。

One of our customers is in urgent need of a stock of rice and soybeans of high quality.

⑫ ***enclosed*** 被附上的，随函所附的，附件的 included within, attached

e. g. 随函附上我方的产品目录，请查收。

Enclosed please find the catalogue of our company.

⑬ ***illustration*** *n.* 图解，图例 visual matter used to clarify or decorate a text, picture

⑭ ***give you information about*** 详细说明，提供信息，让……详细了解 tell a collection of facts or data

e. g. 在我们的报价单里，详细地向你方提供我方现在可供出口的产品的情况。

In our price list, we give you information about the items of our company available for export at present.

⑮ ***T/T*** 电汇 telegraphic transfer, the fastest way of remittance（汇付 sending money by post）which is one of the modes of international payment

Compare:

Among the modes of international payment, T/T, D/A, D/P and L/C are the most common.

T/T is a process that the remitting bank, at the request of the importer, sends a cable to its correspondent bank in the country concerned instructing it to make a certain amount of payment to the payee, which is usually the exporter.

D/P 付款交单。Document against Payment, one of the two ways of collection（托收）, which is one of the modes of international payment. Under D/P, the exporter asks his bank to arrange for payment of the bill overseas. The exporter is to ship the goods ordered and deliver the relevant shipping documents to the buyer abroad through his bank and the collection bank overseas with instructions not to release the documents to the buyer until the full payment is effected by the buyer.

D/A 承兑交单。Document against Acceptance, another way of collection. Under D/A, the exporter asks his bank to arrange for acceptance of the bill overseas. The importer can get the shipping documents and take delivery of the goods after mere acceptance is made on the draft.

L/C 信用证。Letter of Credit. Under L/C, the issuing bank opens a letter of credit in favor of and addressed to the exporter at the request of the importer if the bank is satisfied with its credit rating. This letter pledges to pay the exporter if the merchandise is shipped in accordance with the conditions in the letter of credit—conditions that are based on the contract between the buyer and the seller.

⑯ ***can be sure*** 对……有信心 can be confident, believe

e. g. 对中国丝绸产品的质量，你方请尽可放心。

You can be sure of the quality of Chinese silk products.

请相信我方会在10月底前装运完毕。

You can be sure that the goods should be shipped before the end of October.

⑰ ***trial* order** 试订 order of testing, attempted or advanced order on a provisional or experimental basis

e. g. 如你方能把价格降低5%，我方将试订1000件。

We should place a trial order of 1000 pcs with you, if you could reduce your price, say by 5%.

Exercises

Fill in the following chart by analyzing the given letter.

Dear Sirs,

We are very pleased to receive your letter of September 1, showing your interest in our digital watches and extending the wish to place orders with us.

For your information, we are enclosing a copy of our latest catalogue. As to our terms and conditions, please see page 3 of the catalogue. Please note that this offer remains valid until the end of this month. It is our usual practice that payment should be made by T/T before shipment except for regular customers.

Under separate cover, we are sending you samples of various sizes and the brochure required. It is to your great advantage to place early order at this time of the year. Because of the excellent quality and favorable price, you may be assured that our products will no doubt help you expand your market.

We look forward to a trial order.

Yours faithfully,

Letter of Offer	
Writer: （写信人）	□Seller（卖方） □Buyer（买方）
Receiver: （收件人）	□Seller（卖方） □Buyer（买方）
Purpose: （写信目的）	
Enclosed: （随函附寄）	
Terms of payment: （支付条款）	
Validity: （报盘有效期）	
Advice: （写信人的建议）	
Possible response of the receiver: （收信人处理意见）	

III. Counter-offer and Counter Counter-offer*

Macdonald & Evans Co. , Ltd.

58 Lawton Street, New York, U. S. A.
Tel: 1 -10 -5624 × × × ×
Fax: 1 -10 -5624 × × × ×
E-mail: × × × ×@ msn. com

Sep. 5, 20 × ×

Dear Mr. Wugang,

Thank you for your letter dated August 31, in which you quoted us for embroidered slippers and cotton shoes.

Much we would like to do business with you, we are *regretful* that we can't accept your price, i. e. , FOB Fuzhou USD20 *per* pair for embroidered slippers and FOB Fuzhou USD10 per pair for cotton shoes as *stated* in your catalogue. To accept your prices would *leave us with no profit*. We do not doubt that your quality is good, but we would like to *invite your attention to the fact* that slippers of Indian origin with the same quality are being sold in our area *at a price about* 10% *lower than* yours.

In view of our long friendly business relationship, we suggest that you *reduce* your price at least by 8%. Other *terms and conditions* are *as per* your letter of August 25.

We are looking forward to your early reply.

Yours truly,
Macdonald & Evans Co. , Ltd.

Michael Evans

Michael Evans
Manager

Fujian Shoes Import & Export Corporation

45 Baoding Street, Fuzhou, Fujian, P. R. China

Sep. 10, 20 × ×

Subject: Embroidered Slippers and Cotton Shoes

Dear Mr. Evans,

Thank you for your letter of Sep. 5 and we learn that you find our price for the *captioned* goods is *on the high side*.

Much to our *regret*, we can't reduce our price by 8%. As the price we quoted is *in line with* the *prevailing* market. Embroidered slippers from China are *superior in quality*. In fact, we have already *concluded considerable* business with other customers *at your end*.

We cannot reduce the price to your *level* or even *meet you halfway*. The best we can do is to *create a reduction of* 2%. FOB Fuzhou USD19.6 per pair for embroidered slippers and FOB Fuzhou USD9.8 per pair for cotton shoes. Other terms and conditions are as per our letter dated August 25. This is a *special offer*. It is valid, *subject to* the receipt of your reply before September 30.

It is likely that the material price will *rise*. It would be *to your advantage* to place orders *without delay*.

We are looking forward to your early *acceptance*.

Yours faithfully,

Fujian Shoes Import & Export Corporation

Wugang

Wugang

Manager of the Exporting Department

Notes

1. ***Much we would like to do business with you*** 虽然我方很想与你方做生意 although we would like much to do business with you
2. ***regretful*** *adj.* 遗憾的 sorry, disappointed, full of regret

   e. g. 你方觉得我方报价高，对此我们觉得很遗憾。

   We are regretful for our quotation that you consider high.

   We are regretful that you think our price is on the high side.
3. ***per*** *prep.* 每 for every

   e. g. 汽油的价格曾为40美分每加仑。

   Gasoline once cost 40 cents per gallon.
4. ***state*** *v.* 提及 to mention
5. ***leave sb. with no profit*** 使某人无利可图
6. ***as per*** 按照 according to
7. ***at a price about 10% lower than*** 以比……低10%的价格
8. ***In view of*** 鉴于，为了，考虑到 taking into account, in consideration of

   e. g. 鉴于以往的惠顾，我方本次给予特价优惠。

   In view of your previous order, we are giving you special offer this time.
9. ***reduce*** *v.* 降低，减少 to make reduction, to cut down

   e. g. ① 很遗憾，我方不能把价格降到你方所要的水平。

   We are regretful that we could not reduce our price to your level.

   ② 这是我方的最低价格，我们不能再让了。

   This is our rock-bottom price, so we can't make further reduction.
10. ***terms and conditions*** 条款

    这里由terms与同义词或近义词conditions连用能使措辞准确，避免误解和歧义，其他类似的表达还有：

    ① by and between

    e. g. 本合同经由买卖双方签订。

    This contract is made by and between the buyer and the seller.

    ② fulfill and perform

    e. g. 双方应履行协议所规定的义务。

    Each party shall fulfill and perform any of the obligations stipulated in the agreement.

    ③ furnish and provide

    e. g. 一旦装运，卖方应提供有关装船的详细情况给买方。

    The seller should furnish and provide all the necessary information about shipment once the goods have been loaded on board.

    ④ null and void

    e. g. 不履行义务，合同将无效。

Failure to fulfill the agreement will render it null and void.

11. ***invite sb's attention to sth.*** 提请某人注意某事

e. g. 我方请你方注意合同规定的装运时间。

We'd like to invite your attention to the date of shipment stipulated in the contract.

12. ***on the high side*** 偏高
13. ***captioned*** *adj.* 标题所列的 mentioned in the title
14. ***regret*** *n.* 抱歉 being sorry

e. g. 使我方遗憾的是，你方的报价与本地市场价格不相符合。

Much to our great regret, your quotation is not in accordance with the market price at our end.

15. ***in line with*** 与……相符合 similar to, in agreement with, in consistency with, in accordance with, in conformity with
16. ***prevailing*** 占优势的，现行的 generally current, most frequent or common at a certain time or in a certain place
17. ***superior in quality*** 品质优良

类似结构（*adj.* + *in* + *n.*）短语如下：

excellent in quality 质量优良

low in price 价格低廉

abundant in resource 物产丰富

rich in land 土地肥沃

18. ***conclude*** *v.* 达成，实现 to bring about a final agreement, to reach, to come to

e. g. 如你方有可能将价格降低5%，则有可能成交。

There is a possibility to conclude the deal if you could reduce your price by 5%.

19. ***considerable*** *adj.* 相当大的，相当多的 large in amount, extent, or degree
20. ***at your end*** 在我方市场 in our local market
21. ***level*** *n.* 程度 a relative degree of price

e. g. 我方已与你地其他买主按我们的价格成交了业务。

We've concluded business with other buyers in your area at our level.

22. ***meet sb. halfway*** 折中处理，各让一半，妥协 make a compromise with sb., go halfway

e. g. 为了解决分歧，我方建议各让一半。

Our suggestion is that both sides meet each other halfway so as to settle the dispute.

23. ***create a reduction of 2%*** 降价2% reduce by 2%, cut the price down by 2%
24. ***special offer*** 特殊报价 low price that is put forward
25. ***subject to*** 在……条件下，以……为准，受……约束 under the condition that

e. g. 我方接受你的还盘，条件是你方订购量在10 000件以上。

We accept your counter-offer, subject to your order surpassing 10,000 pcs.

26. ***rise*** *v.* 涨价 to go up, to increase
27. ***acceptance*** *n.* 接受 favorable approval, agreement

28. ***without delay*** 赶快，立刻，毫不延误地 as soon as possible, with the least possible delay
29. ***to sb's advantage*** 对某人有利 to one's benefit or profit

Exercises

Fill in the following chart by analyzing the given letter.

Dear Sirs:

We are in receipt of your letter of May 10 offering us 200 cameras at US $ 500/pc CIF Shanghai.

In reply, we regret to inform you that our customers here find your price too high and out in line with the prevailing market level. You may be aware that some Japanese dealers are lowering their prices. No doubt there is keen competition in the market.

We do not deny that the quality of your digital cameras is slightly better, but the difference in price should, in no case, be as much as 5%. On behalf of our customers, we make counter-offer as follows:

"200 cameras at US $ 480/pc CIF Shanghai, other terms as per your letter of May 10."

As the market is declining, we recommend your acceptance.

Yours faithfully,

Counter-Offer Letter	
Writer: （写信人）	□Seller □Buyer （卖方） （买方）
Receiver: （收件人）	□Seller □Buyer （卖方） （买方）
Purpose: （写信目的）	
Accept or not: （接受与否）	
Reasons: （原因）	
Request: （要求）	
Market: （市场行情）	
Possible response of the receiver: （收信人处理意见）	

IV. Placing Order and Sending S/C*

Macdonald & Evans Co. , Ltd.

58 Lawton Street, New York, U. S. A.
Tel: 1 – 10 – 5624 × × × ×
Fax: 1 – 10 – 5624 × × × ×
E-mail: × × × ×@msn. com

Sep. 20, 20 × ×

Dear Mr. Wugang,

Thank you for your letter of Sep. 10. We really *appreciate* your effort to *pave the way for* our business.

We are pleased to accept your prices and terms *stated* in your previous letter. And our Order No. NE0911 has been *enclosed*. We note that you can *make delivery* by the end of October and we hope that you will *effect* shipment on time.

Please kindly send us contract to conclude this *transaction*.

Yours faithfully,
Macdonald & Evans CO. , LTD.

Michael Evans

Michael Evans
Manager

ORDER

No. : NE0911
September 20, 20 × ×

TO: ***Fujian Shoes Import & Export Corporation***
45 Baoding Street, Fuzhou, Fujian, P. R. China
Please supply the following items:

Quantity (pairs)	Item	Model	Unit Price (per pair) FOB Fuzhou
20,000	EMBROIDERED SLIPPERS	MODEL ES101	USD 19. 60
10,000	COTTON SHOES	MODEL CS203	USD 9. 80

Fujian Shoes Import & Export Corporation

45 Baoding Street, Fuzhou, Fujian, P. R. China

Sep. 22, 20 × ×

Dear Mr. Evans,

Thank you for your letter of Sep. 20 and your Order No. NE0911.

Enclosed is our Sales Confirmation No. CT20125 *in duplicate*. Please *countersign* and return one copy to us *for our file*.

In order to allow us to *stick on* our production schedule and meet the date of delivery, please *remit* 30% by T/T as *down payment* without delay, that is USD147, 000 as down payment *as requested* in our previous letter. Our account No. is 6220 1854 0923 0907 with Bank of China, Fuzhou Branch. We will keep you fully informed of the progress of your order. The rest payment, 70%, is required to be made before the end of October.

Please *rest assured* that we shall effect the shipment in time to satisfy your local market demand.

Yours truly,

Fujian Shoes Import & Export Corporation

Wugang

Wugang

Manager of the Exporting Department

Notes

1. ***appreciate*** *v.* 感谢 to put high value on sth. , to thank sb. for sth.

   e. g. 如蒙你方及时处理这件事，我方将不胜感激。

   Your early attendance to this matter would be highly appreciated.

2. ***pave the way for*** 为……铺平道路，使更容易取得进展

   e. g. 为了定出一个有竞争力的价格，我方已做了市场调研。

   Market research has been done to pave the way for competitive prices.

3. ***stated in your previous letter*** 过去分词后置短语 post attributive phrase modifying "prices and terms"

4. ***enclose*** *v.* 随函附上 to insert into the same envelope or package, attach

   e. g. 随函附上我方的产品目录和价目单。

   Enclosed is our catalogue and price list.

6. ***make delivery*** 交货 ship the goods on board

   e. g. 我方会在合同规定的最迟装运日期前完成交货。

   Delivery will be made before the latest date of shipment stipulated in the S/C.

7. ***effect*** *v.* 实施，实行 to accomplish, to fulfill, to make

   e. g. 在本月底你方装运前，我方将会电汇货款给你方。

   Payment will be effected to you by T/T before you make shipment at the end of this month.

8. ***transaction*** *n.* 交易 business, deal

   e. g. 如果你方能把价格降到我们的水平，双方的交易将会达成。

   Transaction will be concluded if you could reduce the price to our level.

9. ***in duplicate*** 一式两份 in two identical copies

   e. g. 我方寄出合同一式两份，上面已有我方签署，其中一份请会签并返还给我方，另一份由你方留存。

   We are sending you contract with our signature in duplicate, one of which should be countersigned and returned to us and another of which should be kept by your side.

10. ***countersign*** *v.* 会签，确认 to sign (a previously signed document), as for authentication.

    e. g. 若要求在本月底前装运，请你方尽早会签确认合同。

    Your countersignature on the contract would be urgently necessary if goods are to be delivered before the end of this month.

11. ***for our file*** 存档 for records

12. ***stick on*** 保持 remain on

13. ***remit*** *v.* 汇款 to transmit (money) in payment

    e. g. 若本月底前装运，需要你方及早汇款。

    Remittance is highly expected if the goods are to be shipped before the end of this month.

14. ***down payment*** 预付定金，首付 a partial payment made at the time of purchase, with the

balance to be paid later

e. g. 买一套 20 万美元的房子，你可以首付 10%，即 2 万美元，抵押贷款 18 万美元。

You might make a 10% down payment of $20, 000 to buy a home selling for $200, 000 and take an $180, 000 mortgage.

15. ***as requested*** 按照要求 at the request of sb.

e. g. 应你方要求，寄上样本和价目表。

As requested, we are sending you samples and price list.

16. ***rest assured*** 有保证的，确信无疑，放心 be certain, be guaranteed

e. g. ① 你方尽可放心，货物质量与样本完全一致。

You may rest assured that the quality of the goods will be strictly in line with the sample.

② 请放心，我方会按时装运的。

We can assure you that the shipment of the goods would be on time.

Exercises

Fill in the following chart by analyzing the given letter.

Dear Sirs,

We are in receipt of your trial order for 100 boxes of black tea. We are pleased to enclose you our Sales Contract No. 208 in duplicate of which please countersign and return one copy to us for our file.

As required, shipment will be effected before July 10, so long as you remit payment by T/T on time. We will advise you of the name of steamer and the delivery date.

Looking forward to your early reply.

Yours sincerely,

Letter of Sending Contract	
Writer: （写信人）	□Seller　□Buyer （卖方）　（买方）
Receiver: （收件人）	□Seller　□Buyer （卖方）　（买方）
Purpose: （写信目的）	
Enclosed: （随附资料）	
Shipment: （装运日期）	
Condition of shipment: （装运的条件）	
Requirement: （要求）	
Possible response of the receiver: （收信人处理意见）	

销售合同
SALES CONTRACT

编号 **NO.**: CT20125
日期 **DATE**: SEP. 30, 20××
地点 **SIGNED IN**: FUJIAN, CHINA

卖方 FUJIAN SHOES IMPORT & EXPORT CO., LTD.
SELLER 45 BAODING STREET, FUZHOU, FUJIAN, CHINA

买方 MACDONALD & EVANS CO., LTD.
BUYER 58 LAWTON STREET, NEW YORK, U. S. A.

买卖双方同意以下条款达成交易：
This contract is made by and agreed between the BUYER and SELLER, in accordance with the terms and conditions stipulated below.

1. 品名及规格 **Commodity & Specification**	2. 数量 **Quantity**	3. 单价及价格条款 **Unit Price & Trade Terms**	4. 金额 **Amount**
		FOB FUZHOU	
EMBROIDERED SLIPPERS (MODEL ES101)	20,000PAIRS	USD19.60	392,000
COTTON SHOES (MODEL CS203)	10,000PAIRS	USD9.80	98,000
	Total: 30000PAIRS	USD	**490,000**

允许 With 10% 溢短装，由卖方决定 More or less of shipment allowed at the sellers' option

5. 总值 Total Value SAY US DOLLARS FOUR HUNDRED AND NINETY THOUSAND ONLY

6. 包装 Packing
ES101 TO BE PACKED IN CARTONS OF 50 PAIRS EACH
CS203 TO BE PACKED IN CARTONS OF 100 PAIRS EACH
TOTAL: 500 CARTONS

7. 唛头 Shipping Marks
M. E. CO.
CT20125
NEW YORK
C/NO. 1 - 500

8. 装运期及运输方式 Time of Shipment & Means of Transportation TO BE EFFECTED BEFORE THE END OF OCT. 20×× WITH PARTIAL SHIPMENT ALLOWED AND TRANSSHIPMENT ALLOWED.

9. 装运港及目的地 Port of Loading & Destination
FROM: FUZHOU
TO: NEW YORK

10. 保险 Insurance THE BUYER SHALL COVER INSURANCE AGAINST ALL RISKS & WAR RISKS AS PER AND SUBJECT TO THE RELEVANT OCEAN MARINE CARGO CLUASES OF THE PEOPLE'S INSURANCE COMPANY OF CHINA DATED 1/1, 1981.

11. 付款方式 Terms of Payment T/T, 30% IN ADVANCE, AND THE REST 70% BEFORE SHIPMENT

12. 备注 Remarks

The Buyer	**The Seller**
MACDONALD & EVANS CO., LTD.	FUJIAN SHOES IMPORT & EXPORT CO., LTD.
Michael Evans	*Wugang*
(signature)	(signature)

V. Making Commercial Invoice*

FUJIAN SHOES IMPORT & EXPORT CO., LTD. ①

45 BAODING STREET, FUZHOU, FUJIAN, CHINA

COMMERCIAL INVOICE ②

To: MACDONALD & EVANS CO., LTD. ③
58 LAWTON STREET, NEW YORK, U. S. A.

Invoice No.: 20××SDT009 ④
Invoice Date: Oct. 10, 20×× ⑤
S/C No.: CT20125 ⑥
S/C Date: Sep. 30, 20×× ⑦

From: FUZHOU, CHINA **To:** NEW YORK, U. S. A.

Marks and Numbers⑧	Number and kind of package; Description of goods ⑨	Quantity⑩ (pairs)	Unit Price ⑪	Amount⑫
M. E. CO. CT20125 NEW YORK C/NO. 1-500	EMBROIDERED SLIPPERS MODEL ES101	20,000	FOB Fuzhou ⑬ USD 19.60	USD 392,000
	COTTON SHOES MODEL CS203	10,000	USD 9.80	USD 98,000
	TOTAL:	**30,000PAIRS**		**USD490,000**

⑭SAY TOTAL: SAY U. S. DOLLARS FOUR HUNDRED AND NINETY THOUSAND ONLY

FUJIAN SHOES IMPORT & EXPORT CO., LTD.

*Wugang*⑮

Definition

An invoice or bill is a commercial document issued by a seller to the buyer, indicating the products, quantities, and agreed prices for products or services the seller has provided the buyer. An invoice indicates the buyer must pay the seller, according to the payment terms. The buyer has a maximum amount of days to pay these goods and are sometimes offered a discount if paid before.

From the point of view of a seller, an invoice is a sales invoice. From the point of view of a buyer, an invoice is a purchase invoice. The document indicates the buyer and seller, but the term invoice indicates money is owed or owing. In English, the context of the term invoice is usually used to clarify its meaning, such as "We sent them an invoice" (they owe us money) or "We received an invoice from them" (we owe them money).

Commercial invoice is a customs declaration form used in international trade that describes the parties involved in the shipping transaction, the goods being transported, and the value of the goods. It is the primary document used by customs, and must meet specific customs requirements, such as the Harmonized System number and the country of manufacture. It is used to calculate tariffs.

A typical invoice contains

① Name and contact details of the seller 出票人名称和地址
② The word invoice or commercial invoice 发票名称
③ Name and contact details of the buyer 发票抬头人，买方公司名称和地址
④ A unique reference number 发票号码
⑤ Date of the invoice 发票日期
⑥ Referring contract number 合同号码
⑦ Referring contract date 合同日期
⑧ Shipping marks. If there is no mark, "N/M" is printed 唛头
⑨ Description of the product(s): name of commodity, specification and packing 商品描述
⑩ Quantity of the commodity in pairs, pieces, dozens, etc. 商品数量
⑪ Unit price(s) of the product(s) 商品单价
⑫ Total amount charged 总金额小写
⑬ Payment terms 成交方式
⑭ Total amount written in words 总金额大写
⑮ Company's name and signature of the person in charge 出票人落款及签章

Exercises

Fill in the following invoice according to the given Contract No. 00123（表 1－1 销售确认书）.

COMMERCIAL INVOICE

To:

Invoice No.: ____________

Invoice Date: ____________

S/C No.: ____________

S/C Date: ____________

From: **To:**

Marks & Nos.	Description of Goods	Quantity	Unit Price	Amount

TOTAL:

SAY TOTAL:

表1-1 销售确认书

EASTERN FOODS CORP.

Room 501, Jiafa Mansion, Beijing East Road, Nanjing 21005, P. R. China

SALES CONFIRMATION

Messrs:	Carters Trading Company P. O. Box 8935, New Terminal, Lata, Vista, Ottawa, Canada	**No.**	00123
		Date:	20××-08-19

Dear Sirs,

We are pleased to confirm our sale of the following goods on the terms and conditions set forth below.

Product No.	**Description**	**Quantity**	**Unit**	**Unit Price**	**Amount**
01005	CANNED SWEET CORN 3060G × 6TINS/CTN	800	CARTON	FOB Nanjing USD 14	USD11200
	Total:	800	CARTON		USD11200

Say Total:	SAY U. S. DOLLARS ELEVEN THOUSAND TWO HUNDRED ONLY	
Payment:	T/T	(50% down payment immediately after contract signing, another 50% payment before shipment)
Packing:	3060G × 6TINS/CTN	
Port of Shipment:	Nanjing	
Port of Destination:	Toronto	
Shipment:	All the goods will be shipped on or before Sep. 20, 20×× subject to full payment reaching the seller before shipment. Partial shipment and transshipment are not allowed.	
Shipping Mark:	CANNED SWEET CORN CANADA C/NO. 1-800 MADE IN CHINA	
Quality:	As per sample submitted by seller	
Insurance:	To be covered by the buyer	
Remarks:	The buyers are requested to sign and return one copy of this Sales Confirmation immediately after receipt of the same.	

BUYERS	**SELLERS**
Carters Trading Company ×××	Eastern Foods Corp. ×××
(Manager Signature)	(Manager Signature)

VI. Making Packing List*

FUJIAN SHOES IMPORT & EXPORT CO. , LTD. ①

45 BAODING STREET, FUZHOU, FUJIAN, CHINA

PACKING LIST②

To: **MACDONALD & EVANS CO. , LTD.** ③
58 LAWTON STREET, NEW YORK, U. S. A.

Invoice No.: 20××SDT009④
Invoice Date: Oct. 10, 20××
P/L No.: 2009PK889⑤
P/L Date: Oct. 12, 20××

From: FUZHOU, CHINA
To: NEW YORK, U. S. A.

Marks and Numbers⑥	Number and kind of package Description of goods⑦	Quantity⑦	Package⑦	G. W⑧	N. W⑧	Meas. ⑧
M. E. CO. CT20125 NEW YORK C/NO. 1-500	EMBROIDERED SLIPPERS MODEL ES101 (IN CARTONS OF 50 PAIRS EACH)	20, 000PAIRS	400 CARTONS	@3KGS 1200KGS	@2. 5KGS 1000KGS	@40×30×30CM 14. 4CBMS
	COTTON SHOES MODEL CS203 (IN CARTONS OF 100 PAIRS EACH)	10, 000PAIRS	100 CARTONS	@4KGS 400KGS	@3KGS 300KGS	@40×30×30CM 3. 6CBMS
	⑨TOTAL:	30, 000PAIRS	500CARTONS	1600KGS	1300KGS	18. 0CBMS

SAY TOTAL: SAY FIVE HUNDRED CARTONS ONLY⑩

FUJIAN SHOES IMPORT & EXPORT CO. LTD.

⑪ *Wugang*

Definition

Packing List is a document made out by a seller when a sale is effected in international trade. It shows numbers and kinds of packages being shipped, total gross weight, net weight and measurement of the packages, as well as marks and numbers on the packages. It is used to make up the deficiency of an invoice. It also enables the consignee to declare the goods at customs office, distinguish and check the goods when they arrive at the port of destination, thus, facilitates the clearance of goods through customs. What's more, packing lists can facilitate settling insurance claims in case of loss or damage.

A typical packing list contains

① Name of the issuer 出单人的名称和地址

② The words Packing List, though sometimes the words Weight List, Weight Memo or Measurement List could be used. 装箱单名称

③ Name and contact details of the buyer 买方公司名称和地址

④ No. and date of the relevant invoice 发票号码和日期

⑤ No. and issuing date of packing list. Issuing date can be usually after the date of invoice or the same date as invoice. 装箱单号码和日期

⑥ Marks and numbers, usually the shipping marks that distinguish the goods from others. 唛头

⑦ Quantity and description, usually the name of the commodity, and the quantity of cases or cartons of the goods 数量与商品描述

⑧ Net weight, gross weight and measurement, usually mentioning the fact of each package and the total packages respectively 净重、毛重和体积

⑨ Total figures, usually summing up the fact of above-mentioned commodity (s) 总计

⑩ Total amount of packages in words 总计大写

⑪ Signature of issuer, usually of the same person as the invoice 出单人落款及签章

Exercises

Fill in the following packing list according to Contract No. 00123 signed between Eastern Foods Corp. and Carters Trading Company.（见表 1－1 销售确认书）

PACKING LIST

To：______________

Invoice No.：______________

Invoice Date：______________

Marks and Numbers	Number and Kind of Packages Description of Goods	Weight（Kgs）		Measurement（M^3）
		Net	Gross	
			20KGS/CTN	0. 08CBMS/CTN
			16, 000KGS	64CBMS

TOTAL：______________ 16, 000KGS 64CBMS

SAY TOTAL：____________________

VII. Certificate of Origin

ORIGINAL①

<table>
<tr><td>1. Exporter②
FUJIAN SHOES IMPORT & EXPORT CO., LTD.
45 BAODING STREET, FUZHOU, FUJIAN, CHINA</td><td rowspan="2">③ Certificate No. CZC1/120 × ×

CERTIFICATE OF ORIGIN
OF
THE PEOPLE'S REPUBLIC OFCHINA</td></tr>
<tr><td>2. Consignee④
MACDONALD & EVANS CO., LTD.
58 LAWTON STREET, NEW YORK, U. S. A.</td></tr>
<tr><td>3. Means of transport and route⑤
FROM FUZHOU, CHINA TO NEW YORK BY SEA</td><td rowspan="2">5. For certifying authority use only⑦</td></tr>
<tr><td>4. Country / region of destination⑥
U. S. A.</td></tr>
</table>

6. Marks and numbers⑧	7. Number and kind of packages; description of goods ⑨	8. H. S. Code⑩	9. Quantity⑪	10. Number and date of invoices⑫
M. E. CO. CT20125 NEW YORK C/NO. 1 - 500	400 (FOUR HUNDRED) CTNS OF EMBROIDERED SLIPPERS 100 (ONE HUNDRED) CTNS OF COTTON SHOES ********************⑮	6402. 2000. 00 6307. 9000. 90	20, 000 PAIRS 10, 000 PAIRS	Oct. 10, 20 × × 20 × × SDT009

<table>
<tr><td>11. Declaration by the exporter⑬
The undersigned hereby declares that the above details and statements are correct, that all the goods were produced in China and that they comply with the Rules of Origin of the People's Republic of China.

FUJIAN SHOES IMPORT & EXPORT CO., LTD. 45 BAODING STREET, FUZHOU, FUJIAN, CHINA
福建鞋业进出口有限公司
FUZHOU, CHINA OCT. 20, 20 × ×
×××（签名）

Place and date, signature and stamp of authorized signatory</td><td>12. Certification⑭
It is hereby certified that the declaration by the exporter is correct.

中国国际贸易促进委员会福州分会
CHINA COUNCIL FOR THE PROMOTION OF INTERNATIONAL TRADE, FUZHOU
FUZHOU, CHINA OCT. 23, 20 × ×
×××（签名）

Place and date, signature and stamp of certifying authority</td></tr>
</table>

Definition

A document stating the country in which a product was manufactured. Many countries require certificates of origin as part of the paperwork necessary for importing goods. This is because most nations give certain other nations preferential or detrimental treatment with regard to trade. That is, it may charge no or very low tariffs on some countries while charging very high tariffs on others. A certificate of origin lets customs agents know what fees are applicable to a given shipment of goods.

In our country, Certificate of Origin is issued by one of the following three governmental or trade organizations:

MOFCOM, which is Ministry of Commerce;

CIQ, meaning China Exit and Entry Inspection and Quarantine Bureau under the administration of AQSIQ, General Administration of Quality Supervision, Inspection and Quarantine;

CCPIT, which stands for China Council for the Promotion of International Trade.

A General Certificate of Origin Contains

① The word Original 产地证正本字样

② Name and contact details of Exporter 出口方名称和地址

③ Certificate Number issued by the certifying organization 产地证号码

④ Name and contact details of Consignee, i. e. the importer of the international trade 收货方名称和地址

⑤ Means of transport and route, the way the goods go directly as "From Port A to Port B by vessel", or indirectly as "From Port A to Port C VIA Port B by Steamer" 运输方式和路线

⑥ Country/Region of Destination, the final destination of the goods 目的地国家/地区

⑦ For certifying authority use only. It is left for the issuing authority for remarks. 签证机构用栏

⑧ Marks and numbers, the same as what is mentioned in commercial invoice and packing list 唛头与号码

⑨ Number and kind of packages; description of goods, usually as stated in the S/C or L/C 商品名称、包装数量及种类

⑩ H. S. Code, a ten-digit Harmonized System Code, which can be obtained in the customs' website: http://service.customs.gov.cn/default.aspx?tabid=9409 商品编码

⑪ Quantity of the goods 商品数量

⑫ Number and date of invoices. The date of invoice is earlier than the date of C/O. 发票号码及日期

⑬ Declaration by the exporter, usually with official stamp of the exporting company and signature of the authorized person 出口方声明及签字

⑭ Certification, usually with the official stamp of issuing institute, such as MOFCOM, CIQ and CCPIT. The date of certifying is later than the date of invoice and the date of applying. 签

证机构证明及签署

⑮ A row of " * " is used in blank space when necessary so as to avoid any malicious replenishment. 以下空白，防止篡改

⑯ China Council for the Promotion of International Trade is China Chamber of International Commerce. 中国国际贸易促进委员会，即中国国际商会。

Exercises

Fill in the following packing list according to Contract No. 00123 signed between Eastern Foods Corp. and Carters Trading Company.（见表 1－1 销售确认书）

<table>
<tr><td colspan="2">1. Exporter</td><td colspan="3">Certificate No.</td></tr>
<tr><td colspan="2">2. Consignee</td><td colspan="3">CERTIFICATE OF ORIGIN
OF
THE PEOPLE'S REPUBLIC OF CHINA</td></tr>
<tr><td colspan="2">3. Means of transport and route</td><td colspan="3" rowspan="2">5. For certifying authority use only</td></tr>
<tr><td colspan="2">4. Country/region of destination</td></tr>
<tr><td>6. Marks and numbers</td><td>7. Number and kind of packages; description of goods</td><td>8. H. S. Code
2005800000</td><td>9. Quantity</td><td>10. Number and date of invoices</td></tr>
<tr><td colspan="2">11. Declaration by the exporter
The undersigned hereby declares that the above details and statements are correct, that all the goods were produced in China and that they comply with the Rules of the People's Republic of China.
Place and date, signature and stamp of authorized signatory</td><td colspan="3">12. Certification
It is hereby certified that the declaration by the export is Correct.
中国国际贸易促进委员会南京分会
CHINA COUNCIL FOR THE PROMOTION OF INTERNATIONAL TRADE, NANJING
NANJING SEP. 10, 20 × × * * * *
Place and date, signature and stamp of certifying authority</td></tr>
</table>

VIII. Pressing for Payment and Urging Shipment*

Fujian Shoes Import & Export Corporation

45 Baoding Street, Fuzhou, Fujian, P. R. China

Oct. 26, 20××

Subject: Embroidered Slippers and Cotton Shoes

Dear Mr. Evans,

Thank you for your Order No. NE0911 and your countersigning on our S/C No. CT20125, which led to our preparation for the goods *in question*.

Needless to say that as a buyer, you *are responsible for* remittance of the amount needed for this order. Although we received your down payment, USD147,000, a month ago in September, we haven't got any news of the rest 70% of the total amount yet. In fact, we have got the goods ready for shipment for quite some days. *As contracted*, the rest 70% payment, i. e. USD 343,000, should reach us before the end of October. As the *date of delivery* is only several days away, we recommend that you remit the amount needed for the goods without delay. Extra charges and any losses caused by delay of the payment will be *for your account*.

Please make your remittance immediately, enabling us to effect shipment of the goods in time. Your *prompt attention* to this matter will be highly appreciated.

We are looking forward to your reply *by return*.

Yours truly,

Fujian Shoes Import & Export Corporation

Wugang

Wugang

Manager of the Exporting Department

Macdonald & Evans
Co. , Ltd.

58 Lawton Street, New York, U. S. A.
Tel: 1 - 10 - 5624 × × × ×
Fax: 1 - 10 - 5624 × × × ×
E-mail: × × × ×@ msn. com

Oct. 26, 20 × ×

Dear Mr. Wugang,

Thank you for your letter dated Oct. 26, in which you *reminded* us *of* the prompt payment of the remaining amount of the S/C No. CT20125.

We are sorry to say that our financial staff was so *preoccupied* by routine affairs that they hardly remember to send remittance to you. Please be assured that our financial manager will *see to it that* the rest 70% of the amount of the S/C No. CT20125 will be telegraphically remitted to you before the closing of the bank, today.

Actually, the goods are in great need here in our local market. We would appreciate it if you could do your best to *dispatch* the *consignment* within the stipulated shipment period.

We are looking forward to your early shipment.

Yours truly,

Macdonald & Evans Co. , Ltd.

Michael Evans

Michael Evans

Manager

Notes

1. ***in question*** 被谈及的，正在谈论的 under consideration or discussion
2. ***Needless to say*** 不用说 obviously

   e. g. 不用说，我方本该核查货物的数量，但是没有做到。

   Needless to say, we should have double checked the quantity of the goods, but we just didn't have it.
3. **be *responsible for*** 为……负责 *be liable for*
4. ***as contracted*** 按合同规定 according to the stipulation of the contract
5. ***date of delivery*** 装运日期 date of shipment
6. ***for sb's account*** 费用由……承担，由……来赔偿 compensated by sb, sb has to bear the responsibility of

   e. g. 你方额外需要的样本将用快递寄出，费用由你方承担。

   Extra samples that you want would be sent to you by courier for your account.
7. ***prompt*** *adj.* 迅速的，即时的，立刻的 carry out or perform without delay

   e. g. 期待着你方的即刻回复。

   We are anticipating your prompt reply.
8. ***attention*** *n.* 关注 concentration of the mental powers upon sth, consideration

   e. g. 我们已经考虑了你方提出的各让一半的建议。

   Your suggestion of meeting each other halfway has come to our attention.
9. ***by return*** (***of post***) 立即回复 by the next post back to the sender

   e. g. 本账单过期未结，请立即开来支票结清。

   Since this bill is overdue, would you kindly send us your check by return mail?
10. ***remind*** *v.* 提醒 to cause to remember, to prompt

    e. g. 我方想提醒你方，在去年的一次交易中，由于双方妥协，最终达成了一笔大宗的业务。

    Our suggestion is to remind you of one of our last-year's transactions, in which we both compromised and finally reached a considerable transfer of goods.
11. ***preoccupy*** *v.* 过分关注某事，过于忙于某事 to be excessively concerned with something, to be busily engaged in sth.

    e. g. 索赔的事占据了她全部的时间，她没有时间去想别的了。

    The matter of claiming preoccupies her completely. She cannot think of anything else.
12. ***see to it that*** 确保 be careful or certain to do something, make certain of something

    e. g. 请确保交货质量必须与样本质量一致。

    Please see to it that the quality of the goods to be delivered must be in strict accordance with the sample.
13. ***dispatch*** *v.* 发送 to send
14. ***consignment*** *n.* （货物的）交托，交货 a shipment of goods consigned

e. g. 最后一批的毛衣昨天到达我方港口时，发现有水渍。

The last consignment of sweaters arrived at our port yesterday, only to find that they were contaminated by sea water.

Exercises

Fill in the following chart by analyzing the given letter.

Dear Sirs,

With reference to the 4,000 dozen Shirts under our Sales Confirmation No. C215, we would draw your attention to the fact that the date of delivery is approaching, but we still have not received any of your covering payment.

As stipulated in the S/C, 30% as down payment should be made 30 days before shipment, the rest 70% payment 10 days before shipment. Unfortunately, neither full payment nor down payment has been received by us till now. The latest date of shipment is only several days away. We cannot but ask you to make 100% payment for this transaction. We reserve the right to cancel the order unless you remit by T/T the full amount of the goods within 48 hours. Please do your utmost to send your remittance promptly so that we may execute your order smoothly.

We hope to receive your payment soon.

Yours faithfully,

Urging Letter	
Writer: （写信人）	□Seller （卖方） □Buyer （买方）
Receiver: （收件人）	□Seller （卖方） □Buyer （买方）
Purpose: （写信目的）	
Reason: （写信原因）	
Requirement: （要求）	
Possible response of the receiver: （收信人处理意见）	

IX. Making Export Commodities Inspection Certificate*

中华人民共和国出入境检验检疫

出境货物报检单

报检单位（加盖公章）:	福建鞋业进出口有限公司	*编号	FZ20××10AC1134

报检单位登记号:	52304125596	联系人:	××	电话:	0591－5869××××	报检日期:	OCT. 23, 20××

发货人	（中文）	福建鞋业进出口有限公司
	（外文）	FUJIAN SHOES IMPORT & EXPORT CO., LTD.
收货人	（中文）	
	（外文）	MACDONALD & EVANS CO., LTD.

货物名称（中/外文）	H. S. 编码	产地	数/重量	货物总值	包装种类及数量
绣花拖鞋 EMBROIDERED SLIPPERS	6402.2000.00	广东汕头	20,000 PAIRS	USD 392,000	400 纸箱
棉鞋 COTTON SHOES	6307.9000.90		10,000 PAIRS	USD 98,000	100 纸箱
运输工具名称号码	NANGXING V.086	贸易方式	一般贸易	货物存放地点	福州
合同号	CT20125	信用证号	T/T	用途	－－－－

发货日期	20××. 10. 30	输往国家（地区）	美国	许可证/审批号	－－－－
启运地	福州	到达口岸	纽约	生产单位注册号	－－－－
集装箱规格、数量及号码	1×20'（CBHU2264001）				

合同、信用证订立的检验检疫条款或特殊要求	标记及号码	随附单据（划"✓"或补填）	
	M. E. CO. CT20125 NEW YORK C/NO. 1－500	√合同 □信用证 √发票 □换证凭单 √装箱单 □厂检单	□包装性能结果单 □许可/审批文件 □ □ □

需要证单名称（划"✓"或补填）				*检验检疫费
□品质证书	_正_副	□植物检疫证书	_正_副	总金额（人民币元）
□重量证书	_正_副	√熏蒸/消毒证书	1正1副	
□数量证书	_正_副	□出境货物换证凭单	_正_副	
□兽医卫生证书	_正_副	□		计费人
□健康证书	_正_副	□		
□卫生证书	_正_副	□		收费人
□动物卫生证书	_正_副	□		

报验人郑重声明:	领取证单	
1. 本人被授权报检。 2. 上列填写内容正确属实，货物无伪造或冒用他人的厂名、标志、认证标志，并承担货物质量责任。 签名: ×××	日期	
	签名	

注：有"＊"号栏由出入境检验检疫机关填写

◆国家出入境检验检疫局制

Definition

Export Commodity Inspection Application is a document certifying the result of commodity inspection issued by a third party generally as surveyor. In China, the Exit and Entry Inspection and Quarantine Bureau (CIQ) is the main governmental authority to carry out supervision and inspection and quarantine of goods in foreign trade business, while in other countries supervision and inspection and quarantine of this kind might be performed by individual authoritative organizations, such as SGS, or other trade associations.

出境货物报检单包括以下内容：

1. 报检单位登记号：指在检验检疫机构的登记号码。

2. 发货人：根据不同情况填写。预验时，可以填写生产单位，出口报检外贸合同中的卖方或信用证受益人。

3. 报检单位、H. S. 编号、货物的总值、贸易方式、集装箱规格、数量及编号。

4. 货物存放的地点：指本批货物存放的地点。

5. 信用证号：指本批货物所对应信用证的编号。

6. 用途：货物具体用途。

7. 发货日期：指出口装运日期，预验时可不填。

8. 输往国家（地区）：指贸易合同中买方（进口方）所在国家或地区，或货物的最终输往国家或地区。

9. 许可证/审批号：对已实施许可制度/审批制度管理的货物，报检时填写许可证编号或审批单编号。

10. 启运地：指装运本批货物离境的交通工具的启运口岸/地区城市。

11. 到达口岸：最终抵达目的地停靠口岸名称。

12. 生产单位注册号：指生产/加工本批货物的单位在检验检疫机构的卫生编号，如卫生注册、质量许可证号等。

13. 合同、信用证订立的检验检疫条款或特殊要求：指贸易合同或信用证的买方对本批货物特别订立的质量、卫生等条款和报检单位对本批货物检验检疫的要求。

14. 随附单据：按实际提供的单据，在对应的“□”打“✓”。

15. 需要证单名称：根据所需由检验检疫机构出具的证单，在对应的“□”打“✓”，并注明所需证单的正副本数量。

16. 报检人郑重声明：报检人必须亲笔签名。

17. 领取证单：由领证人填写实际领证日期并签名。

18. 检验检疫费：由检验检疫机构人员填写。

Exercises

Fill in the following Commodity Inspection Application according to Contract No. 00123 signed between Eastern Foods Corp. and Carters Trading Company.（见表 1－1 销售确认书）

报检单位（加盖公章）： *编 号＿＿＿＿＿＿

报检单位登记号： 联系人：××× 电话： 报检日期：**20××年×月××日**

发货人	（中文）					
	（外文）					
收货人	（中文）					
	（外文）					
货物名称（中/外文）	H. S. 编码	产地	数/重量	货物总值	包装种类及数量	
	2005800000	**江苏镇江**				
运输工具名称号码	**Hanghai V168**	贸易方式	**一般贸易**	货物存放地点	**南京**	
合同号		信用证号		用途	**其他**	
发货日期		输往国家（地区）		许可证/审批号	－－－－	
启运地		到达口岸		生产单位注册号	－－－－	
集装箱规格、数量及号码	**1×20'（CBHU55693214）**					

合同、信用证订立的检验检疫条款或特殊要求	标 记 及 号 码	随附单据（划"√"或补填）	
		☑合同	□包装性能结果单
		□信用证	□许可/审批文件
		☑发票	□
		□换证凭单	□
		☑装箱单	□
		□厂检单	

需要证单名称（划"✓"或补填）				*检验检疫费	
✓品质证书	1正1副	□植物检疫证书	＿正＿副	总金额（人民币元）	
□重量证书	＿正＿副	□熏蒸/消毒证书	＿正＿副		
□数量证书	＿正＿副	□出境货物换证凭单		计费人	
□兽医卫生证书	＿正＿副	✓出境通关单			
□健康证书	＿正＿副	□		收费人	
□卫生证书	＿正＿副	□			
□动物卫生证书	＿正＿副				

报检人郑重声明：	领 取 证 单	
1. 本人被授权报检。	日期	
2. 上列填写内容正确属实，货物无伪造或冒用他人的厂名、标志、认证标志，并承担货物质量责任。 ×××（签名）	签名	

X. Making the Customs Declaration*

中华人民共和国海关出口货物报关单

预录入编号：06101231 page 1 **海关编号**：

出口口岸 福州海关（3500）	备案号	出口日期 20××. 10. 30	申报日期 20××. 10. 25
经营单位 福建鞋业进出口有限公司（5911245632）	**运输方式** 江海运输	**运输工具名称** NANGXING V. 086	**提运单号** COCS0511861
发货单位 福建鞋业进出口有限公司（5911245632）	**贸易方式** 一般贸易	**征免性质** 一般征税	**结汇方式** 电汇

许可证号	**运抵国（地区）** 美国	**指运港** 纽约	**境内货源地** 广东汕头

批准文号	**成交方式** FOB	运费 – – – –	保费 – – – –	杂费
合同协议号 CT20125	**件数** 500	**包装种类** 纸箱	**毛重（公斤）** 1200	**净重（公斤）** 1000

集装箱号 TEXU2264000	**随附单据** B（出境货物通关单）	**生产厂家** 广东汕头××鞋厂

标记唛码及备注

M. E. CO. CT20125 随附单证号：出境货物通关单（54615512341）

NEW YORK C/NO. 1 – 500 集装箱号 CBHU2264001

项号	商品编号	商品名称、规格型号	数量及单位	最终目的国（地区）	单价	总价	币制	征免
01	6402. 2000. 00	绣花拖鞋 无牌	20, 000 双	美国	19. 6	392, 000	USD	照章
02	6307. 9000. 90	棉鞋 无牌	10, 000 双	美国	9. 8	98, 000	USD	照章

税费征收情况

录入员 **录入单位** ×× 福州××报关有限公司	**兹声明以上申报无讹并承担法律责任**	**海关审单批注及放行日期（签章）**
报关员 ××	福州××报关有限公司 （591001253000） **申报单位（签章）**	**审单** **审价**
		征税 **统计**
单位地址 福州××路75号 **邮编** **电话**	**填制日期** 20××. 10. 25	**查验** **放行**

Definition

Customs Declaration is a document used to declare to the Customs for tax assessment about the goods shipped. The exporter must apply to the customs for declaration of the commodity before shipment. The customs officers hold examination and let go the goods if they are up to the requirements of the authority after declaration.

出口报关单包括以下内容：

1. 预录入编号和海关编号。指预录入单位预录入报关单的编号，用于申报单位与海关之间引用其申报后尚未接受申报的报关单。预录入编号由接受申报的海关决定编号规则，报关单录入凭单的编号规则由申报单位自行决定。

2. 进口口岸/出口口岸。指货物实际进（出）我国关境口岸海关的名称。填报接受申报的海关名称及代码。

3. 备案号。指进出口企业在海关办理加工贸易合同备案或征、减、免税审批备案等手续时，海关给予的编号。

*合同协议号。本栏目应填报进（出）口货物合同（协议）的全部字头和号码。

4. 进口日期/出口日期。进口日期指运载所申报货物的运输工具申报进境的日期。本栏目填报的日期必须与相应的运输工具进境日期一致。出口日期指运载所申报货物的运输工具办结出境手续的日期。本栏目供海关打印报关单证明联用，在申报时免予填报。无实际进出境的报关单填报办理申报手续的日期，以海关接受申报的日期为准。在 H2000 通关系统中，本栏目为 8 位数字，顺序为年（4 位）、月（2 位）、日（2 位）。

5. 申报日期。指海关接受进出口货物的收、发货人或受其委托的报关企业申请的日期。以电子数据报关单方式申报的，申报日期为海关计算机系统接受申报数据时记录的日期。以纸质报关单方式申报的，申报日期为海关接受纸质报关单并对报关单进行登记处理的日期。

在 H2000 通关系统中，本栏目为 8 位数字，顺序为年（4 位）、月（2 位）、日（2 位）。

6. 经营单位。经营单位指对外签订并执行进出口贸易合同的中国境内企业、单位或个体工商户。本栏目应填报经营单位名称及经营单位编码。经营单位编码是经营单位在海关办理注册登记手续时，海关给予的注册登记10 位编码。

7. 运输方式。指载运货物进出关境所使用的运输工具的分类，包括实际运输方式和海关规定的特殊运输方式。本栏目应根据实际运输方式按海关规定的《运输方式代码表》选择填报相应的运输方式。

8. 运输工具名称。指载运货物进出境的运输工具的名称或运输工具编号。本栏目填制内容应与运输部门向海关申报的载货清单所列相应内容一致。根据不同的运输方式，分别填写船只名称及号码，汽车车牌号码及火车的车次，对于空运或邮运的只填“空运”或“邮运”字样。一份报关单只允许填报一种运输工具名称。其中的航次号指载运货物进出境的运输工具的航次编号。

9. 提运单号。指进出口货物提单或运单的编号。本栏目填报的内容应与运输部门向海关申报的载货清单所列相应内容一致。一份报关单只允许填报一个提运单号，一票货物对应多个提运单时，应分单填报。

10. 收货单位/发货单位。收货单位指已知的进口货物在境内的最终消费、使用单位。包括：①自行从境外进口货物的单位；②委托进出口企业进口货物的单位。发货单位指出口货物在境内的生产或销售单位。包括：①自行出口货物的单位；②委托进出口企业出口货物的单位。③备有海关注册编号或加工生产企业编号的收、发货单位。本栏目必须填报其经营单位编码或加工生产企业编号，否则填报其中文名称。加工贸易报关单的收、发货单位应与《加工贸易手册》的“货主单位”一致；减免税货物报关单的收、发货单位应与《征免税证明》的“申请单位”一致。

11. 贸易方式。本栏目应根据实际情况，并按海关规定的《贸易方式代码表》选择填报相应的贸易方式简称或代码。一份报关单只允许填报一种贸易方式。

12. 征免性质。指海关对进出口货物实施征、减、免税管理的性质类别。本栏目应按照海关核发的《征免税证明》中批注的征免性质填报，或根据实际情况按海关规定的《征免性质代码表》选择填报相应的征免性质简称或代码。加工贸易报关单栏目应按照海关核发的《登记手册》中批注的征免性质填报相应的征免性质简称或代码。一份报关单只允许填报一种征免性质。

13. 征税比例/汇结方式。征税比例仅用于“非对口合同进料加工”贸易方式下（代码“0715”）进口料件的进口报关单，填报海关规定的实际应征税比率，例如5%填报5，15%填报15。出口报关单应填报结汇方式，即出口货物的发货人或其代理人收结外汇的方式。本栏目应按海关规定的《结汇方式代码表》选择填报相应的结汇方式名称或代码。

14. 许可证号。应申领进（出）口许可证的货物，必须填报商务部及其授权发证机关签发的进（出）口货物许可证的编号，不得空出。一份报关单只允许填报一个许可证号。

15. 起运国（地区）/运抵国（地区）。起运国（地区）指进口货物直接运抵或者在运输中转国（地）未发生任何商业性交易的情况下运抵我国的起始发出的国家（地区）。运抵国（地区）指出口货物离开我国关境直接运抵或者在运输中转国（地）未发生任何商业性交易的情况下最后运抵的国家（地区）。

对发生运输中转的货物，如中转地未发生任何商业性交易，则起运＼运抵地不变，如中转地发生商业性交易，则以中转地为起运/运抵国（地区）填报。本栏目应按海关规定的《国别（地区）代码表》选择填报相应的起运国（地区）或运抵国（地区）中文名称或代码。无实际进出境的，本栏目填报“中国”（代码“142”）。

16. 装货港/指运港。装货港指进口货物在运抵我国关境前的最后一个境外装运港。指运港指出口货物运往境外的最终目的港；最终目的港不可预知的，可按尽可能预知的目的港填报。本栏目应根据实际情况按海关规定的《港口航线代码表》选择填报相应的港口中文名称或代码。无实际进出境的，本栏目填报“中国境内”（代码“0142”）。

17. 境内目的地/境内货源地。境内目的地指已知的进口货物在国内的消费、使用地或最终运抵地。境内货源地指出口货物在国内的产地或原始发货地。本栏目应根据进口货物的收货单位、出口货物生产厂家或发货单位所属国内地区，并按海关规定的《国内地区代码表》选择填报相应的国内地区名称或代码。

18. 批准文号。出口报关单本栏目用于填报《出口收汇核销单》编号。

* 成交方式。本栏目应根据实际成交价格条款按海关规定的《成交方式代码表》选择填报相应的成交方式代码。无实际进出境的，进口填报 CIF 价，出口填报 FOB 价。

19. 费用。

（1）运费。本栏目用于成交价格中不包含运费的进口货物或成交价格中含有运费的出口货物，应填报该份报关单所含全部货物的国际运输费用。可按运费单价、总价或运费率三种方式之一填报，同时注明运费标记，并按海关规定的《货币代码表》选择填报相应的币种代码，如港元为 110、日元为 116、英镑为 303、美元为 502 等。运保费合并计算的，运保费填报在本栏目。运费标记“1”表示运费率，“2”表示每吨货物的运费单价，“3”表示运费总价。例如：运费 502/2400/3 表示运费总价为 2 400 美元。

H2000 通关系统：①运费标记填写在运费标记处；②运费价格填写在运费价格处；③运费币制填写在运费币制处。

（2）保费。本栏目用于成交价格中不包含保险费的进口货物或成交价格中含有保险费的出口货物，应填报该份报关单所含全部货物国际运输的保险费用。可按保险费总价或保险费率两种方式之一填报，同时注明保险费标记，并按海关规定的《货币代码表》选择填报相应的币种代码。运保费合并计算的，运保费填报在运费栏中。保险费标记“1”表示保险费率，“3”表示保险费总价。

H2000 通关系统：①保费标记填写在保费标记处；②保费总价填写在保费总价处；③保费币制填写在保费币制处。

（3）杂费。指成交价格以外的、按照《中华人民共和国进出口关税条例》相关规定应计入完税价格或应从完税价格中扣除的费用，可按杂费总价或杂费率两种方式之一填报，同时注明杂费标记，并按海关规定的《货币代码表》选择填报相应的币种代码。应计入完税价格的杂费填报为正值或正率，应从完税价格中扣除的杂费填报为负值或负率。杂费标记“1”表示杂费率，“3”表示杂费总价。

H2000 通关系统：①杂费标记填写在杂费标记处；②杂费总价填写在杂费总价处；③杂费币制填写在杂费币制处。

20. 合同协议号。本栏目应填报进（出）口货物合同（协议）全部字头和号码。

21. 件数、包装种类。

（1）件数。本栏目应填报有外包装的进（出）口货物的实际件数。特殊情况下填报要求如下：①舱单件数为集装箱（TEU）的，填报集装箱个数；②舱单件数为托盘的，填报托盘数。

本栏目不得填报为零，裸装货物填报为 1。

（2）包装种类。本栏目应根据进（出）口货物的实际外包装种类，按海关规定的《包装种类代码表》（另文发布）选择填报相应的包装种类代码。

22. 毛重（千克）、净重（千克）。

（1）毛重。指货物及其包装材料的重量之和。本栏目填报进（出）口货物实际毛重，计量单位为千克，不足 1 千克的填报为 1。

（2）净重（千克）。指货物的毛重减去外包装材料后的重量，即商品本身的实际重量。本栏目填报进（出）口货物的实际净重，计量单位为千克，不足 1 千克的填报为 1。

23. 集装箱号。集装箱号是在每个集装箱箱体两侧标示的全球唯一的编号。本栏目用于填报和打印集装箱编号及数量。集装箱数量四舍五入填报整数，非集装箱货物填报为 0。H2000 通关系统下，填报在集装箱表中，一个集装箱填一条记录，分别填报集装箱号、规格和自重。

24. 随附单据。指随进（出）口货物报关单一并向海关递交的单证或文件。合同、发票、装箱单、许可证等必备的随附单证不在本栏目填报。H2000 通关系统下，本栏目分为随附单据代码和随附单据编号两项，其中代码栏应按海关规定的《监管证件名称代码表》选择填报相应证件的代码，如 B 为出境货物通关单，编号栏应填报许可证件编号。

*另外，用途/生产厂家情况，进口货物填报用途，应根据进口货物的实际用途按海关规定的《用途代码表》选择填报相应的用途代码，如以产顶进，就填 13。生产厂家指出口货物的境内生产企业，本栏目在必要时手工填写。

25. 标记唛码及备注。H2000 通关系统：①标记唛码中除图形以外的文字、数字；②受外商投资企业委托代理其进口投资设备、物品的外贸企业名称；③与本报关单有关联关系的，同时在业务管理规范方面又要求填报的备案号，如加工贸易结转货物及凭《征免税证明》转内销货物，其对应的备案号应填报在“关联备案”栏；④与本报关单有关联关系的，同时在业务管理规范方面又要求填报的报关单号，应填报在“关联报关单”栏。

加工贸易结转类的报关单，应先办理进口报关，并将进口报关单号填入出口报关单的关联报关单号栏。

26. 项号。本栏目分两行填报及打印。第一行打印报关单中的商品排列序号；第二行专用于加工贸易等已备案的货物，填报和打印该项货物在《登记手册》中的项号。加工贸易合同项下进出口货物，必须填报与《登记手册》一致的商品项号，所填报项号用于核销对应项号下的料件或成品数量。

27. 商品编号。指按商品分类编码规则确定的进（出）口货物的商品编号。此栏目分为商品编号和附加编号两栏，其中商品编号栏应填报《中华人民共和国海关进出口税则》8 位税则号列，附加编号栏应填报商品编号附加的第 9、10 位附加编号。加工贸易《登记手册》中商品编号与实际商品编号不符的，应按实际商品编号填报。

28. 商品名称、规格型号、数量。本栏目分两行填报及打印。第一行打印进（出）口货物规范的中文商品名称，第二行打印规格型号，必要时可加注原文。

（1）数量及单位。指进（出）口商品的实际数量及计量单位。本栏目分三行填报及打印。进出口货物必须按海关法定计量单位填报，法定第一计量单位及数量打印在本栏目第一行。凡海关列明第二计量单位的，必须报明该商品第二计量单位及数量，打印在本栏目第二行。无第二计量单位的，本栏目第二行为空。成交计量单位及数量应当填报并打印在第三行。

（2）原产国（地区）/最终目的国（地区）。原产国（地区）指进口货物的生产、开采或加工制造国家（地区）。最终目的国（地区）指已知的出口货物的最终实际消费、使用或进一步加工制造国家（地区）。本栏目应按海关规定的《国别（地区）代码表》选择填报相应的国家（地区）名称或代码。

29. 价格。

（1）单价。本栏目应填报同一项号下进（出）口货物实际成交的商品单位价格。海关估价时，应在H2000通关系统“海关单价”栏修改。无实际成交价格的，本栏目填报货值。

（2）总价。本栏目应填报同一项号下进（出）口货物实际成交的商品总价。海关估价时，应在H2000通关系统“海关总价”栏修改。无实际成交价格的，本栏目填报货值。

（3）币制。指进（出）口货物实际成交价格的币种。本栏目应根据实际成交情况按海关规定的《货币代码表》选择填报相应的货币名称或代码，如《货币代码表》中无实际成交币种，需转换后填报。

（4）征免。指海关对进（出）口货物进行征税、减税、免税或特案处理的实际操作方式。本栏目应按照海关核发的《征免税证明》或有关政策规定，对报关单所列每项商品选择填报海关规定的《征减免税方式代码表》中相应的征减免税方式。

加工贸易报关单应根据《登记手册》中备案的征免规定填报。

30. 税费征收情况。本栏目供海关批注进（出）口货物税费征收及减免情况。

（1）录入员。本栏目用于记录预录入操作人员的姓名并打印。

（2）录入单位。本栏目用于记录并打印电子数据报关单的录入单位名称。

（3）填制日期。指报关单的填制日期。电子数据报关单的填制日期由计算机自动打印。在H2000通关系统中，本栏目为8位数字，顺序为年（4位）、月（2位）、日（2位）。

31. 申报单位。本栏目指报关单左下方用填报申报单位有关情况的总栏目。申报单位指对申报内容的真实性直接向海关负责的企业或单位。自理报关的，应填报进（出）口货物的经营单位名称及代码；委托代理报关的，应填报经海关批准的专业或代理报关企业名称及代码。本栏目还包括报关单位地址、邮编和电话等分项目，由申报单位的报关员填报。

另外，在海关审单批注栏中，该栏目指供海关内部作业时签注的总栏目，由海关关员手工填写在预录入报关单上。其中“放行”栏填写海关对接受申报的进出口货物做出放行决定的日期。

Exercises

Fill in the following Customs Declaration according to Contract No. 00123 signed between Eastern Foods Corp. and Carters Trading Company.（见表1-1销售确认书）

出口口岸 南京海关（2300）	备案号 – – – –	出口日期 **20××.9.20**	申报日期 **20××.9.13**
经营单位	运输方式	运输工具名称 **MARRYLAND 225**	提运单号 **CSNJ325641**
发货单位	贸易方式 **一般贸易**	征免性质 **一般征税**	结汇方式
许可证号 – – – –	运抵国（地区）	指运港	境内货源地 **江苏镇江**

批准文号 – – – –	成交方式	运费 – – – –	保费 – – – –	杂费
合同协议号	件数	包装种类	毛重（公斤）	净重（公斤）

集装箱号 **1×20'（CBHU55693214）**	随附单据	生产厂家 **江苏××罐头食品厂**

标记唛码及备注　　　　随附单证号：

项号	商品编号	商品名称、规格型号	数量及单位	最终目的国（地区）	单价	总价	币制	征免
								照章

税费征收情况

合计总价：

录入员　录入单位 报关员	兹声明以上申报无讹并承担法律责任	海关审单批注及放行日期(签章) 审单　　审价
单位地址：________	申报单位：________	征税　　统计
邮编：________　电话：________	填制日期：________	查验　　放行

Business Letter Writing Stylistics 商务函电修辞技巧（I）

1. 英语函电属正式文体，倾向于多用介词短语、名词化结构、分词短语、被动语态等

（1）**Through the courtesy of** Tokyo Chamber of Commerce and Industry, we **are given to understand** that you are one of the leading importers of textile products in your country.

（2）**On the recommendation of** Fort & William Co., Ltd, we get to know that you are producing Chinese toys **for export.**

（3）**We are indebted for** your address to the Commercial Counselor's Office of the Algerian Embassy in Beijing.

（4）We are writing to you **with a keen desire** to establish business connections with you.

→We are desirous to enter into business relations with you.

（5）It's on this subject that we approach you today **in the hope that** we will establish mutually beneficial trading relations.

（6）**We are informed** that you are **in the market for** various Chinese textile products.

（7）The L/C to be opened must **be strictly in conformity with** the S/C signed between us.

→When you apply to open the L/C, you should make sure that it must conform to the contract already signed between us.

（8）**Payment should be made** by confirmed, irrevocable L/C at sight in our favor.

（9）**A fair comparison** between the quality of our products and that of other sources will convince you of **the reasonableness of our quotation**.

→If you compare the quality of our products with that of other sources, you will get to believe that our price is quite reasonable.

（10）**In view of** our long friendly relations, **we are prepared** to give you this special offer.

（11）We will put the offer out **in the event of** your not being interested.

2. 英汉对照，有利于学习外贸函电句子的表达技巧

2.1 汉语先发生的先说，英语语序则十分灵活

（1）从南京经香港转运到纽约。

The vessel will go to New York from Nanjing with transshipment at Hong Kong.

（2）从天津经过香港、新加坡再到悉尼。

This freighter goes to Sydney from Tianjin after a stopover at Hong Kong and another at Singapore.

The cargo ship heads to Sydney from Tianjin with two stopovers, first at Hong Kong and then at Singapore.

The steamer ship leaves Tianjin for Hong Kong before going on to Sydney, with a stop at Singapore.

（3）上次合作以后，几个月已经过去了。

Months had lapsed since we last traded.

（4）收到订单后叫来工人连夜开工。

Summoning its workers, our company began to manufacture on the evening of the day when we received your order.

Having received your order, we began to produce that very evening when workers came upon notification.

2.2 汉语先说事后表态，英语则先表态后说事

(1) 如蒙早日回复，不胜感激。

① We shall be grateful if you could reply at an early date.

② We shall be obliged if you could make a reply at your earliest convenience.

③ We would appreciate it if you could reply as soon as possible.

④ It would be highly appreciated if you could reply without delay.

(2) 如蒙你方对我方的询盘给予答复，我方将不胜感激。

① We would appreciate it if you could respond to our enquiries.

② We greatly appreciate your help in providing answers to our inquiries.

(3) 收到你方来函，获知你方欲与我方建立业务关系，十分高兴。

① We are glad to learn from your letter that you wish to enter into business connections with us.

② With reference to your letter of September 24, we are glad to learn that you wish to establish business relations with us.

(4) 收到你方续订，十分高兴。

It is a great pleasure to receive your repeat order.

(5) 能与你方达成一笔实质性的交易，我方感到非常高兴。

① We are very happy to have concluded a substantial business with you today.

② We are greatly honored today *to have the* pleasure of finalizing a real transaction with you.

(6) 久无联系之后，收到你方大额订单，十分高兴。

We are very pleased to get such a good order from you, although it was after a lapse of much too long a time.

(7) 对于你方的谅解，我方先表示感谢。

We thank you in advance for your understanding in this respect.

(8) 你方研发了一个新产品，我方十分感兴趣。

We are all interested in the latest product you have successfully developed recently.

Drill (I) 实训操作

训练要求：

1. 根据所给的合同与补充资料写出双方为了达成这笔交易从认识到签约所往来的函电（共8个），如下图所示。
2. 根据所给的合同与补充资料制作出卖方履行合同所必备的5份单据，如下图所示。
3. 往来的空白信笺和空白单据请见电子文本附件。

函电 1—2：建立业务关系
函电 3—4：询盘、发盘
函电 5—6：还盘、再还盘
函电 7—8：下订单、寄送合同

单据 1：商业发票
单据 2：装箱单
单据 3：原产地证书
单据 4：报检单
单据 5：报关单

卖方公司：

SHANGHAI TIANYE TOOLS MANUFACTURE CO. , LTD.
GUANXIANG TOWN, JINSHAN DISTRICT, SHANGHAI, CHINA
TEL：0086 - 21 - 6575 × × × ×
FAX：0086 - 21 - 6575 × × × ×

买方公司：

PT. HYCO LANGGENG
310 VTRA SEMARANG INDONESIA

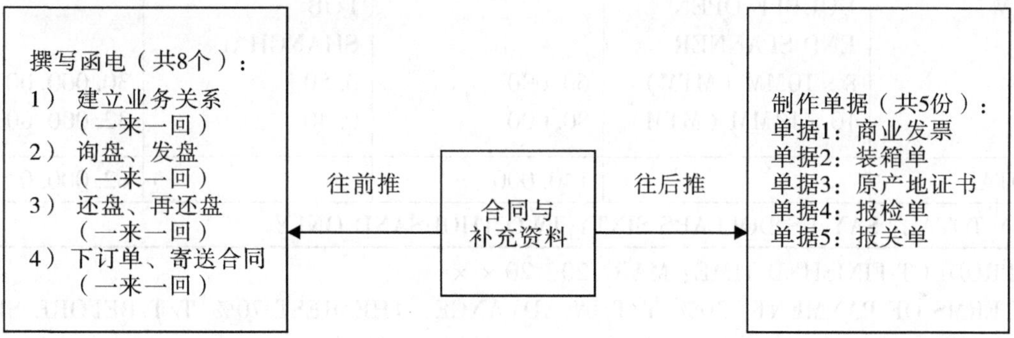

SHANGHAI TIANYE TOOLS MANUFACTURE CO., LTD.

GUANXIANG TOWN, JINSHAN DISTRICT, SHANGHAI, CHINA

TEL: 0086-21-6575××××　　S/C NO.: 20××1166

FAX: 0086-21-6575××××　　DATE: JAN. 15, 20××

SALES CONTRACT

TO: PT. HYCO LANGGENG
310 VTRA SEMARANG INDONESIA

Dear Sirs,

We hereby confirm having sold to you the following goods on terms and conditions as specified below:

SHIPPING MARK	DESCRIPTION OF GOODS	QUANTITY (PCS)	UNIT PRICE (USD)	AMOUNT (USD)
N/M	DOUBLE OPEN END SPANNER		FOB SHANGHAI	
	8×10MM (MTM)	60,000	0.50	30,000.00
	10×12MM (MTM)	80,000	0.40	32,000.00
TOTAL		140,000		62,000.00
SAY TOTAL: SAY US DOLLARS SIXTY TWO THOUSAND ONLY				

1. PRODUCT FINISHED TIME: MAR. 20, 20××
2. TERMS OF PAYMENT: 30% T/T IN ADVANCE, THE REST 70% T/T BEFORE SHIPMENT.
3. PORT OF DEPARTURE: SHANGHAI, CHINA
4. PORT OF DESTINATION: SEMARANG, INDONESIA
5. LATEST DATE OF SHIPMENT: MAY 10, 20××

OUR BANK INFORMATION IS AS FOLLOWS:
BENEFICIARY: SHANGHAI TIANYE TOOLS MANUFACTURE CO., LTD.
BENEFICARY ADDRESS: NO. 3188, JINGZHANG ROAD, GANXIANG TOWN, JINSHAN DISTRICT, SHANGHAI, CHINA
BANK NAME: BANK OF CHINA SHANGHAI BRANCH JINSHAN SUB-BRANCH
ACCOUNT NO.: RMB80456861
BANK ADDRESS: NO. 98, WEILING ROAD, SHIHUA, JINSHAN DISTRICT, SHANGHAI, CHINA

THE BUYER:　　THE SELLER:
PT. HYCO LANGGENG　　SHANGHAI TIAN YE TOOLS MANUFACTURE CO., LTD.

ROGERT TAN　　**CHEN GANG**

补充资料

1）INVOICE NO.：TY068

2）PACKING　　G. W.　　N. W.　　MEAS.

Double Open End Spanner			
8 × 10MM（MTM）	2KGS/CTN	1. 8KGS/CTN	0. 02CBM/CTN
Packed in 1 carton of 100 pcs each			
10 × 12MM（MTM）	2. 5KGS/CTN	2. 2KGS/CTN	0. 01CBM/CTN
Packed in 1 carton of 100 pcs each			

PACKED IN ONE 20' CONTAINER（装入一个20英尺的集装箱里）

3）H. S. CODE：8204. 1100

4）CERTIFICATE OF ORIGIN NO.：500511266

5）FREIGHT：USD 2400. 00

6）B/L NO. B050588661

7）B/L DATE：MAY. 01，20 × ×

8）报检单位登记号：1367768841

9）报检单编号：T006688451

10）生产单位注册号：SH186674

11）申请单位注册号：YT68114622

12）发货人账号：045686

13）外币账号：MY5684321321

14）海关编号：8328866457

15）境内货源地：上海

16）生产厂家：上海××工具制造有限公司（3105226441）

17）代理报关公司：上海××报关公司（3122668874）

地址：上海××路100号

电话：6575××××

18）随附单据：出口货物通关单（5461786256）

Module 2

Business Correspondence and Documents under L/C + CIF

Learning Objectives

Following are the goals for this module. Read them and consider your personal goals.

1. To strengthen the understanding of business letter writing.
2. To further practice writing correspondence according to specific situations under L/C + CIF.
3. To review and consolidate the understanding of documents learned in the previous module.
4. To master the making of such documents as insurance policy, GSP Form A, bill of lading and bill of exchange.

Case Study of Transaction under L/C + CIF

A business of unbleached kraft linerboard under L/C + CIF had been concluded between WONDER INTERNATIONAL COMPANY LIMITED, located at NO. 529, QIJIANG ROAD, HEDONG DISTRICT, NANJING, CHINA and JAE & SONS PAPERS COMPANY located at 203 HILTON HOTEL 8 - 8, UMEDA 1 - CHOME, KITA - KU, OSAKA, JAPAN. Letters had been exchanged between them as they went through the several stages of establishing business relations, enquiry and offer, counter-offer and counter counter-offer, placing orders and sending S/C before the deal was finally done successfully. These letters are successively displayed for study in full format, followed by notes and exercises in this respect. Different from the case in Module 1 is the fact that this transaction is concluded under L/C, which involves more business letters and documents. All letters and documents concerning the transaction are showcased in full layout, followed by notes and exercises in this respect. Highlighted here in this module are the letters and documents related to L/C.

L/C + CIF is another way of transaction, mostly practiced in international trade. Letter of credit is a letter issued by a bank authorizing the bearer to draw a stated amount of money from the issuing bank, its branches, or other associated banks or agencies. It is a document issued by a bank that guarantees the payment of a customer's draft. L/C is a pledge of a bank in the importing country at the request of the importer. It will be opened when the bank is satisfied with its customer's credit rating. The L/C pledges to pay the exporter if the merchandise is shipped in conformity with the conditions in the credit—conditions that are based on the contract between the buyer and seller. On the other hand, L/C does not pay unless and until the goods and documents sent by the seller meet the requirement of its terms. Thus L/C guarantees the buyer to be able to receive the goods stipulated in the agreement between the two parties. L/C issued by the opening bank backs up the business transaction between importer and exporter. CIF, which abbreviates cost, insurance and freight in international trade, is a type of contract of sale agreement for the transport of goods by sea. Under the terms of CIF, the price of a commodity is set to include the cost of the commodity itself, insurance costs, and costs of transport to the port of destination. CIF means that the seller is responsible for chartering a liner, loading the goods on the liner at the stipulated time in the contract, and in addition procuring marine insurance against the risks of losses, damages to the goods during the carriage.

I. Establishing Business Relations of Both Sides

WONDER INTERNATIONAL COMPANY LIMITED

NO. 529, QIJIANG ROAD,
HEDONG DISTRICT,
NANJING, CHINA
Tel: 86 - 25 - 8825 × × × ×
Fax: 86 - 25 - 8825 × × × ×
E-mail: sales@ wonder. com. cn

AUG. 2, 20 × ×

Mr. Jae Smith
JAE & SONS PAPERS COMPANY
203 HILTON HOTEL 8 - 8, UMEDA 1 - CHOME, KITA - KU, OSAKA, JAPAN

Dear Mr. Smith,

Through the courtesy of Tokyo Chamber of Commerce and Industry, we *are given to understand* that you are one of the leading importers of kraft linerboard in your country. As this item *falls within* the *scope* of our business activities, we are writing to you *with a keen desire* to enter into business connections with you.

We specialize in the exportation of Chinese kraft linerboard, such as raw kraft, bleached kraft linerboard and unbleached kraft linerboard. We can also design and produce according to customers' needs. Our products are excellent in quality and reasonable in price. *To give you a general idea of* our business *lines*, we enclose a copy of our export list, *showing* the main items now *in supply* and we hope that you would *contact* us if any item is *of interest to* you.

We look forward to receiving your early reply, and *assure* you that your requirements will *have our best and prompt attention.*

Yours faithfully,
WONDER INTERNATIONAL COMPANY LIMITED

Wonder Li

Wonder Li
Manager of the Sales Department

JAE & SONS PAPERS COMPANY
203 HILTON HOTEL 8 – 8, UMEDA 1 – CHOME, KITA – KU, OSAKA, JAPAN
Tel: 81 – 6 – 2256 × × × × Fax: 81 – 6 – 2256 × × × ×
Email: purchase@jaeandsons.com

AUG. 3, 20××

WONDER INTERNATIONAL COMPANY LIMITED
NO. 529, QIJIANG ROAD, HEDONG DISTRICT, NANJING, CHINA

Dear Mr. Li,

We *acknowledge* with thanks the receipt of your letter dated Aug. 2, and *take the pleasure of establishing* business relations with your corporation.

Your kraft products are so attractive that we are *confident* of securing large orders for you. We shall be *obliged* if you could send us quotations and sample books.

We look forward to your *favorable reply*.

Yours faithfully,

Jae Smith

Jae Smith
Manager of the purchase department

Notes

1. ***through the courtesy of*** 承蒙……介绍 thanks to someone's willingness or generosity in providing the information
2. ***are given to understand*** 获悉 get to know
3. ***fall within*** 属于 belong to
4. ***scope*** *n.* 范围 the area covered by a given activity or subject, range
   scope of our business activities 我们的业务范围
5. ***with a keen desire*** 渴望 desirously, anxiously
6. ***to give you a general idea of*** 为了使你方大致了解 in order to brief you on sth.
7. ***line*** *n.* 行当，业务，经营范围 business scope, range
8. ***showing*** 显示，说明 indicating, mentioning
9. ***in supply*** 可供应的 suppliable
10. ***contact*** *v.* 接洽 to get in touch with
11. ***of interest*** 使某人感兴趣 be interesting to sb.
12. ***assure*** *v.* 向……保证 to remove doubt, to cause to feel sure
    e. g. 请放心我方一定会在规定的装运日前装运的。
    Please be assured that we will deliver the goods before the stipulated date of shipment.
13. ***have our best and prompt attention*** 得到我方的及时处理 We handle it very quickly.
14. ***acknowledge*** *v.* 表示对……的感谢或感激 to express thanks or gratitude for
15. ***take the pleasure of*** 荣幸 be delighted, be pleased
16. ***establish*** *v.* 建立 to set up, to build up
17. ***confident*** *adj.* 有信心的 sure
    e. g. 你方应对我方的商业信誉有信心。
    You should be confident of our commercial integrity.
18. ***obliged*** *adj.* 感激的 grateful, thankful
19. ***favorable reply*** 给予答复，佳音 response granting what has been desired or requested.

Exercises

1. Choose the best answer.

1) Will you __________ a fountain pen this Sunday?
   A. to purchase B. buying C. be in the market for D. market
2) We would like to __________ you __________ a number of our clients are interested in Chinese walnut meat.
   A. inform; of B. advise; X C. inform; that D. advice; that

3) We desire to establish __________ beneficial business relations.

A. mutual B. mutually C. each other D. both

4) It is our __________ policy to __________ foreign countries on the principle of equality.

A. business; trade with B. trade; business with

C. trade; trade in D. trade; trade with

5) We are a state-operated corporation __________ both the import and export of textiles.

A. handling in B. trading C. dealing with D. dealing in

2. Complete the sentences by translating Chinese into English.

1) Please inform us 你们目前对什么商品感兴趣。(be interested in)

2) We approach you today 看看你们是否要我们进一步提供情况。(supply)

3) We are given to understand that 你公司是独家经营化工产品的国营公司。(state-operated)

4) 在平等、互利、互通有无的基础上 we have established business relations with firms in over one hundred countries. (based on)

5) 一旦收到你方具体询盘, we will do all the necessary things. (upon receipt of)

3. Complete the following letter by translating Chinese into English.

Dear Sirs,

收到你方 2022 年 12 月 2 日来信, from which we learn that you wish to 与本公司建立业务关系 in the line of canned goods.

根据你方要求, we are sending you by air a catalogue together with a range of pamphlets for your reference.

如目录中任何一种商品使你方感兴趣的话, please let us have your specific enquiry.

Looking forward to your early reply.

Yours faithfully,

II. Enquiry and Offer

JAE & SONS PAPERS COMPANY

203 HILTON HOTEL 8 – 8, UMEDA 1 – CHOME, KITA – KU, OSAKA, JAPAN

Tel: 81 – 6 – 2256 × × × × Fax: 81 – 6 – 2256 × × × ×

Email: purchase@jaeandsons.com

AUG. 5, 20 × ×

Mr. Wonder Li
WONDER INTERNATIONAL COMPANY LIMITED
NO. 529, QIJIANG ROAD, HEDONG DISTRICT, NANJING, CHINA

Re: Unbleached Kraft Linerboard

Dear Mr. Li,

A customer of our *firm* is *in the market for the subject commodity*, so we shall be glad if you will make an *offer* as soon as possible.

We must point out, however, that it is essential to *quote moderate prices*, *purchasing power* in our local market being rather low. We shall, however, be *in a position* to give you *substantial* orders if your quotations are reasonable. Some slight *concession* in price would, we feel sure, bring you in sufficient profit to make this business *worth* your *while*. *We shall appreciate it if* you will arrange for shipment to be made as early as possible by direct steamer for Osaka, Japan.

We are looking forward to receiving your *favorable* offer.

Yours faithfully,

Jae Smith

Jae Smith
Manager of the purchase department

WONDER INTERNATIONAL COMPANY LIMITED

NO. 529, QIJIANG ROAD,
HEDONG DISTRICT,
NANJING, CHINA
Tel: 86 - 25 - 8825 × × × ×
Fax: 86 - 25 - 8825 × × × ×
E-mail: sales@ wonder. com. cn

AUG 5, 20 × ×

Mr. Jae Smith
JAE & SONS PAPERS COMPANY
203HILTON HOTEL 8 - 8, UMEDA 1 - CHOME, KITA - KU, OSAKA, JAPAN

Dear Mr. Smith,

Thank you for your *specific enquiry* today.
We are glad to quote with *engagement* as follows:
Article: unbleached kraft linerboard
Time of shipment: During September — October
Package: 0. 5 MT to a wooden case
Payment: by *confirmed irrevocable L/C available by draft at sight*
Unit price: USD 420 per metric ton CIF Osaka

We are willing to allow a 5% *discount* for all orders over 50 *metric tons*.
We would appreciate a prompt reply, since we will *put the offer out in the event of* your not being interested.

Yours faithfully,
WONDER INTERNATIONAL COMPANY LIMITED
Wonder Li

Wonder Li
Manager of the Sales Department

Notes

1. ***firm*** *n.* 公司 company, corporation
2. ***in the market for*** 想买 interested in buying something

   e. g. 我方目前不想买轿车。

   We are not in the market for cars at the moment.
3. ***the subject commodity*** 谈及的货物 goods concerning which something is said, the above-mentioned goods appearing in the headline
4. ***offer*** *n.* 报价 quotation
5. ***quote*** *v.* 报价 to state a price for goods
6. ***moderate prices*** 中等价位 medium-ranged prices
7. ***purchasing power*** 购买力 the ability to purchase
8. ***in a position*** 能够 able

   e. g. 我方不能把生产的成本告诉你方。

   We are not in a position to reveal the cost of our production.
9. ***substantial*** *adj.* 实际上的；相当大的 real or ample
10. ***concession*** *n.* 让步 something, such as a point previously claimed in argument, that is later conceded, the act of yielding
11. ***worth*** *adj.* 值得的 deserving of

    e. g. 我们双方合作达成交易是值得的。

    It is worth for us to come together and make a deal.
12. **while** *n.* 费时，费工夫 the time, effort, or trouble taken in doing something

    e. g. 这样好的货色值得你花工夫的。

    Such a good item is worth your while.
13. ***We shall appreciate it if*** 如蒙你方……我方将不胜感激 We shall be grateful to you if you could do sth. for us.

    e. g. 如果你方能把价格降低5%，我方将不胜感激。

    We shall appreciate it if you could lower the price by 5%.
14. ***favorable*** *adj.* 表示同意的 manifesting approval, granting what has been desired or requested, propitious

    favorable reply 佳音
15. ***specific enquiry*** 具体询盘 request for particular business information, not just price lists, catalogue, samples, but more important details about the goods and trade terms

    e. g. 收到具体询盘以后，作为惯例卖方应立即回复。

    It is a regular practice that the exporter should reply to the specific enquiry without delay.
16. **engagement** *n.* 诺言 promise, commitment

    to quote with engagement 报实盘，有约束力的报盘
17. ***confirmed irrevocable L/C available by draft at sight*** 保兑的、不可撤销的即期信用证

confirmed L/C 保兑信用证

The security provided by an irrevocable credit may be further enhanced if the bank in the exporter's country (advising bank) is requested by the issuing bank to add its "confirmation", thus making it a confirmed letter of credit. The exporter, then has a confirmed irrevocable letter of credit and he is then double guaranteed against payment by both confirming and issuing bank.

irrevocable L/C 不可撤销信用证

Once the credit is issued it cannot be cancelled or amended before the expiry date without the agreement of the beneficiary. Under such a credit, the exporter can rely on payment being made as soon as he has shipped the goods and produced the shipping documents called for in accordance with the terms of the letter of credit. Because of its greater security to the exporter it is very commonly used in the international trade.

L/C available by draft at sight 即期信用证

It means sight letter of credit or letter of credit by sight draft. Under sight credit, the negotiating bank makes payment immediately upon the presentation of the sight draft and shipping documents as stipulated in the letter of credit by the seller. Similarly, when the negotiating bank delivers the sight draft and the documents to the opening bank, the latter also makes reimbursement at once.

18. ***discount*** *n.* 折扣 a reduction from the full or standard amount of a price
19. ***metric tons*** abbreviated as MT 公吨，缩写成 MT a unit of mass or weight in the metric system equal to 1,000 kilograms
20. ***put the offer out*** 取消报价 get rid of the quotation, cancel the offer
21. ***in the event of*** 万一……的话，如果是……的话 if something happens, on the chance that something happens

e. g. 如遇货物延迟到达，请与船公司联系。

In the event of the late arrival of the consignment, please call the shipping company.

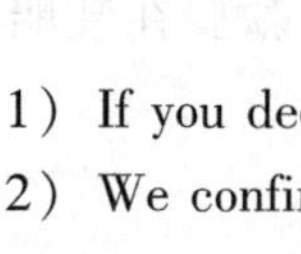

Exercises

1. Choose the proper words given below to fill in the blanks.

delay	offer	subject to	take
occurred	anticipating	confirmation	acceptable

1) If you decide to __________ advantage of our offer, kindly send us your acceptance.
2) We confirm your enquiry of July 3, asking us to make you a (an) __________ for our products.
3) In reply to your previous fax, we are making you an offer subject to our __________ .
4) We are making you the offer, __________ your acceptance before May 5.

5) We trust the offer will be __________ to you and wait for your order with keen interest.

6) It has __________ to us that Type 32 might suit your purpose just as well.

7) As the market is declining, we advise you to place an order without __________.

8) We are __________ that you will place a trial order in the near future.

2. Translate the following sentences into English.

1) 行市上涨，如你们立即确认订货，我们愿意给你方优惠价格。
(confirm, give favorable terms)

2) 我们得知你方是生产铁钉的厂商，想知道你方能否供应圆形铁钉。(note, supply)

3) 我们一位顾客对你方产品感兴趣，想得到你方关于下述货物的报价。(offer for)

4) 请向我方发盘，说明包装、规格、可供应的数量及最早的装运期。
(indicate, the earliest date of shipment)

5) 我们期待你方价格优惠，否则没有成交的可能。(anticipate, favorable, get business done)

6) 由于库存的丝绒有限，需求却很大，此发盘有效期只为一个星期。
(limited supply, heavy demand, firm)

7) 我们渴望尽一切所能，帮助你方开拓新的业务，并很乐意给你方优惠的价格。
(establish new business, be prepared to)

8) 我们的报盘以报盘当日汇率为准。(subject to, foreign exchange rate)

3. Translate the following letter into English.

先生：

感谢贵公司5月4日的询盘，应你方要求，报盘如下，以贵公司的答复于6月3日前到达有效。

商品：混合动力摩托车（hybrid motorcycle） 价格：每台500美元，上海离岸价

数量：200台 装运期：20××年6月

包装方式：木箱，每箱1台 付款条件：装运前电汇付清全部货款

希望以上条件能为贵公司接受，期盼您的订单。

谨上

4. Translate the following offer into English.

熊猫牌男式衬衫，65%涤纶（Dacron又名的确良），35%棉，长袖，长领，一个胸口袋，各种颜色、各种尺寸，每件用塑料袋装，6件装一个盒子，每10打装一个木箱，共1000打。每打7.5英镑，含佣金5%，科威特到岸价，装船期10至11月，付款要在装船前开出不可撤销的信用证。

III. Counter-offer and Counter Counter-offer

JAE & SONS PAPERS COMPANY

203 HILTON HOTEL 8 -8, UMEDA 1 - CHOME, KITA - KU, OSAKA, JAPAN
Tel: 81 -6 -2256 × × × × Fax: 81 -6 -2256 × × × ×
Email: purchase@jaeandsons. com

AUG. 7, 20 × ×

Mr. Wonder Li
WONDER INTERNATIONAL COMPANY LIMITED
NO. 529, QIJIANG ROAD, HEDONG DISTRICT, NANJING, CHINA

Re: Unbleached Kraft Linerboard

Dear Mr. Li,
Thank you for your offer dated Aug. 5 for the above-mentioned goods. We appreciate the good quality of your goods, but unfortunately we are not in a position to *accept* the offer *on your terms*. Your prices appear to be rather *on the high side*. We are obtaining the same quality through another *channel* at a much lower price than that you quoted us.
Our order will be about 100 metric tons. May we suggest that you make a reduction of, *say* 10%, on your quoted prices so as to help us push the sales of your goods on our market? If you can do so, we will possibly *take up* your entire *stock* of the goods. We hope you will not lose this chance so that you will *benefit* from the expanding market.
We will appreciate it very much if you will consider our counter-offer most favorably and *confirm* us your acceptance *as soon as possible*.

Yours faithfully,

Jae Smith

Jae Smith
Manager of the purchase department

WONDER INTERNATIONAL COMPANY LIMITED

NO. 529, QIJIANG ROAD,
HEDONG DISTRICT,
NANJING, CHINA
Tel: 86 - 25 - 8825 × × × ×
Fax: 86 - 25 - 8825 × × × ×
E-mail: sales@ wonder. com. cn

AUG. 8, 20 × ×

Mr. Jae Smith
JAE & SONS PAPERS COMPANY
203 HILTON HOTEL 8 - 8, UMEDA 1 - CHOME, KITA - KU, OSAKA, JAPAN

Subject: Unbleached Kraft Linerboard

Dear Mr. Smith,

In reply to your letter of Aug. 7 requesting a 10% reduction in price, we *regret* we find it very difficult to *comply with*.

The prices we quoted are closely calculated. Thanks to the excellent quality of our products, considerable business has been done with many customers in European markets at these prices. We believe a fair *comparison* of quality between our products and similar articles from other sources will *convince* you of the *reasonableness* of our quotation. However, in order to help you develop business in this *line*, we *are prepared to* allow you a special offer of USD390 per metric ton *provided* your order *calls for* a *minimum* quantity of 100 MT. If you think our proposal *acceptable*, please let us have your order as soon as possible.

We are *anticipating* your early reply.

Yours faithfully,
WONDER INTERNATIONAL COMPANY LIMITED

Wonder Li

Wonder Li
Manager of the Sales Department

Notes

1. ***accept*** *v.* 接受（acceptance *n.* acceptable *adj.*）to receive officially, to regard as proper
2. ***on sb's terms*** 按照某人的条件、意见或定价 according to the conditions set forth by someone
3. ***on the high side*** 偏高
4. ***channel*** *n.* 途径 a course or passage through which something may move or be directed
5. ***say*** *adv.* 比方说 for instance
6. ***take up*** 认购 occupy by purchasing
7. ***stock*** *n.* 库存 the total merchandise kept on hand
8. ***benefit*** *v.* 获利 to derive advantage from something

   e. g. 他从股票的分割受益。

   He benefited from the stock split.
9. ***confirm*** *v.* 确认 to affirm the truth, accuracy, or genuineness of something, declare positively or firmly
10. ***as soon as possible*** 尽快 in the least amount of time there can be

    e. g. 库存不多，请尽快下订单。

    Because of the limited stock, it would be to your advantage to place an order as soon as possible.
11. ***in reply to*** 答复 as answer made in words
12. ***regret*** *v.* 遗憾，抱歉 to feel sorry, disappointed, or distressed about
13. ***comply with*** 遵从，答应 act in accordance with another's request
14. **comparison** *n.* 比较，对照 the act of comparing or the process of being compared

    comparison shopper 被派往竞争的同业店中去购买东西，以探听行情、广告方式以及营业情况等的零售商店的雇用人员
15. ***convince*** *v.* 使信服 to bring by the use of argument or evidence to firm belief or a course of action, persuade
16. ***line*** *n.* 系列商品 merchandise of a similar or related nature

    e. g. 本公司包揽了小工具的全部商品。

    We carry a complete line of small tools.
17. ***reasonableness*** *n.* 合理性，公道 the state of being fair

    reasonable prices 公道的价格
18. ***are prepared to*** 打算 to intend to
19. ***provided*** *conj.* 在……的条件下，如果，倘若 on the condition that

    e. g. 如果本次货物能在本月底前装运，我方将会再次订购一批货物。

    We will probably make a repeat order provided the shipment of the consignment will be made before the end of this month.

20. ***call for*** 要求，需要 to make a demand on

e. g. 国际贸易中需要确保买卖双方的权益。

International trade calls for protection of rights of the two parties concerned.

21. ***minimum*** *n.* 最小值 the least possible quantity

22. ***acceptable*** *adj.* 可接受的，合意的 adequate to satisfy a need or requirement, satisfactory

23. ***anticipate*** *v.* 期望，期待 to look forward to, to expect with pleasure

Exercises

1. Fill in the blanks with proper forms of given words.

reduce

1) Buyers ask for a __________ in price.

2) In order to close this deal we shall further __________ our price.

3) Our closely calculated price cannot be further __________.

regret

1) It is __________ to decline your counter offer. However, we can not but do so.

2) We are __________ that we did not advise you earlier.

3) We __________ to say that the quality does not measure up to the contracted standard.

approval

1) We have tried our best to meet with your __________ in this business.

2) Your request has been __________ of after our discussion.

3) We __________ of the fact that the price of raw material is declining, so our quotation will be slightly reduced.

handle

1) To give you a general idea of our products, we enclose a complete set of leaflets showing various products being __________ by this corporation.

2) What items do you mainly __________?

3) We are the leading importer of electronics in Lagos, mainly __________ the import of the electronic goods.

2. Translate the following sentences into English.

1) 我们希望能按比你们现在所报价格低 10% 的价格成交。（conclude business, price … lower than）

2）虽然我们尽力说服买主，但他们仍未接受。（while）

3）如你方能在报价上减少 2%，我们将立即接受。（reduce）

4）由于所报价格很低，我们不可能再让步，否则我们无利可图。（make concession, leave sb. with a small profit）

5）我们同意将价格从原来的每公吨 1000 美元降至现在的每公吨 990 美元。（reduce from…to）

6）从目前迹象来看，行市将继续下降。（present indications）

7）如你方能设法减价，比方说 3%，我们准备再向你订购 500 台蝴蝶牌缝纫机，即期装运。（reduce, be prepared to, place another order, prompt shipment）

8）虽然我们很乐意利用你方所报的盘，但我方认为不能接受，因为你方价格比一般价格高 10%。（price…higher）

3. Translate the following letter into English.

先生：

贵公司 5 月 10 日函悉，报盘 200 台数码相机，单价为 500 美元，上海到岸价。

兹复，很遗憾，我处客户认为你方价格过高，且与现行行市不一致。贵公司可能知道，一些日本商人正在削价销售，毋庸置疑，市场竞争激烈。

我们不否认贵公司的数码相机质量稍好，但差价绝不至于高达 5%。我们谨代表客户还价如下：

"200 台数码相机，每台 480 美元上海到岸价，其他条件按你方 5 月 10 日函办理。"

由于行情下跌，建议你方早日接受。

盼早复。

IV. Placing Order and Sending S/C

JAE & SONS PAPERS COMPANY

203 HILTON HOTEL 8 - 8, UMEDA 1 - CHOME, KITA - KU, OSAKA, JAPAN
Tel: 81 - 6 - 2256 × × × × Fax: 81 - 6 - 2256 × × × ×
Email: purchase@jaeandsons. com

AUG. 9, 20 × ×

Re: Unbleached Kraft Linerboard

We thank you for your quotation dated Aug. 8. Both the prices and the quality are satisfactory, and we are pleased to *confirm* the letters previously exchanged between us and to enclose our Order No. UKL321. Now the deal has been successfully *put through*. The goods are *urgently* needed and shipment before October is essential.

Yours faithfully,

Jae Smith

Jae Smith
Manager of the purchase department

Encl. Order No. UKL321

ORDER

No. UKL321
Date: AUG. 9, 20 × ×

WONDER INTERNATIONAL COMPANY LIMITED
NO. 529, QIJIANG ROAD, HEDONG DISTRICT, NANJING, CHINA

Please supply

Quantity	Description	Unit Price	Amount	Delivery
100 MT	Unbleached Kraft Linerboard	CIF Osaka USD 390. 00 per MT	USD 39, 000	Before October 2, 20 × ×

Packing: 0. 5 MT to a strong wooden case
Payment: By L/C at sight
Insurance: For 110% of invoice value All Risks and War Risk

We will *instruct* our bank to open the L/C for the amount of this order. You will soon hear from your bank.

Jae Smith

Jae Smith
Manager of the purchase department

WONDER INTERNATIONAL COMPANY LIMITED

NO. 529, QIJIANG ROAD,
HEDONG DISTRICT,
NANJING, CHINA
Tel: 86 – 25 – 8825 × × × ×
Fax: 86 – 25 – 8825 × × × ×
E-mail: sales@ wonder. com. cn

AUG. 10, 20 × ×

Mr. Jae Smith
JAE & SONS PAPERS COMPANY
203 HILTON HOTEL 8 – 8, UMEDA 1 – CHOME, KITA – KU, OSAKA, JAPAN

Subject: Order No. UKL321

Dear Mr. Smith,

Many thanks for your order No. UKL321 for 100 *metric tons* unbleached kraft linerboard. We are very glad to confirm *the captioned* order and will make efforts to effect *the subject* dealing to your satisfaction. We hope that we will be able to *count* you among our regular customers. *Under separate cover* we are sending you the Sales Contract No. ST05 – 016 *in duplicate* by EMS. If you agree to the *terms and conditions* in the contract, please countersign it and send back one copy to us *by return*. In order to *carry out* the order smoothly, you are requested to *open* the letter of credit in time. On our part, the goods will be shipped *in good time* to meet your requirements.

Please be assured that we will fulfill your order to your entire satisfaction and look forward to *further orders* from you.

Yours faithfully,
WONDER INTERNATIONAL COMPANY LIMITED

Wonder Li

Wonder Li
Manager of the Sales Department

Notes

1. ***confirm*** *v.* 确认 to establish the certainty, to verify
2. ***put through*** 做成，搞成 to bring to a successful end
3. ***urgently*** *adv.* 迫切地，急切地 with great urgency, desperately
4. ***L/C*** 信用证 letter of credit
5. ***instruct*** *v.* 指示 to direct
6. ***metric tons*** 公吨，千克（MTs）1000kgs per MT
7. ***further orders*** 续订 repeat orders
8. ***the captioned*** 标题所示的 something stated in the subject line
9. ***the subject*** 标题 something that is being indicated in the headline
10. ***count*** *v.* 认为 to consider to be, to deem
11. ***under separate cover*** 另封邮寄 by a separate mail
12. ***in duplicate*** 一式两份 in two copies
13. ***EMS*** 特快专递 express mail service
14. ***by return*** 马上，立即 immediately
15. ***terms and conditions*** 条款 detailed stipulations stated in the agreement
16. ***carry out*** 实行，履行 to put into practice, effect
17. ***open*** *v.* 开立 to establish letter of credit, to apply to the bank for the establishment of an L/C
18. ***on sb's part*** 就某一特定的人而言 on the part of sb., regarding or with respect to the one specified
19. ***in good time*** 及时地，迅速地 in a reasonable length of time, quickly
20. ***be assured*** 放心 to feel confident
21. ***fulfill*** *v.* 履行，实现计划 to bring into actuality, to effect

售货确认书 SALES CONFIRMATION

卖方（Sellers）: Contract No.: ST05 - 016
WONDER INTERNATIONAL COMPANY LIMITED Date: AUG. 10, 20 × ×
NO. 529, QIJIANG ROAD, HEDONG DISTRICT, NANJING, CHINA Signed at: NANJING, CHINA

买方（Buyers）:
JAE & SONS PAPERS COMPANY
203 HILTON HOTEL 8 - 8, UMEDA 1 - CHOME, KITA - KU, OSAKA, JAPAN

This Sales Contract is made by and between the Sellers and Buyers, whereby the sellers agree to sell and the buyers agree to buy the under-mentioned goods according to the terms and conditions stipulated below:

品名及规格 NAME OF COMMODITY & SPECIFICATION	单价 UNIT PRICE	数量 QUAN	金额及术语 AMOUNT & PRICE TERMS
UNBLEACHED KRAFT LINERBOARD	CIF OSAKA USD 390. 00 PER MT	100 MT	CIF OSAKA USD 39, 000. 00
		TOTAL	USD 39, 000. 00

TOTAL VALUE: SAY U. S. DOLLARS THIRTY NINE THOUSAND ONLY

PAYMENT TERM: BY IRREVOCABLE L/C AT SIGHT

PACKING: TO BE PACKED IN STRONG WOODEN CASES, SUITABLE FOR LONG DISTANCE OCEAN TRANSPORTATION. 0. 5MT PER WOODEN CASE

SHIPPING MARKS: THE SELLER SHALL MARK EACH PACKAGE WITH FADELESS PAINT PACKAGE NUMBER, GROSS WEIGHT, MEASUREMENT AND THE WORDING: "KEEP AWAY FROM MOISTURE", "HANDLE WITH CARE", ETC. AND THE SHIPPING MARK: ST05 - 016/OSAKA JAPAN

TIME OF SHIPMENT: BEFORE OCTOBER 02, 20 × ×

PORT OF SHIPMENT: MAIN PORTS OF CHINA

PORT OF DESTINATION: OSAKA, JAPAN

INSURANCE: FULL SET OF NEGOTIABLE INSURANCE POLICY ENDORSED FOR 110 PCT OF INVOICE VALUE COVERING ALL RISKS AND WAR RISK AS PER AND SUBJECT TO OMCC OF PICC DATED 1/1, 1981

DOCUMENTS:
+ SIGNED INVOICE INDICATING L/C NO. AND CONTRACT NO.
+ FULL SET (3/3) OF CLEAN ON BOARD OCEAN BILL OF LADING MARKED "FREIGHT PREPAID" MADE OUT TO ORDER OF ISSUING BANK, BLANK ENDORSED AND NOTIFY THE APPLICANT
+ PACKING LIST / WEIGHT LIST INDICATING QUANTITY / GROSS AND NET WEIGHT
+ CERTIFICATE OF ORIGIN GSP CHINA FORM A, ISSUED BY THE ADMINISTRATION OF EXIT AND ENTRY OF INSPECTION AND QUARANTINE OR OTHER AUTHORITY DULY ENTITLED FOR THIS PURPOSE
+ NO QUALITY OR QUANTITY CERTIFICATE ISSUED BY MANUFACTURER

OTHER CONDITIONS REQUIRED IN L/C:
+ ALL BANKING CHARGES OUTSIDE THE OPENING BANK ARE FOR BENEFICIARY'S ACCOUNT
+ DO NOT MENTION ANY SHIPMENT MARKS IN YOUR L/C
+ PARTIAL AND TRANSSHIPMENT ALLOWED

Arbitration: All disputes arising from the execution of or in connection with this contract shall be settled amicably by negotiation. In case settlement can not be reached through negotiation the case shall then be submitted to China International Economic & Trade Arbitration Commission in Nanjing for arbitration in act with its sure of procedures. The arbitral award is final and binding upon both parties for setting the Dispute. The fee for arbitration shall be borne by the losing party unless otherwise awarded.

REMARKS: The last date of L/C opening: 20 August, 20 × ×

THE SELLERS: × × × THE BUYERS: *Jae Smith*
WONDER INTERNATIONAL COMPANY LIMITED JAE & SONS PAPERS COMPANY

Exercises

1. Fill in the blanks with proper forms of given words.

exchange

1) We adhere to the principle of equality, mutual benefit and ________ what one has for what one needs.

2) Our ________ of cables has resulted in the conclusion of transaction successfully.

3) The ________ rate has been changed a lot.

conclude

1) The ________ of this transaction will mark the beginning of our long friendly business relations.

2) If you should make us a bid, we trust there is a possibility of ________ the business.

3) We've ________ business with other buyers at your end at our level.

duly

1) The consignment will leave Tianjin by S. S. "Eastwind", ________ to arrive at Hamburg sometime in early May.

2) We inform you that we'll execute the order ________.

3) We enclosed a copy of your purchase order No. 308 ________ signed by us.

establish

1) We are arranging for the ________ of the relative letter of credit with the Bank of China.

2) We are looking forward to ________ direct business relations with you.

3) It is understood that a letter of credit in our favor covering the above-mentioned goods will be ________ immediately.

advise

1) We write you this letter, ________ the establishment of L/C.

2) Please ________ us if you can not ship the goods as requested.

3) As has been ________ to you, we will effect the shipment before May 15.

2. Please write a business letter on the basis of the following.

a. confirming the order for 100 boxes of black tea.

b. sending the contract (No. 208) and asking for counter-signature.

c. reminding of opening L/C

V. Pressing for Opening L/C and Urging Shipment*

WONDER INTERNATIONAL COMPANY LIMITED

NO. 529, QIJIANG ROAD,
HEDONG DISTRICT,
NANJING, CHINA
Tel: 86 – 25 – 8825 × × × ×
Fax: 86 – 25 – 8825 × × × ×
E-mail: sales@ wonder. com. cn

August 19, 20 × ×

Mr. Jae Smith
JAE & SONS PAPERS COMPANY
203 HILTON HOTEL 8 – 8, UMEDA 1 – CHOME, KITA – KU, OSAKA, JAPAN

Re: L/C Covering Order No. UKL321

Dear Mr. Smith,

We *refer to* our letter dated Aug. 10, confirming the acceptance of your order No. UKL321 for 100 metric tons unbleached kraft linerboard and enclosing our S/C No. ST05 – 016, which *stipulates* shipment be made before October 2 and the L/C be opened before August 20.
But until now we haven't received your L/C. Please *promptly* instruct your banker to open an *irrevocable* L/C *at sight in our favor*, so that we can make arrangement for shipment. If your L/C can't be received within 10 days, we are afraid that we may not be able to ship the goods *as agreed upon*.
In order to make shipment on time, please *rush* your L/C *without delay*. We are looking forward to receiving your early reply.

Yours faithfully,
WONDER INTERNATIONAL COMPANY LIMITED

Wonder Li

Wonder Li
Manager of the Sales Department

JAE & SONS PAPERS COMPANY

203 HILTON HOTEL 8 – 8, UMEDA 1 – CHOME, KITA – KU, OSAKA, JAPAN

Tel: 81 – 6 – 2256 × × × × Fax: 81 – 6 – 2256 × × × ×

Email: purchase@jaeandsons. com

Aug. 20, 20 × ×

Mr. Wonder Li
WONDER INTERNATIONAL COMPANY LIMITED
NO. 529, QIJIANG ROAD, HEDONG DISTRICT, NANJING, CHINA

Re: L/C No. S200 – 108

Dear Mr. Li,

Thank you for your letter of Aug. 19. We hereby *draw your attention to the fact* that application has been made to the Industrial Bank of Japan Limited, Osaka for the establishment of an irrevocable L/C at sight in your favor. *It is to our belief* that the L/C will reach you later today. Please *see to it* that shipment of this order is *effected* before October 2, since *punctual shipment* is one of the important considerations in dealing with our market. Please fax us your shipping advice immediately after the departure of the *vessel*.

As called for in our S/C, please mark in *fadeless paint* all the wooden cases *conspicuously* with the shipping mark "ST05 – 016/OSAKA JAPAN" and the warning sign "KEEP AWAY FROM MOISTURE", "HANDLE WITH CARE" as well as the package number, gross weight, and measurement. Your *compliance in this respect* will do much to *facilitate* our taking delivery of the goods on arrival.

Yours faithfully,

Jae Smith

Jae Smith
Manager of the purchase department

Notes

1. ***refer to*** 提到，谈及 to mention or talk about something
2. ***stipulate*** *v.* 规定 to lay down as a condition of an agreement
3. ***promptly*** *adv.* 马上，立刻地 immediately, at once
4. ***irrevocable*** *adj.* 不可撤销的 impossible to retract or revoke
5. ***at sight*** 即期的 as soon as seen, or presented to sight
6. ***in sb.'s favor*** 以……为受益人 inscribed or made out to the benefit of

   e. g. a check in favor of the exporter 以一个出口商为受款人的票据
7. ***as agreed upon*** 商定好的 on which a contract has been reached
8. ***rush*** *v.* 加速，赶紧做 to perform with great haste, to expedite
9. ***without delay*** 赶快，立刻 as soon as possible
10. ***draw sb.'s attention to the fact*** 提请某人注意某事 to direct one's interest to sth.
11. ***It is to our belief*** 我方相信 We believe that
12. ***see to it*** 确保 make sure
13. ***effect*** *v.* 履行 to perform, to carry out
14. ***punctual shipment*** 准时装运 delivery on time
15. ***vessel*** *n.* 货船 steamer, cargo ship
16. ***fadeless paint*** 不易褪色的油漆 liquid mixture not subject to fading

    fadeless fabric 不褪色织物
17. ***conspicuously*** *adv.* 显眼地，在明显位置 obviously, noticeably
18. ***compliance*** *n.* 按要求做，顺从 the act of complying with a request
19. ***in this respect*** 在这一方面 in this particular aspect
20. ***facilitate*** *v.* 使容易，促进 to make easier

    e. g. 环银电协的应用大大促进了各国银行间资金的流转。

    SWIFT has greatly facilitated the financial flow among the banks in all countries of the world.

Exercises

1. Fill in the following blanks with the given words in their proper forms.

press　　favor　　open　　deliver

1) The L/C No. 246 has been opened in the __________ of ABC company.

2) It's difficult for us as our customers are __________ us for assurance of prompt shipment.

3) We shall __________an L/C within 7 working days upon receipt of the contract countersigned by you.

4) The sales season is drawing near, so please make __________ as agreed.

5) We write this letter in order __________ you for establishment for the required L/C.

6) We hasten to inform you that we have today been advised by the Bank of China of the ______ ____of an L/C in our favor to the amount of $100,000 available on or before April 30.

7) In whose __________ the L/C is issued in this cotton transaction?

8) According to your request for __________ an L/C, we are pleased to inform you that we have airmailed today through the Bank of China an irrevocable L/C for $200,000 in favor of the New York Trading Co., Inc.

9) You cannot expect us to make __________ in less than a month without receipt of irrevocable L/C promptly.

10) We are arranging for the __________ of the relative L/C with the Bank of China, Shanghai and shall let you know by fax.

2. Fill in the blanks with proper prepositions.

1) The application __________ the L/C covering the following goods to the amount of $1,200 has been made __________ the Citibank.

2) We have pressed issuing bank __________ opening an L/C covering the goods.

3) The L/C is valid __________ Mar.

4) Any charges appeared outside issuing bank are to be __________ your account.

5) Application __________ establishing an L/C has been made 3 days ago.

6) The date of shipment is approaching. Please expedite the issuance of L/C to the amount of $2,000 and send us reply __________ return as possible as you can.

7) If there are any losses arising __________ the delay of the L/C, you should be responsible for compensation.

8) The shipment is ________ great need, so please arrange to ship without any delay.

3. Translate the following letter into English.

本公司欲以每台300美元价格（拉各斯到岸价），订购500台伊琳娜262型号电动打字机，于7—8月装运。

该项交易款额高达150,000美元，本公司只是适量现金储备，占用资金3—4个月将造成麻烦，故建议用30日期的信用证付款。

承蒙贵公司一向照顾，若能继续给予优惠，本公司感激不尽。如同意上述建议，烦请赐寄合约，即开立信用证。

谨上

VI. Making Commercial Invoice

万达国际有限公司

WONDER INTERNATIONAL COMPANY LIMITED

NO. 529, QIJIANG ROAD, HEDONG DISTRICT, NANJING, CHINA

Tel: 86 -25 -8825 × × × × Fax: 86 -25 -8825 × × × × E-mail: sales@wonder.com.cn

COMMERCIAL INVOICE

To: JAE & SONS PAPERS COMPANY
203 HILTON HOTEL 8 -8, UMEDA 1 -CHOME, KITA -KU,
OSAKA, JAPAN

Invoice No.: JSP0810
Invoice Date: AUG. 19, 20 × ×
S/C No.: ST05 -016
S/C Date: AUG. 10, 20 × ×

From: NANJING, CHINA To: OSAKA, JAPAN

Letter of Credit No.: S200 -108 Issued By: INDUSTRIAL BANK OF JAPAN LIMITED, OSAKA

Marks and Numbers	Number and kind of package; Description of goods	Quantity	Unit Price	Amount
ST05 -016 OSAKA JAPAN	CIF OSAKA 100 MT UNBLEACHED KRAFT LINERBOARD ***************************	100 MT	USD 390.00	USD39,000.00

TOTAL: 100 MT USD39,000.00

SAY TOTAL: U. S. DOLLARS THIRTY NINE THOUSAND ONLY.

WONDER INTERNATIONAL COMPANY LIMITED

× × ×（签名）

Exercises

Make out the relevant invoice with the following information from the L/C.

……

Doc. Credit Number	*20	:	M0756510NS0023000
Date of issue	31C	:	SEPT. 08, 20××
Expiry	*31D	:	Date NOV. 30, 20×× Place CHINA
Applicant	*50	:	CHANG JI TRADING CO., 305, SEONG CHANG BLDG., 2972 SEOKCHON DONG, SEOUL, KOREA
Beneficiary	*59	:	HUAYUE MEDICINE & HEALTH PRODUCTS IMP. AND EXP. CORP. 196 TIANHE ROAD, GUANGZHOU, CHINA
Amount	*32B	:	Currency USD Amount 45, 600.00

……

Partial Shipments	43P	:	ALLOWED
Transshipment	43T	:	PROHIBITED
Loading in Charge	44A	:	CHINA PORT
For Transport to...	44B	:	INCHON, KOREA
Latest Date of Ship	44C	:	NOV. 15, 20××
Descript. of Goods	45A	:	

CINNAMON WHOLE 8.64MT @ USD2, 250.00/MT AS PER INDENT NO. 57152

CINNAMON BROKEN 12 MT @ USD2, 180.00/MT AS PER INDENT NO. 57151

C AND F INCHON

Documents required 46A :

*SIGNED COMMERCIAL INVOICE IN QUADRUPLICATE

Additional Cond. 47A :

*SHIPPING MARK CHANGJI

INCHON

SHOULD BE INDICATED ON BOTH SIDES OF PACKING CARTONS

Some useful information:

Port of Loading: Yantian	Port of Discharge: Inchon
S. S.: CHANGYUN V. 346	B/L Date: Nov. 8, 20××
Sales Confirmation No.: 05MHS14635	Invoice No.: 05327MK72

VII. Making Packing List

万达国际有限公司

WONDER INTERNATIONAL COMPANY LIMITED

NO. 529, QIJIANG ROAD, HEDOND DISTRICT, NANJING, CHINA

Tel: 86 - 25 - 8825 × × × × Fax: 86 - 25 - 8825 × × × × E-mail: sales@ wonder. com. cn

PACKING LIST

To: JAE & SONS PAPERS COMPANY
203 HILTON HOTEL 8 - 8, UMEDA 1 - CHOME,
KITA - KU, OSAKA, JAPAN

Invoice No.: JSP0810
Invoice Date: AUG. 19, 20 × ×
S/C No.: ST05 - 016
S/C Date: AUG. 10, 20 × ×

From: NANJING, CHINA
To: OSAKA, JAPAN
Letter of Credit No.: S200 - 108
Date of Shipment: BEFORE OCT. 02, 20 × ×

Marks and Numbers	Number and kind of package Description of goods	Quantity	Package	G. W	N. W	Meas.
ST05 - 016 OSAKA JAPAN	UNBLEACHED KRAFT LINERBOARD (PACKED IN WOODEN CASES OF 0.5 MT EACH)	100 MT	200 WOODEN CASES	@0.6MT 120 MT	@0.5MT 100 MT	@3 × 2 × 1M 1,200CBMS
TOTAL:		100 MT	200 WOODEN CASES	120 MT	100MT	1,200 CBMS

SAY TOTAL: SAY TWO HUNDRED WOODEN CASES ONLY

WONDER INTERNATIONAL COMPANY LIMITED

× × × (签名)

Exercises

Make out the relevant Packing List with the following information from the L/C.

……

Doc. Credit Number	* 20	:	M0756510NS0023000
Date of issue	31C	:	SEPT. 08, 20 × ×
Expiry	* 31D	:	DATE NOV. 30, 20 × × Place CHINA
Applicant	* 50	:	CHANG JI TRADING CO., 305, SEONG CHANG BLDG., 2972 SEOKCHON DONG, SEOUL, KOREA
Beneficiary	* 59	:	HUAYUE MEDICINE & HEALTH PRODUCTS IMP. AND EXP. CORP. 196 TIANHE ROAD, GUANGZHOU, CHINA
Amount	* 32B	:	CURRENCY USD AMOUNT 45, 600. 00

……

Partial Shipments	43P	:	ALLOWED
Transshipment	43T	:	PROHIBITED
Loading in Charge	44A	:	CHINA PORT
For Transport to…	44B	:	INCHON, KOREA
Latest Date of Ship	44C	:	NOV. 15, 20 × ×
Descript. of Goods	45A	:	

CINNAMON WHOLE 8. 64MT @ USD2, 250. 00/MT AS PER INDENT NO. 57152

CINNAMON BROKEN 12 MT @ USD2, 180. 00/MT AS PER INDENT NO. 57151

C AND F INCHON

Documents required 46A :

* PACKING/WEIGHT LIST IN QUADRUPLICATE

Additional Cond. 47A :

* SHIPPING MARK CHANGJI
INCHON

SHOULD BE INDICATED ON BOTH SIDES OF PACKING CARTONS

Some other useful information:

Cinnamon whole: 216 cartons of 40kgs net each, gross weight: 42. 5kgs/CTN

Cinnamon broken: 300 cartons of 40 kgs net each, gross weight: 42. 5kgs/CTN

M: 45 × 30 × 20CM/Carton

Sales Confirmation No.: 05MHS14635

Loading Port: Yantian, China

B/L Date: NOV. 8, 20 × ×

VIII. Insurance Policy*

中保财产保险有限公司

The People's Insurance (Property) Company of China, Ltd.
No. of Original, one

发票号码 JSP0810 保险单号次 PICC34321P
②Invoice No. ①Policy No

海 洋 货 物 运 输 保 险 单
MARINE CARGO TRANSPORTATION INSURANCE POLICY

被保险人 **WONDER INTERNATIONAL COMPANY LIMITED** ③
NO. 529, QIJIANG ROAD, HEDOND DISTRICT, NANJING, CHINA

Insured:

中保财产保险有限公司（以下简称本公司）根据被保险人的要求，及其所缴付约定的保险费，按照本保险单承保险别和背面所载条款与下列条款承保下述货物运输保险，特签发本保险单

This POLICY of Insurance witnesses that The People's Insurance (Property) Company of China, Ltd. (hereinafter called "The Company"), at the request of the Insured and in consideration of the agreed premium paid by the Insured, undertakes to insure the under-mentioned goods in transportation subject to the conditions of this Policy as per the Clauses printed overleaf and other special clauses attached hereon.

保险货物项目 Descriptions of Goods	包装 单位 数量 Packing Unit Quantity	保险金额 Amount Insured
UNBLEACHED KRAFT LINERBOARD④	200 WOODEN CASES 100 MT⑤	USD 42, 900 ⑥

承保险别：⑦

COVERING ALL RISKS AND WAR RISK INCLUDING W/W CLAUSE AS PER AND SUBJECT TO THE RELEVANT OCEAN MARINE CARGO CLAUSES OF THE PEOPLE'S INSURANCE (PROPERTY) COMPANY OF CHINA DATED 1/1, 1981

货 物 标 记
Marks of Goods⑧
ST05 - 016
OSAKA
JAPAN

总保险金额
Total Amount Insured: ⑨SAY US DOLLARS FOURTY TWO THOUSAND NINE HUNDRED ONLY

保 费 运 输 工 具 开航日期
Premium: As Arranged⑩ Per Conveyance S. S. YANGFAN 882⑪ Slg. On or abt. OCT. 1, 2022⑫

起运港 ⑬ 目的港
From NANJING, CHINA To OSAKA, JAPAN

所保货物，如发生本保险单项下可能引起索赔的损失或损坏，应立即通知本公司下述代理人查勘。如有索赔，应向本公司提交保险单正本（本保险单共有 份正本）及有关文件。如一份正本已用于索赔，其余正本则自动失效。

In the event of loss or damage which may result in a claim under this Policy, immediate notice must be given to the Company's Agent as mentioned hereunder. Claims, if any, one of the Original Policy which has been issued in Original(s) together with the relevant documents shall be surrendered to the Company. If one of the Original Policy has been accomplished, the others to be void.

⑭中 保 财 产 保 险 有 限 公 司
THE PEOPLE'S INSURANCE (PROPERTY) COMPANY OF CHINA LTD.

赔付地点
Claim payable at OSAKA, JAPAN ⑮

日期 ⑯ 在
Date AUG. 19, 20×× at NANJING, CHINA

地址
Address

(Endorsement overleaf) ⑰

Definition

Insurance Policy is an agreement between the insured and the insuring company, detailing the types of coverage and outlining what risks are insured. It is a document, usually made out in the name of the policyholder. It certifies contracts for property insurance. The insurance policy is given to the insured (the company in whose interest insurance is provided) after the premium is paid. The policy establishes the basic terms of the insurance. These include the type and object of coverage and the life of the contract. They also include the amount of the insurance and information about the policyholder and the underwriter. Under CIF, it is the exporter who is responsible to have the cargo insured before the steamer sets sail. Under FOB or CFR, it is the importer who is to have its own cargo insured before the ship leaves the port of loading.

A general Insurance Policy contains

① Policy Number, which is given by the insurance company 保险单号次

② Invoice Number, the same as what the commercial invoice indicates 发票号码

③ Name of the Insured 被保险人

Unless otherwise stated, under CIF, insurance should be covered by exporter, so the insured should be the beneficiary in the L/C.

④ Description of Goods, as what stated in the S/C or L/C 被保货物项目

Usually, it is the general name of goods.

⑤ Packing, Unit, Quantity 包装、单位、数量

It is the number of the biggest package and the number of total units. Total gross weight or net weight should be indicated if total units are not available.

⑥ Amount Insured 保险金额（小写）

It will be 110% of the invoice value under CIF according to the general practice of international trade. Example: If the CIF invoice value is USD39, 000, then the amount insured is $USD39,000 \times 1.1 = USD429,000$.

⑦ Conditions 承保险别

Usually the insurance company should stamp the insurance risks and clauses at the requirements of the insured. Three insurance clauses are generally accepted worldwide:

a. 中国保险条款（CIC）: OCEAN MARINE CARGO CLAUSES OF THE PEOPLE'S INSURANCE COMPANY OF CHINA DATED 1/1, 1981 (abbreviated to OMCC OF PICC DATED 1/1, 1981) with basic risks being called All Risks（一切险）, W. P. A. （水渍险）, F. P. A. （平安险）.

b. 伦敦保险协会条款（ICC）: INSTITUTE CARGO CLAUSES DATED 1/1, 1982 with basic risks being called ICC （A）, ICC （B）, ICC （C）.

c. 美国协会条款（AICC）: AMERICAN INSTITUTE CARGO CLAUSES DATED 1/1, 1996

W/W CLAUSE 仓至仓条款（Warehouse to Warehouse Clause）即保险责任自被保险人货物远离保险单上所载明的启运地仓库或储存处所开始，包括正常运输中的海上、陆上、内河和驳船运输在内，直至该项货物运抵保险单所载明的目的地收货人的最后仓库或储存处所，或被保险人用作分配、分派或非正常运输时的其他存储处所为止。When the goods are delivered to the consignee's warehouse at the destination named in the policy, the insurance shall terminate. It should be noted that the cover is limited to 60 days upon discharge of the insured goods from seagoing vessel at the final port of discharge before the insured goods reach the consignee's warehouse.

⑧ Marks of Goods 装运标志，唛头

It should be the shipping marks of the goods, the same as that in the L/C and the invoice.

⑨ Total Amount Insured 保险金额（大写）

It should be the total amount of insurance in words with the writing pattern being SAY U. S. DOLLARS ... ONLY.

⑩ Premium 保费

The amount paid for an insurance policy. "As Arranged" is usually printed in the insurance policy so as not to let the exact fare expose unless otherwise the L/C calls for details of it.

⑪ Per Conveyance S. S. 运输工具

The name of the vessel as per B/L

⑫ Sailing on or about 开航日期

It is the date of B/L.

⑬ From...To... 起运港……目的港

It should be from the port of departure to the port of destination. In case of transshipment, port of transshipment should be filled in, such as:

From Guangzhou, China to New York, U. S. A. via Hong Kong.

From Guangzhou, China to New York, U. S. A. with transshipment at Hong Kong.

From Guangzhou, China to New York, U. S. A. W/T Hong Kong.

⑭ Insurer 保险人

It should be the stamp of the insurance company with the signature of the person in charge.

⑮ Claim Payable at 赔付地点

It is usually the port of destination for the purpose of claim. The currency should also be indicated.

⑯ Date...at... 出单日期和出单地点

It should be the issuing date of insurance policy and the locating city of the insurance company. The date of insurance should not be later than the date of B/L.

⑰ Endorsement overleaf 背书

Under CIF terms, the consignor, which is the exporter, should make an endorsement on the overleaf so as to transfer all rights of the policy to the consignee, usually the importer.

Exercises

Make out the relevant Insurance Policy with the following information from the L/C.

Doc. Credit Number	*20	:	67893EIUR567
Date of issue	31C	:	APRIL 10, 20 × ×
Expiry	*31D	:	Date JUNE 30, 20 × × Place CHINA
Applicant	*50	:	WING HENG INTERNATIONAL TRADING CO. …… HONGKONG.
Beneficiary	*59	:	HUAYUE MEDICINE & HEALTH PRODUCTS IMP. AND EXP. CORP. 196 TIANHE ROAD, GUANGZHOU, CHINA
Amount	*32B	:	Currency USD Amount 12, 600. 00
Partial Shipments	43P	:	PROHIBITED
Transshipment	43T	:	PROHIBITED
Loading in Charge	44A	:	CHINA PORT
For Transport to…	44B	:	LOS ANGELES
Latest Date of Ship	44C	:	JUNE 15, 20 × ×
Descript. of Goods	45A	:	

CINNAMON WHOLE 5. 6MT @ USD2, 250. 00/MT CIF LOS ANGELES
AS PER SALES CONFIRMATION NUMBER. 583665

Documents required 46A :

+ INSURANCE POLICY/CERTIFICATE COVERING F. P. A. AND S. R. C. C. FOR 110% OF INVOICE VALUE AS PER CIC

CLAIMS, IF ANY, PAYABLE AT PORT OF DESTINATION IN CURRENCY OF DRAFT

Additional Cond. 47A :

* SHIPPING MARK F. V. T. L. (IN A TRIANGLE)
LOS ANGELES
CTN/NO. 1 - UP

SHOULD BE INDICATED ON BOTH SIDES OF PACKING CARTONS

Some useful information:

Cinnamon whole: 140 cartons of 40kgs net each, Gross Weight: 42. 5KGS/CTN
M: 45 × 30 × 20CM/CARTON
Port of Loading: Yantian Port of Discharge: LOS ANGELES
S. S. : YUANHONG V. 465 B/L Date: JUN. 3, 20 × ×
Invoice No. : 09832/NM

IX. GSP Certificate of Origin Form A*

<table>
<tr><td colspan="3">1. Goods consigned from (Exporter's business name, address, country)
WONDER INTERNATIONAL COMPANY LIMITED
NO. 529, QIJIANG ROAD, HEDONG DISTRICT
NANJING, CHINA</td><td colspan="3" rowspan="2">Reference No. CCPIT558833CO

GENERALIZED SYSTEM OF PREFERENCES
CERTIFICATE OF ORIGIN
(Combined declaration and certificate)
FORM A
issued in THE PEOPLE'S REPUBLIC OF CHINA
(Country)
See Notes overleaf</td></tr>
<tr><td colspan="3">2. Goods consigned to (Consignee's name, address, country)
JAE & SONS PAPERS COMPANY
203 HILTON HOTEL 8 - 8, UMEDA 1 - CHOME,
KITA - KU, OSAKA, JAPAN</td></tr>
<tr><td colspan="3">3. Means of transport and route (as far as known)
FROM NANJING, CHINA TO OSAKA, JAPAN BY SEA ON OCT. 1, 20 × ×</td><td colspan="3">4. For official use ①</td></tr>
<tr><td>5. Item Number ②</td><td>6. Marks and numbers of packages</td><td>7. Number and kind of packages; description of goods</td><td>8. Origin Criterion (see Notes overleaf) ③</td><td>9. Gross Weight or other quantity</td><td>10. Number and date of invoices</td></tr>
<tr><td>1</td><td>ST05 -016
OSAKA
JAPAN</td><td>200 (TWO HUNDRED) WOODEN CASES OF UNBLEACHED KRAFT LINERBOARD</td><td>"P"</td><td>120 MT</td><td>JSP0810
AUG. 19, 20 × ×</td></tr>
<tr><td colspan="3">11. Certification
It is hereby certified, on the basis of control carried out, that the declaration by the exporter is correct

南京出入境检验检疫局
NANJING ADMINISTRATION OF EXIT AND ENTRY INSPECTION AND QUARANTINE

NANJING AUG. 24. , 20 × × × × ×
Place and date, signature and stamp of certifying authority</td><td colspan="3">12. Declaration by the exporter
The undersigned hereby declares that the above details and statements are correct; that all the goods were produced in
CHINA ④
And that they comply with the origin requirements specified for those goods in the Generalized System of Preferences for goods exported to
JAPAN
(importing country)

WONDER INTERNATIONAL COMPANY LIMITED
NANJING AUG. 19, 20 × × × × ×
Place and date, signature of authorized signatory</td></tr>
</table>

Definition

普惠制原产地证（Generalized System of Preferences Certificate of Origin），简称“GSP 产地证”，也称“FORM A”（格式 A）。普遍优惠制度是发达国家给予发展中国家出口制成品或半制成品（包括某些初级产品）普遍的、非歧视性的、非互惠的一种关税优惠制度。普惠制原产地证就是一种受惠国有关机构（检验检疫局）向给惠国出口受惠商品而签发的用以证明原产地的文件。我国出口商在对给惠国出口“可受惠商品”时，不管信用证是否要求提供 GSP 产地证，都应向口岸的检验检疫机构申领此证交收货人，使其能享受普惠制的待遇。2003 年全球有 32 个给惠国，近年来，除了美国、匈牙利、保加利亚三国对我国未给此种待遇外，其他 29 个国家均给予中国产品以普惠制待遇。欧洲国家有德国、比利时、英国、波兰、荷兰、卢森堡、法国、意大利、丹麦、爱尔兰、希腊、西班牙、葡萄牙、奥地利、芬兰、挪威、瑞典、瑞士、捷克、斯洛伐克、俄罗斯、白俄罗斯、乌克兰等；亚洲国家有日本、土耳其、哈萨克斯坦；大洋洲国家有澳大利亚、新西兰；北美洲国家有加拿大。

普惠制原产地证包括以下主要内容

① For official use 官方填写

② Item number 项目编号，按每一项商品归类品种编写“1”、“2”

“1”，“2” … are marked depending on different varieties of goods being declared.

③ Origin criterion 原产地标准

填报代码	出口国家	原产地标准
P	所有给惠国家	完全原产品
W + H. S. CODE	欧盟、挪威、瑞士、日本	产品列入给惠国“加工清单”并符合其加工厂条件； 产品未列入“加工清单”但产品使用的进口原料和零部件经过充分加工，产品 H. S. 号不同于原材料或零部件的 H. S. 号
F	加拿大	有进口成分，但进口成分价值未超过产品出厂价的 40%
W + H. S. CODE	波兰	有进口成分，但进口成分价值未超过离岸价的 50%
Y + 进口成分	白俄罗斯、乌克兰、哈萨克斯坦、捷克、斯洛伐克	有进口成分，但进口成分价值未超过离岸价的 50%

④ Declaration by the exporter 出口方申明（需要填写出口国和进口国名称）

Names of country of origin and importing country should be marked in the corresponding place in the column.

Exercises

Make out the relevant Certificate of Origin with the following information from the L/C.

: TO 0944 26 BKCHCNBJANNG01851
: FM: 1566 25VRBPIT2VAXXX32463
VRBPIT2VXXX
+BANK POLOLARE DI CAERANO
+CAERANO
……
: 20 DOC. CREDIT NUMBER: TT456643132
: 31C: DATE OF ISSUE: OCT. 5, 20 × ×
: 31D: EXPIRY: DATE: DEC. 15, 20 × ×
PLACE: CHINA
: 50: APPLICANT: SAINT MARCO SUITCASE CORP.
320, VIA MAZZINI
310310 CAERANO, SAN MARCO, ITALY
: 59: BENEFICIARY: CHINA NATIONAL ARTS & CRAFTS
IMP. AND EXP. CO. ZHAOQING BRANCH
168 XIHU ROAD, DUANZHOU DISTRICT
ZHAOQING, GUANGDONG, CHINA
……
: 45B: SHIPMENT OF GOODS:
1000PCS TRAVEL SUITCASE MODEL: 27002 AT USD 20. 00/PC
2000PCS TRAVEL SUITCASE MODEL: 43708 AT USD 30. 00/PC
CIF VENICE, ITALY LESS 3% DISCOUNT
PACKED IN CARTONS AS PER S/C NO. P070GAB
SHIPPING MARK: SAINT MARCO SUITCASE/VENICE/CTN NO. /MADE IN CHINA
: 44A: LOADING IN CHARGE: ANY PORT IN CHINA
: 44B: FOR TRANSPORT TO…: VENICE, ITALY
: 44C: LATEST DATE OF SHIP. : NOV. 30, 20 × ×
: 44D: PARTIAL SHIPMENT: NOT ALLOWED
: 44E: TRANSSHIPMET: ALLOWED
: 46B: DOCUMENTS REQUIRED:
G) CERTIFICATE OF ORIGIN GSP FORM A
47A: ADDITIONAL COND. :

A) L/C NO. SHOULD BE INDICATED IN ALL DOCUMENTS PRESENTED FOR NEGOTIATION

Some messages from S/C:

Packed in cartons of 300 cartons total, 100 suitcases each carton

G. W.: 3.5KG/CTN N. W.: 3.3KG/CTN M.: 140×138×120CM/CTN

Port Of Loading: Shenzhen, China Port Of Transshipment: Singapore

Name Of Vessel: Maria V598/Concord Date Of B/L: Nov. 27, 20××

Invoice Number: KU8458×××× Dated: Nov. 17, 20××

X. Asking Amendment to L/C and Expecting Shipment*

有不符点的信用证:

INDUSTRIAL BANK OF JAPAN LIMITED, OSAKA

SEQUENCE OF TOTAL	27: 1/1
FORM OF DOC. CREDIT	40A: IRREVOCABLE
DOC. CREDIT NUMBER	20: S200-108
DATE OF ISSUE	31C: 20××0819
DATE AND PLACE OF EXPIRY	31D: DATE: 20××1001 PLACE: BENEFICIARY'S COUNTRY
APPLICANT	50D: JAE & SONS PAPERS COMPANY 203 HILTON HOTEL 8-8, UMEDA 1-CHOME, KITA-KU, OSAKA, JAPAN
BENEFICIARY	59: WONDER INTERNATIONAL CO MPANY LIMITED NO. 529, QIJIANG ROAD, HEDONG DISTRICT NANJING, CHINA
AMOUNT	32B: CURRENCY HKD AMOUNT 39,000.00 10% MORE OR LESS ARE ALLOWED
AVAILABLE WITH/BY	41D: ANY BANK IN CHINA BY NEGOTIATION
DRAFTS AT…	42C: DRAFT AT SIGHT FOR FULL INVOICE COST
DRAWEE	42A: INDUSTRIAL BANK OF JAPAN LIMITED, OSAKA
PARTIAL SHIPMENT	43P: NOT ALLOWED
TRANSSHIPMENT	43T: NOT ALLOWED
LOADING ON BOARD	44A: MAIN PORTS OF CHINA
FOR TRANSPORTATION TO…	44B: OSAKA, JAPAN
LATEST DATE OF SHIPMENT	44C: 20××1002
DESCRIPT OF GOODS	45A: COMMODITY: UNBLEACHED KRAFT LINERBOARD

UNIT PRICE: USD 390.00/ MT
TOTAL: 100 MT ±10% ARE ALLOWED
PRICE TERMS: CIF BUSAN KOREA
COUNTRY OF ORIGIN: P. R. CHINA
PACKING: TO BE PACKED IN STRONG WOODEN CASES

DOCUMENTS REQUIRED 46A:

+COMMERCIAL INVOICE IN 3 COPIES INDICATING L/C NO. & CONTRACT NO. ST05 - 016

+FULL SET OF CLEAN ON BOARD OCEAN BILLS OF LADING, MADE OUT TO ORDER OF ISSUING BANK AND BLANK ENDORSED, MARKED FREIGHT PREPAID AND NOTIFY APPLICANT.

+PACKING LIST/WEIGHT LIST IN 3 COPIES INDICATING QUANTITY / GROSS AND NET WEIGHTS

+CERTIFICATE OF ORIGIN GSP CHINA FORM A IN 3 COPIES ISSUED BY THE ADMINISTRATION OF EXIT AND ENTRY INSPECTION AND QUARANTINE

+NO SOLID WOOD PACKING CERTIFICATE ISSUED BY MANUFACTURER

+BENEFICIARY'S CERTIFICATE CERTIFYING THAT ONE SET OF SHIPPING DOCUMENTS HAS BEEN FAXED TO APPLICANT WITHIN 1 DAY AFTER SHIPMENT

ADDITIONAL COND. 47B: ALL DOCUMENTS ARE TO BE PRESENTED TO US IN ONE LOT BY COURIER / SPEED POST

DETAILS OF CHARGES 71B: ALL BANKING CHARGES OUTSIDE OF OPENING BANK ARE FOR ACCOUNT OF BENEFICIARY

PERIOD OF PRESENTATION 48: DOCUMENTS TO BE PRESENTED WITHIN 21 DAYS AFTER THE DATE OF SHIPMENT BUT WITHIN THE VALIDITY OF THE CREDIT

WONDER INTERNATIONAL COMPANY LIMITED

NO. 529, QIJIANG ROAD,
HEDONG DISTRICT,
NANJING, CHINA
Tel: 86 - 25 - 8825 × × × ×
Fax: 86 - 25 - 8825 × × × ×
E-mail: sales@ wonder. com. cn

August 21, 20 × ×

Mr. Jae Smith
JAE & SONS PAPERS COMPANY
203 HILTON HOTEL 8 - 8, UMEDA 1 - CHOME, KITA - KU, OSAKA, JAPAN

Subject: L/C No. S200 - 108

Dear Mr. Smith,

We refer to the 100 MT unbleached kraft linerboard under S/C No. ST05 - 016, but we regret that there are several points in the L/C not *in conformity with* what stipulated in the contract. We, therefore, would like you to *amend* the L/C as follows:
(1) The kind of currency is not correct. The total amount is CURRENCY USD AMOUNT 39, 000 *instead of* CURRENCY HKD AMOUNT 39, 000.
(2) Please delete the *wording* "NOT" *in the terms of* partial shipment and transshipment, since partial shipment and transshipment are all allowed according to the *S/C*.
(3) Please *extend* the *validity* date of the L/C to October 17, 20 × ×. It would be impossible for us to *dispatch* the goods since your L/C *expiration predates* the latest date of shipment as stated in the S/C.
As we can do nothing until the above L/C is *duly* amended, we would advise you to *attend to the matter with the least possible delay*.

Yours faithfully,
WONDER INTERNATIONAL COMPANY LIMITED

Wonder Li

Wonder Li
Manager of the Sales Department

JAE & SONS PAPERS COMPANY

203 HILTON HOTEL 8 - 8, UMEDA 1 - CHOME, KITA - KU, OSAKA, JAPAN

Tel: 82 - 51 - 2256 × × × × Fax: 81 - 51 - 2256 × × × ×

Email: purchase@jaeandsons.com

Sep. 21, 25, 20××

Mr. Wonder Li
WONDER INTERNATIONAL COMPANY LIMITED
NO. 529, QIJIANG ROAD, HEDONG DISTRICT, NANJING, CHINA

Re: Shipment of Unbleached Kraft Linerboard under L/C No. S200 - 108

Dear Mr. Li,

As regards our Order No. UKL321 and L/C No. S200 - 108 for 100 MT unbleached kraft linerboard, it is to our belief that you had been *advised* of the *amendment* to L/C by the bank 30 days ago. However, we have not received any information from your company about its shipment.

As the sales season is rapidly *approaching* and the demand *at our end* is *heavy*, any delay in shipment will *involve us in* no small difficulty. If the goods cannot be on the market on time to *cater for* the *end-users'* satisfaction, every effort we made before is meaningless.

We have to draw your attention to the fact that any loses caused by shipment delay should be *compensated* according to the stipulations in the contract. What you should do urgently at present is to *do your utmost* to dispatch the goods in question without delay.

Thank you *in advance* for your cooperation.

Yours faithfully,

Jae Smith

Jae Smith
Manager of the purchase department

修改好的信用证（与合同一致）：

INDUSTRIAL BANK OF JAPAN LIMITED, OSAKA

SEQUENCE OF TOTAL	27：1/1
FORM OF DOC. CREDIT	40A：IRREVOCABLE
DOC. CREDIT NUMBER	20：S200 – 108
DATE OF ISSUE	31C：20 × ×0819
DATE AND PLACE OF EXPIRY	31D：DATE：20 × ×1017 PLACE：BENEFICIARY'S COUNTRY
APPLICANT	50D：JAE & SONS PAPERS COMPANY 203 HILTON HOTEL 8 – 8, UMEDA 1 – CHOME, KITA – KU, OSAKA, JAPAN
BENEFICIARY	59：WONDER INTERNATIONAL COMPANY LIMITED NO. 529, QIJIANG ROAD, HEDONG DISTRICT NANJING, CHINA
AMOUNT	32B：CURRENCY USD AMOUNT 39, 000. 00 10% MORE OR LESS ARE ALLOWED
AVAILABLE WITH/BY	41D：ANY BANK IN CHINA BY NEGOTIATION
DRAFTS AT…	42C：DRAFT AT SIGHT FOR FULL INVOICE COST
DRAWEE	42A：INDUSTRIAL BANK OF JAPAN LIMITED, OSAKA
PARTIAL SHIPMENT	43P：ALLOWED
TRANSSHIPMENT	43T：ALLOWED
LOADING ON BOARD	44A：MAIN PORTS OF CHINA
FOR TRANSPORTATION TO…	44B：OSAKA, JAPAN
LATEST DATE OF SHIPMENT	44C：20 × ×1002
DESCRIPT OF GOODS	45A：COMMODITY：UNBLEACHED KRAFT LINERBOARD UNIT PRICE：USD 390. 00/ MT TOTAL：100 MT ±10% ARE ALLOWED PRICE TERMS：CIF OSAKA JAPAN COUNTRY OF ORIGIN：P. R. CHINA PACKING：TO BE PACKED IN STRONG WOODEN CASES
DOCUMENTS REQUIRED	46A：

+COMMERCIAL INVOICE IN 3 COPIES INDICATING L/C NO. & CONTRACT NO. ST05 – 016

+FULL SET OF CLEAN ON BOARD OCEAN BILLS OF LADING, MADE OUT TO ORDER OF ISSUING BANK AND BLANK ENDORSED, MARKED FREIGHT PREPAID AND NOTIFY APPLICANT.

+PACKING LIST/WEIGHT LIST IN 3 COPIES INDICATING QUANTITY / GROSS AND NET WEIGHTS

+CERTIFICATE OF ORIGIN GSP CHINA FORM A IN 3 COPIES ISSUED BY THE ADMINISTRATION OF EXIT AND ENTRY INSPECTION AND QUARANTINE

+NO SOLID WOOD PACKING CERTIFICATE ISSUED BY MANUFACTURER
+BENEFICIARY'S CERTIFICATE CERTIFYING THAT ONE SET OF SHIPPING DOCUMENTS HAS BEEN FAXED TO APPLICANT WITHIN 1 DAY AFTER SHIPMENT

ADDITIONAL COND.	47B:	ALL DOCUMENTS ARE TO BE PRESENTED TO US IN ONE LOT BY COURIER / SPEED POST
DETAILS OF CHARGES	71B:	ALL BANKING CHARGES OUTSIDE OF OPENING BANK ARE FOR ACCOUNT OF BENEFICIARY
PERIOD OF PRESENTATION	48:	DOCUMENTS TO BE PRESENTED WITHIN 21 DAYS AFTER THE DATE OF SHIPMENT BUT WITHIN THE VALIDITY OF THE CREDIT

Notes

1. ***in conformity with*** 与……一致 in accordance with, in consistency with
2. ***amend*** *v.* 修改 to remove the faults or errors, to correct
3. ***instead of*** 代替，而不是 in place of, rather than
4. ***wording*** *n.* 措词 style of expressing in words
5. ***in the terms of*** 在……条款上 in the elements of a proposed or concluded agreement
6. ***S/C*** 销售合同，销售确认书 sales contract, sales confirmation
7. ***extend*** *v.* 延期，延展 to stretch or spread (something) out to greater length, to broaden, to expand
8. ***validity*** *n.* 有效 the state of being valid
9. ***dispatch*** *v.* 发货 to deliver, to send, to make shipment
10. ***expiration*** *n.* 期满，终止 the act of coming to a close, termination
11. ***predate*** *v.* 先于 to precede in time
12. ***duly*** *adv.* 按时地 at the expected time
13. ***attend to the matter*** 注意，留心 to take care of the matter, to give attention to the matter
14. ***with the least possible delay*** 毫不迟疑 without delay, as soon as possible
15. ***as regards*** 关于，至于 concerning, in regard to
16. ***advise*** *v.* 通知，告知 to inform, to notify
17. ***amendment*** *n.* 修改，改正 correction, alteration, improvement
18. ***approach*** *v.* 接近 to come nearer in time
19. ***at our end*** 在我方市场 in our local market
20. ***heavy*** *adj.* (需求) 大的 large in number or quantity
21. ***involve sb. in sth.*** 使卷入，使陷入 to engage as a participant, to draw someone into a matter or problem, to embroil

    e. g. 小企业并不想被涉及到大公司的财务困境中去。

    Small enterprises don't usually want to be involved in big companies' financial problems.
22. ***cater for* sth.** 满足 (需要) to attend to the wants or needs of sb.
23. ***end-user*** 终端用户 the person who uses the product, consumer
24. ***compensate*** *v.* 赔偿，补偿 to recompense or reimburse, to make up for

    e. g. 货物灭失，我方获得保险公司的赔偿。

Insurance company compensated us for the goods lost.

25. ***do one's utmost*** 竭力 do one's best

26. ***in advance*** 提前，事先，预先 beforehand

27. **Field names of the *Documentary* L/C** 跟单信用证的栏位名称

Sequence of Total	合计次序
Form of Documentary Credit	跟单信用证类别
Documentary Credit Number	信用证号码
Reference to Pre Advice	预通知的编号
Date of Issue	开证日期
Date and Place of Expiry	到期日及地点
Applicant Bank	申请人银行
Applicant	申请人
Beneficiary	受益人
Currency Code, Amount	币别代号、金额
Percentage Credit Amount Tolerance	信用证金额加减百分率
Maximum Credit Amount	最高信用证金额
Additional Amount Covered	可附加金额
Available with...by...	向……银行押汇，押汇方式为……
Draft at	汇票期限
Drawee	付款人
Mixed Payment Details	混合付款指示
Deferred Payment Details	延迟付款指示
Partial Shipments	分批装运
Transshipment	转运
Loading on Board/Dispatch/Loading in Charge at/from	由……装船/发运/接管
For Transport to	装运至
Latest Date of Shipment	最后装运日
Shipment Period	装运期间
Description of Goods and/or Services	货物及/或服务描述
Documents Required	应具备单据
Additional Conditions	附加条件
Charges	费用
Period for Presentation	提示期间
Confirmation Instructions	保兑指示
Reimbursement Bank	清算银行
Instructions to the Paying/Accepting/Negotiation Bank	对付款/承兑/议付银行之指示
"Advise Through" Bank	收讯银行以外的通知银行
Sender or Receipt Information	银行间的通知

Exercises

1. Translate the following sentences into Chinese.

1) We would like you to make the necessary amendments immediately. As you know shipment will not be made until the above are corrected.

2) The L/C has been received this date but without necessary amendments. Again we must ask you to refer to our letter of February 20 in which our request was made to you regarding the following clauses to be amended.

3) Please amend L/C No. 100 as follows:

a. Amount to be increased up to USD50, 000

b. Validity to be extended to 10th November

c. The words "Transshipment Not Allowed" are to be deleted.

4) We hope that you will take commercial reputation into account in all seriousness and open L/C at once, otherwise you will be responsible for all the losses arising there from.

5) Please notify the buyers that we shall make an amendment in the L/C, using FOB San Francisco instead of CFR New York.

6) For payment, we require 100% invoice value, confirmed and irrevocable L/C with clauses allowing partial shipment and transshipment, available by draft at sight, against surrendering the full set of shipping documents to the negotiating bank here.

2. Translate the following sentences into English.

1) 信用证规定允许分批装运和转船。(stipulate)

2) 请尽快将信用证修改通知书寄给我方。(amend)

3) 经详阅，我们发现信用证中的有效期和合同不符。(on perusal, in conformity with)

4) 按照贵方 12 月 2 日来电，我们将在没有信用证修改书的情况下装运 20,000 码棉布。(amendment)

5) 经核对信用证条款，我们遗憾地发现你方信用证要求 10 月装运，但我方合约规定 11 月份装运。(stipulate for)

3. Write a letter according to the following main points.

a. receive the credit and find the mistakes;

b. amendments: the weight should be 2, 000 MT;

c. partial shipment and transshipment allowed;

d. ask for cable amendment.

XI. Making Export Commodity Inspection Application

中华人民共和国出入境检验检疫
出境货物报检单

报检单位(加盖公章)：WONDER INTERNATIONAL COMPANY LIMITED

*编　　号__________　　报检单位登记号：－－－－　　联系人：李××

电话：××××　　报检日期：20××年9月21日

发货人	（中文）万达国际有限公司						
	（外文）WONDER INTERNATIONAL COMPANY LIMITED						
收货人	（中文）						
	（外文）JAE & SONS PAPERS COMPANY						
货物名称（中/外文）	H. S. 编码	产地	数/重量	货物总值	包装种类及数量		
未漂白牛皮卡纸 UNBLEACHED KRAFT LINERBOARD	4707100000	江苏南京	100MT	USD39, 000	200WOODEN CASES		
运输工具名称号码	YANGFAN 882	贸易方式	一般贸易	货物存放地点	南京		
合同号	ST05－016	信用证号	S200－108	用途	其他		
发货日期	SEP. 30, 20××	输往国家（地区）	日本	许可证/审批号	－－－－		
启运地	江苏南京	到达口岸	大阪	生产单位注册号	－－－－		
集装箱规格、数量及号码	50×40'（ZCSU2270001～ZCSU2270050）						
合同、信用证订立的检验检疫条款或特殊要求	标 记 及 号 码	随附单据（划“√”或补填）					
	ST05－016 OSAKA JAPAN	☑合同 ☐信用证 ☑发票 ☐换证凭单 ☑装箱单 ☐厂检单	☐包装性能结果单 ☐许可/审批文件 ☐ ☐ ☐				

需要证单名称（划“✓”或补填）				*检验检疫费	
✓品质证书	1正1副	☐植物检疫证书	__正__副	总金额（人民币元）	
✓重量证书	1正1副	☐熏蒸/消毒证书	__正__副		
☐数量证书	__正__副	☐出境货物换证凭单		计费人	
☐兽医卫生证书	__正__副	✓出境通关单			
☐健康证书	__正__副	☐		收费人	
☐卫生证书	__正__副	☐			
☐动物卫生证书	__正__副				

报检人郑重声明：	领 取 证 单	
1. 本人被授权报检。	日期	
2. 上列填写内容正确属实，货物无伪造或冒用他人的厂名、标志、认证标志，并承担货物质量责任。　签名：李××	签名	

注：有“*”号栏由出入境检验检疫机关填写　　◆国家出入境检验检疫局制

Exercises

Make out the relevant Application for Inspection according to the information from the L/C.

……

Doc. Credit Number	* 20	:	M0756510NS0023000
Date of issue	31C	:	SEPT. 08, 20 × ×
Expiry	* 31D	:	DATE NOV. 30, 20 × × PLACE CHINA
Applicant	* 50	:	CHANG JI TRADING CO., 305, SEONG CHANG BLDG., 2972 SEOKCHON DONG, SEOUL, KOREA
Beneficiary	* 59	:	HUAYUE MEDICINE & HEALTH PRODUCTS IMP. AND EXP. CORP. 196 TIANHE ROAD, GUANGZHOU, CHINA
Amount	* 32B	:	CURRENCY USD AMOUNT 45, 600. 00

……

Partial Shipments	43P	:	ALLOWED
Transshipment	43T	:	PROHIBITED
Loading in Charge	44A	:	CHINA PORT
For Transport to…	44B	:	INCHON, KOREA
Latest Date of Ship	44C	:	NOV. 15, 20 × ×
Descript. of Goods	45A	:	

CINNAMON WHOLE 8. 64MT @ USD2, 250. 00/MT AS PER INDENT NO. 57152
CINNAMON BROKEN 12 MT @ USD2, 180. 00/MT AS PER INDENT NO. 57151
C AND F INCHON

Additional Cond. 47A :

* SHIPPING MARK CHANGJI
INCHON
SHOULD BE INDICATED ON BOTH SIDES OF PACKING CARTONS

Some messages from Shipping Order:
Cinnamon whole: 216 cartons of 40kgs net each, Gross Weight: 42. 5KGS
Cinnamon broken: 300 cartons of 40kgs net each, Gross Weight: 42. 5KGS
M: 45 × 30 × 20CM/CARTON
Loading Port: YANTIAN, CHINA
B/L DATE: NOV. 8, 20 × ×
S. S.: CHANGYUN V. 346
Sales Confirmation No.: 05MHS14635
Tariff No.: 0906100000
Legal Unit: kg
Container No.: EMCU3254752/40'/LE3222

XII. Making the Customs Declaration

中华人民共和国海关出口货物报关单

预录入编号： 海关编号：（由海关填写）

出口口岸 南京海关（2300）	备案号	出口日期 20××-9-30	申报日期 20××-9-23

经营单位 南京万达国际有限公司 （3222456321）	运输方式 江海运输	运输工具名称 YANGFAN 882	提运单号 CSCLNJ5858490
发货单位 南京万达国际有限公司 （3222456321）	贸易方式 一般贸易	征免性质 一般征税	结汇方式 信用证

许可证号	运抵国（地区） 日本	指运港 大阪	境内货源地 江苏南京

批准文号	成交方式 CIF	运费 502/2400/3	保费 502/1100/3	杂费
合同协议号 ST05-016	件数 200	包装种类 木箱	毛重（公斤） 120, 000 KGS	净重（公斤） 100, 000 KGS

集装箱号 50×40'（ZCSU2270001 ～ZCSU2270050）	随附单据 B	生产厂家

标记唛码及备注　　随附单证号：出口货物通关单（5441252564）
ST05-016
OSAKA JAPAN

项号	商品编号	商品名称、规格型号	数量及单位	最终目的国（地区）	单价	总价	币制	征免
1	4707100000	未漂白牛皮卡纸 UNBLEACHED KRAFT LINERBOARD	100 MT	日本大阪	390 per MT	39, 000	美元	照章

税费征收情况
合计总价：

录入员 ××× 录入单位 南京××报关行	兹声明以上申报无讹并承担法律责任	海关审单批注及放行日期(签章)
报关员 ×××	申报单位 南京××报关行 （3211254691）	审单 审价
		征税 统计
单位地址 南京××路53号 邮编 210000 电话 5288××××	填制日期 20××-9-23	查验 放行

Exercises

Make out the relevant Export Customs Declaration with the following information from the L/C.

Doc. Credit Number	* 20	:	M0756510NS0023000
Date of issue	31C	:	SEPT. 08, 20 × ×
Expiry	* 31D	:	DATE NOV. 30, 20 × × PLACE CHINA
Applicant	* 50	:	CHANG JI TRADING CO., 305, SEONG CHANG BLDG., 2972 SEOKCHON DONG, SEOUL, KOREA
Beneficiary	* 59	:	HUAYUE MEDICINE & HEALTH PRODUCTS IMP. AND EXP. CORP. 196 TIANHE ROAD, GUANGZHOU, CHINA
Amount	* 32B	:	CURRENCY USD AMOUNT 45, 600. 00
……			
Partial Shipments	43P	:	ALLOWED
Transshipment	43T	:	PROHIBITED
Loading in Charge	44A	:	CHINA PORT
For Transport to…	44B	:	INCHON, KOREA
Latest Date of Ship	44C	:	NOV. 15, 20 × ×
Descript. of Goods	45A	:	

CINNAMON WHOLE 8. 64MT @ USD 2, 250. 00/MT AS PER INDENT NO. 57152
CINNAMON BROKEN 12 MT @ USD 2, 180. 00/MT AS PER INDENT NO. 57151
C AND F INCHON

Additional Cond. 47A :

* SHIPPING MARK CHANGJI
INCHON

SHOULD BE INDICATED ON BOTH SIDES OF PACKING CARTONS

Some messages from Shipping Order:

Cinnamon whole: 216 cartons of 40kgs net each, Gross Weight: 42. 5KGS/CTN
Cinnamon broken: 300 cartons of 40kgs net each, Gross Weight: 42. 5KGS/CTN
M: 45 × 30 × 20CM/CARTON
Loading Port: YANTIAN, CHINA

B/L Date: NOV. 8, 20 × ×	S. S.: CHANGYUN V. 346
Sales Confirmation No.: 05MHS14635	B/L NO.: TE984 × × ×
Tariff No.: 0906100000	Legal Unit: kg
Container No.: EMCU3254752/40'/LE3222	Freight: USD400/FCL

XIII. Making Shipping Advice*

WONDER INTERNATIONAL COMPANY LIMITED①

NO. 529, QIJIANG ROAD,
HEDONG DISTRICT,
NANJING, CHINA
Tel: 86 - 25 - 8825 × × × ×
Fax: 86 - 25 - 8825 × × × ×
E-mail: sales@wonder.com.cn

SEP. 30, 20 × ×②

Mr. Jae Smith
③JAE & SONS PAPERS COMPANY
203 HILTON HOTEL 8 - 8, UMEDA 1 - CHOME, KITA - KU, OSAKA, JAPAN

Dear Mr. Smith,

Ref: ④ Shipping Advice Covering Order No. UKL 321⑤

We hereby inform you that the following shipment is effected by us. Please arrange to collect the goods.

FROM: NANJING, CHINA TO OSAKA, JAPAN⑥
SHIPPING MARKS: ⑦ ST05 - 016/OSAKA JAPAN
QUANTITIES AND DESCRIPTIONS: ⑧ 100 MT UNBLEACHED KRAFT LINERBOARD
PACKING: ⑨ 0.5MT PER WOODEN CASE, TOTAL ⑩ 200 WOODEN CASES
NAME OF VESSEL: YANGFAN 882 ⑪
ETD: SEP. 30, 20 × × ⑫
ETA: OCT. 14, 20 × × ⑬
B/L NO.: CSCLNJ5858490 ⑭

We hope that the above-mentioned goods will reach you on time and in good condition.

Yours faithfully,
WONDER INTERNATIONAL COMPANY LIMITED ⑮

Wonder Li

Wonder Li
Manager of the Sales Department

Definition

Shipping Advice is the advice that the exporter sends to the importer before or shortly after the shipment, informing of the particulars of shipment. Receiving the shipping advice, the importer can get ready for payment and to collect the goods. Under FOB or CFR terms, it is the Shipping Advice that enables the importer to cover the insurance of the goods in due time.

A Shipping Advice contains

① Exporter 出口商名称

It will indicate the name, address and detail information of the exporter.

② Date 通知书日期

It should be the issuing date of the Shipping Advice. Under FOB or CFR terms, the advice date should predate the relative shipping documents, thus enabling the importer to cover insurance of the goods prior to the departure of the vessel.

③ To 进口商名称

The name of the importer should be indicated. It is the applicant of the L/C or the person named in the L/C.

④ Shipping Advice 标题

The title catches the immediate attention of the importer.

⑤ Order No. /Contract No. /Letter of Credit No. 订单号/合同号/信用证号

Any of the numbers should be consistent with relative documents.

⑥ From... To... 从……至……

It should be the port of shipment and port of destination and transshipment if any.

⑦ Shipping Marks 唛头

It should be identical with what the packing list indicates.

⑧ Quantities and Descriptions 货物数/重量描述

It should be filled in according to the stipulations of the L/C. Usually the name of the goods, specification, quantity can be indicated.

⑨ Packing 货物包装

It should be the outer packing and number of packages.

⑩ Total 货物总数

It should be the total quantity or total weight of the goods.

⑪ Name of the Vessel 货船名称

It should be the name of the cargo steamer with the second ship in case of transshipment.

⑫ ETD 预计装运日期 estimated time of departure

Date of Shipment should be indicated if the time of departure has been set specifically. Date of shipment is the same as the date of B/L.

⑬ ETA 预计装运日期 estimated time of arrival

It may not be indicated, for it is a rough calculation.

⑭ B/L No. 提单号码

It should be indicated in strict accordance with the requirements in the L/C.

⑮ Signature 出单人落款签章

It is the exporter's name and the signature of the person in charge.

Exercises

Make out the relevant Shipping Advice with the following information from the L/C.

Doc. Credit Number	*20	:	M0756510NS0023000
Date of Issue	31C	:	SEPT. 08, 20××
Expiry	*31D	:	DATE NOV. 30, 20×× Place CHINA
Applicant	*50	:	CHANG JI TRADING CO., 305, SEONG CHANG BLDG., 2972 SEOKCHON DONG, SEOUL, KOREA
Beneficiary	*59	:	HUAYUE MEDICINE & HEALTH PRODUCTS IMP. AND EXP. CORP. 196 TIANHE ROAD, GUANGZHOU, CHINA
Amount	*32B	:	CURRENCY USD AMOUNT 45,600.00
Partial Shipments	43P	:	ALLOWED
Transshipment	43T	:	PROHIBITED
Loading in Charge	44A	:	CHINA PORT
For Transport to...	44B	:	INCHON, KOREA
Latest Date of Ship	44C	:	NOV. 15, 20××
Descript. of Goods	45A	:	

CINNAMON WHOLE 8.64MT @ USD2,250.00/MT AS PER INDENT NO. 57152

CINNAMON BROKEN 12 MT @ USD2,180.00/MT AS PER INDENT NO. 57151

C AND F INCHON

Additional Cond. 47A :

* SHIPPING MARK CHANGJI
INCHON

SHOULD BE INDICATED ON BOTH SIDES OF PACKING CARTONS

* BENEFICIARY'S FAX SENT TO APPLICANT WITHIN 48 HOURS AFTER SHIPMENT INDICATING CONTRACT NO., L/C NO., GOODS NAME, QUANTITY, INVOICE VALUE, VESSEL'S NAME, LOADING PORT, SHIPPING DATE AND ETA. COPY OF WHICH SHOULD BE PRESENTED AS ONE OF THE NEGOTIATION DOC.

Some useful information:

Cinnamon whole: 216 cartons of 40kgs net each, Gross Weight: 42.5KGS/CTN

Cinnamon broken: 300 cartons of 40kgs net each, Gross Weight: 42.5KGS/CTN

M: 45 × 30 × 20CM/Carton

Port of Loading: Yantian

Port of Discharge: Inchon

S. S.: CHANGYUN V. 346

B/L Date: Nov. 8, 20 × ×

Sales Confirmation No.: 05MHS14635

ETA: XXX B/L No.: TE984 × × ×

XIV. Bill of Lading*

1. Shipper ②
WONDER INTERNATIONAL COMPANY LIMITED
NO. 529, QIJIANG ROAD, HEDONG DISTRICT
NANJING, CHINA

B/L NO CSCLNJ5858490

中海集装箱运输上海有限公司

①

CHINA SHIPPING CONTAINER LINERS (SHANGHAI) CO., LTD.

Port-to-Port or Combined Transport

BILL OF LADING

ORIGINAL

2. Consignee ③
TO ORDER OF
INDUSTRIAL BANK OF JAPAN LIMITED, OSAKA

3. Notify Party (Carrier not to be resposible for failure to notify) ④
JAE & SONS PAPERS COMPANY
203 HILTON HOTEL 8 - 8, UMEDA 1 - CHOME, KITA - KU
OSAKA, JAPAN

4. Pre-carriage by	5. Place of Receipt ⑧
6. Ocean Vessel ⑩ YANGFAN 882	7. Port of Loading ⑤ NANJING, CHINA

8. Port of Discharge ⑥	9. Port of Delivery ⑦	10. Final Destination (of the goods not the ship) ⑨
OSAKA, JAPAN		

11. Marks & Nos. ⑪	12. No. of Containers Or Packages. ⑫	13. Kind of Packages; Description of Goods	14. G. W. (kgs) ⑬	15. Measurement ⑭
ST05 - 016 OSAKA JAPAN	50 × 40' (ZCSU2270001 ~ ZCSU2270050)	200 WOODEN CASES UNBLEACHED KRAFT LINERBOARD	120 MT	1,200CBMS

16. Description of Contents for Shipper's Use Only (CARRIER NOT RESPONSIBLE)

17. TOTAL NO. CONTAINERS OR PACKAGES (IN WORDS) ⑮
SAY TWO HUNDRED WOODEN CASES ONLY

18. FREIGHT & CHARGES⑯	19. Revenue Tons	20. Rate	21. Paid	22. Prepaid ⑯	23. Collect
AS ARRANGED				FREIGHT PREPAID	

24. Ex. Rate:	25. Prepaid at	26. Payable at	27. Place and Date of Issue ⑰ NANJING, SEP. 30, 20 × ×
	28. Total prepaid in	29. No. of Original B/L (S) 3	Signed for the Carrier ⑱ CHINA SHIPPING CONTAINER LINES

Definition

Bill of lading is a document issued by a carrier to a shipper, listing and acknowledging receipt of goods for transport and specifying terms of delivery. There are three functions for it. First, it is a cargo receipt, which symbolizes that the shipping company has received certain packages of goods on board of the ship. Second, it is an evidence of carriage contract, for which the shipping company undertakes to ship the goods from port of loading to port of destination. Third, it is a document of title, only against which the shipping company will release the goods to its legal owner at the port of destination.

A typical bill of lading contains

① **Carrier**, usually the shipping company or its agent 承运人，运输公司

② **Shipper**, the seller in fact, also called consignor, which is the beneficiary of the L/C 托运人或发货人

③ **Consignee**, the name of which should be in strict accordance with the L/C. "To order" or "To order of sb." is requested in many cases according to the L/C. 收货人

④ **Notify Party**, the contact person at the port of destination. It will be highly necessary for the shipping company to notify the arrival of the ship when the title of goods is sold and transferred from the importing company to another corporation. 通知方

⑤ **Port of Loading**, which is the port of exporting country 装运港

⑥ **Port of Discharge**, the Destination in case of direct shipment; the stopover port in case of transshipment 卸货港

⑦ **Port of Delivery**, the final port of destination in case of transshipment 目的港

⑧ **Place of Receipt**, the inland place to pick the goods up if requested for the shipping company 接货地点

⑨ **Final Destination**, the interior place to send by truck the goods to door if needed for the shipping company 最终目的地

⑩ **Ocean Vessel**, the name and the voyage number of the ship 船名和船次

⑪ **Marks and Numbers**, the shipping marks for transportation 唛头与号码

⑫ **Number and Kind of Packages**, **Description of Goods**, the name and the package in figure of the goods shipped 货物件数、包装种类、货物描述

⑬ **Gross Weight**, in kilogram of the goods shipped 毛重

⑭ **Measurement**, in cubic meter of the goods volume 体积

⑮ **Number of Package in Words**, number in words besides in figures 箱数大写

⑯ **Freight & Charges**, it must be inconsistent with the stipulations of the L/C. "Freight Prepaid (运费已付)" means that the exporter has already paid for the sea transportation. "Freight to Collect (运费到付)" means that the shipper has not yet paid for the sea transportation, leaving the shipping company to collect the freight from the consignee. "As arranged" is indicated to show no revelation of the exact charges. 运费

⑰ **Date and Place of Issue**, the time when the B/L is issued and the port where the goods is shipped 签发地点和日期

⑱ **Signature of the Carrier**, the authorized signature of the person in charge in the shipping company 承运人签章

Exercises

Make out the relevant Bill of Lading with the following information from the L/C.

Doc. Credit Number	*20	:	M0756510NS0023000
Date of issue	31C	:	SEPT. 08, 20××
Expiry	*31D	:	DATE NOV. 30, 20×× Place CHINA
Applicant	*50	:	CHANG JI TRADING CO., 305, SEONG CHANG BLDG., 2972 SEOKCHON DONG, SEOUL, KOREA
Beneficiary	*59	:	HUAYUE MEDICINE & HEALTH PRODUCTS IMP. AND EXP. CORP. 196 TIANHE ROAD, GUANGZHOU, CHINA
Amount	*32B	:	CURRENCY USD AMOUNT 45,600.00
……			
Partial Shipments	43P	:	ALLOWED
Transshipment	43T	:	PROHIBITED
Loading in Charge	44A	:	CHINA PORT
For Transport to…	44B	:	INCHON, KOREA
Latest Date of Ship	44C	:	NOV. 15, 20××
Descript. of Goods	45A	:	

CINNAMON WHOLE 8.64MT @ USD2,250.00/MT AS PER INDENT NO. 57152
CINNAMON BROKEN 12 MT @ USD2,180.00/MT AS PER INDENT NO. 57151
C AND F INCHON

Documents required 46A :

* FULL SET OF CLEAN ON BOARD OCEAN BILL OF LADING MADE OUT TO ORDER OF SHIPPER AND BLANK ENDORSED, MARKED FREIGHT PREPAID, NOTIFYING THE APPLICANT.

Additional Cond. 47A :

* SHIPPING MARK CHANGJI

INCHON

SHOULD BE INDICATED ON BOTH SIDES OF PACKING CARTONS

Some messages from Shipping Order:
CINNAMON WHOLE: 216 cartons of 40kgs net each, Gross Weight: 42.5KGS/CTN
CINNAMON BROKEN: 300 cartons of 40 kgs net each, Gross Weight: 42.5KGS/CTN
M: 45 × 30 × 20CM/CARTON

Loading Port: YANTIAN, CHINA	B/L Date: NOV. 8, 20 × ×
S. S.: CHANGYUN V. 346	B/L No.: TE984 × × ×

XV. Making Beneficiary's Certificate*

万达国际有限公司

WONDER INTERNATIONAL COMPANY LIMITED①

NO. 529, QIJIANG ROAD, HEDONG DISTRICT, NANJING, CHINA
Tel: 86 − 25 − 8825 × × × × Fax: 86 − 25 − 8825 × × × × E-mail: sales@wonder.com.cn

BENEFICIARY'S CERTIFICATE②

Invoice No.: ④	JSP0810	**Date:** ③	SEP. 30, 20 × ×
Invoice Date:	AUG. 19, 20 × ×	**L/C No.:** ④	S200 − 108

WE CERTIFY HEREBY THAT ONE SET OF SHIPPING DOCUMENTS HAS BEEN FAXED TO APPLICANT WITHIN 1 DAY AFTER SHIPMENT. ⑤

WONDER INTERNATIONAL COMPANY LIMITED⑥
李 × ×（签名）

Definition

Beneficiary's Certificate is a document issued by the beneficiary of the L/C to certify that he has already performed certain duty in accordance with the requirements of the L/C.

A beneficiary's certificate contains:

① Issuer 证明人

It is the beneficiary who addresses to the bank, certifying that he has already carried out his obligation stipulated in the L/C.

② Name of Certificate 证明书标题

As stipulated in the L/C, one of the following names could be used as a title:

Beneficiary's Certificate

Beneficiary's Declaration

Beneficiary's Statement

③ Date 出单日期

It is the date when the exporter has just finished his responsibilities.

④ Number of L/C, Number of Invoice, Date of Invoice 信用证号码、发票号码、发票日期

Unless otherwise stipulated, Beneficiary's Certificate should bear the number of L/C, S/C and invoice as well as the date of invoice.

⑤ Statement 证明文句

The content of the statement should comply with the stipulation in the L/C. Instead of stating "The beneficiary or they have done sth.", "We have done sth." should be used. Likewise, instead of showing "Sth. will be done" as written in the L/C, "Sth. has been done" should be used.

⑥ Signature of Issuer 证明人签章

It should be the company name of the exporter and the signature of the person in charge.

Exercises

Make out the relevant Beneficiary's Certificate with the following information from the L/C.

……

Doc. Credit Number	*20	:	M0756510NS0023000
Date of issue	31C	:	SEPT. 08, 20 × ×
Expiry	*31D	:	DATE NOV. 30, 20 × × PLACE CHINA
Applicant	*50	:	CHANG JI TRADING CO.
			305, SEONG CHANG BLDG.,

			2972 SEOKCHON DONG, SEOUL, KOREA
Beneficiary	*59	:	HUAYUE MEDICINE & HEALTH PRODUCTS IMP. AND EXP. CORP. 196 TIANHE ROAD, GUANGZHOU, CHINA
Amount	*32B	:	CURRENCY USD AMOUNT 45, 600. 00

……

Partial Shipments	43P	:	ALLOWED
Transshipment	43T	:	PROHIBITED
Loading in Charge	44A	:	CHINA PORT
For Transport to…	44B	:	INCHON, KOREA
Latest Date of Ship	44C	:	NOV. 15, 20 × ×
Descript. of Goods	45A	:	

CINNAMON WHOLE 8. 64MT @ USD 2, 250. 00/MT AS PER INDENT NO. 57152
CINNAMON BROKEN 12 MT @ USD 2, 180. 00/MT AS PER INDENT NO. 57151
C AND F INCHON

Documents required 46A :

* BENEFICIARY'S CERTIFICATE CERTIFYING THAT THEY WILL GIVE THE BUYER AN IMMEDIATE NOTICE ABOUT SHIPPING PARTICULAR WITHIN 48 HOURS FROM THE EXACT SHIPPING DATE.

……

Some useful information:

B/L Date: Nov 8, 20 × × S/C No. 05MHS14635

XVI. Making Bill of Exchange*

BILL OF EXCHANGE			
凭 Drawn Under	INDUSTRIAL BANK OF JAPAN LIMITED, OSAKA(1)	不可撤销信用证 Irrevocable L/C No.	S200-108 (2)
日期 Date	20××0819 (3)	支取 Payable with Interest @ (4) % 按 息 付款	
号码 No.	JSP0810 (5)	汇票金额 Exchange for US$39,000 (6)	南京 Nanjing OCT. 6, 20×× NANJING, CHINA (7)
	见票 at ---- (8)	日后（本汇票之副本未付）付交 sight of this FIRST of Exchange (Second of Exchange	
Being unpaid) Pay to the order of	BANK OF CHINA, NANJING BRANCH (9)		
金额 The Sum of	SAY U.S. DOLLARS THIRTY NINE THOUSAND ONLY (10)		
此致 To	INDUSTRIAL BANK OF JAPAN LIMITED, OSAKA (11)	WONDER INTERNATIONAL COMPANY LIMITED (12) ×××（签名）	

Definition

Bill of exchange, also called draft or bill, is a written order for payment of money. Under sight L/C, it is addressed by the drawer, which is the exporter, to the drawee, which is the issuing bank, requiring the drawee to pay on demand a certain amount of money to the payee, usually his negotiating bank.

The relationship among these parties concerned in a bill of exchange may be described as a triangle.

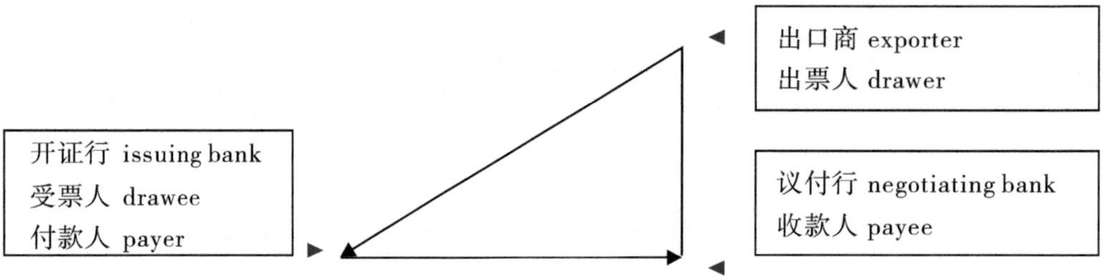

A typical bill of exchange usually contains

1. Drawing under 出票依据

   Under L/C, it consists of three aspects: the name of the opening bank, the number of the L/C and the date of issue.

   Under collection, contract No. and specific goods should be indicated in the place of the name of the opening bank. Examples:

Drawn under Contract No. LK - 4855 - 43

Covering 500 cartons of garments shipped from Xingang to Hong Kong under Contract No. XG155D

2. Number of L/C 信用证号码

It can be located in the letter of credit.

3. Date of L/C 信用证开证日期

It is the issue date of the credit.

4. Interest Rate 年息

It is usually filled in by the bank to clear the interest between the bank and the enterprise.

5. Number of Draft 汇票号码

Invoice number is used here for the convenience of checking.

6. Amount of the Draft 汇票金额

It should be the same as the amount in the invoice.

7. Date and Place of Issue 出票日期和出票地点

It is the date when beneficiary presents the draft as well as all other documents to the bank for negotiation. It is usually filled in by the negotiating bank.

8. Tenor 付款期限

If it is a sight draft, the mark of " ×××× " or " - - - - " should be filled in. It then means "at sight".

If it is a time draft, one of the following ways should be used to specify the actual days:

At ×××× days after date

At ×××× days after sight

At ×××× days after date of B/L

9. Payee 收款人

It is named by the drawer. Usually it should be the negotiating bank according to the L/C or collecting bank or even the drawer itself on collection basis. One of the following ways should be used to indicate the payee directly or indirectly:

PAY ××× ONLY 限制性抬头 This kind of draft can not be negotiable.

PAY TO THE ORDER OF ××× or PAY TO ××× OR ORDER 指示性抬头 This kind of bill can be negotiable after endorsement.

PAY BEARER 来人抬头 This kind of draft is negotiable only by holding out but without endorsement.

10. Amount in Words 金额大写

It should be in accordance with the figure amount of the draft, bearing the expression of "Say...Only" with the type of currency usually preceding the amount in words.

11. Drawee 受票人，付款人

Drawee is the payer of the draft. Under L/C, it is the issuing bank or a bank designated by it.

12. Signature of the Drawer 出票人及签章

Under L/C, it should be the beneficiary and the signature of the person in charge. On collection basis, the drawer is the principal.

Exercises

Make out the relevant Draft with the following information from the L/C.

Application Header 0 700 1411 050523 HSBCHKHHDHKH 0760 552387 050523 1411 N
* FIRST BANK OF KOREA, SOUEL
* SOUEL, KOREA

Doc. Credit Number	*20	:	M0756510NS0023000
Date of issue	31C	:	SEPT. 08, 20××
Expiry	*31D	:	DATE NOV. 30, 20×× PLACE CHINA
Beneficiary	*59	:	HUAYUE MEDICINE & HEALTH PRODUCTS IMP. AND EXP. CORP. 196 TIANHE ROAD, GUANGZHOU, CHINA
Amount	*32B	:	CURRENCY USD AMOUNT 45, 600. 00
Available with/by	*41D	:	ANY BANK BY NEGOTIATION
Drafts at...	42C	:	AT SIGHT FOR FULL INVOICE OF GOODS
Drawee	42D	:	ISSUING BANK
Latest Date of Ship	44C	:	NOV. 15, 20××
Descript. of Goods	45A	:	

CINNAMON WHOLE 8. 64MT @ USD2, 250. 00/MT AS PER INDENT NO. 57152
CINNAMON BROKEN 12 MT @ USD2, 180. 00/MT AS PER INDENT NO. 57151
C AND F INCHON

Some useful information:

Invoice No.: 05327MK72 Date of B/L: Nov. 8, 20××

Negotiating bank: China Construction Bank, Guangzhou

XVII. Claim and Settlement*

JAE & SONS PAPERS COMPANY

203 HILTON HOTEL 8 - 8, UMEDA 1 - CHOME, KITA - KU, OSAKA, JAPAN

Tel: 81 - 6 - 2256 × × × × Fax: 81 - 6 - 2256 × × × ×

Email: purchase@jaeandsons.com

Oct. 16, 20 × ×

Mr. Wonder Li
WONDER INTERNATIONAL COMPANY LIMITED
NO. 529, QIJIANG ROAD, HEDONG DISTRICT, NANJING, CHINA

Re: CONTRACT NO. ST05 - 016 FOR 100MT UNBLEACHED KRAFT LINERBOARD

Dear Mr. Li,

Thank you for your shipping the captioned goods, 200 wooden cases of which arrived at Osaka port on Oct. 14.

However, *on inspection*, we found at the *terminal* that eight out of 200 wooden cases had *distorted* and the contents, totaling 4MT, were *irretrievably* wet. We then *proceeded* to have a *survey report* made. The report, which you can see in the *enclosure*, has confirmed our *initial findings*. *On the strength of* the survey report, we *have no choice but to lodge our claim* against you for the total amount of USD1, 600 as follows:

Four MT of unbleached kraft linerboard in eight wooden cases unusable and useless at USD1, 560

Survey charges at USD40

Total claimed USD1, 600

Either a check or remittance from your side in full and final *settlement* of the above claim should be urgently needed.

We trust that this unfortunate *happening* will not *adversely* affect our further trade ties.

Yours faithfully,

Jae Smith

Jae Smith
Manager of the purchase department

WONDER INTERNATIONAL COMPANY LIMITED

NO. 529, QIJIANG ROAD,
HEDONG DISTRICT,
NANJING, CHINA
Tel: 86 - 25 - 8825 × × × ×
Fax: 86 - 25 - 8825 × × × ×
E-mail: sales@ wonder. com. cn

Oct. 16, 20 × ×

Mr. Jae Smith
JAE & SONS PAPERS COMPANY
203 HILTON HOTEL 8 - 8, UMEDA 1 - CHOME, KITA - KU, OSAKA, JAPAN

Subject: Wet Contents of 4MT Unbleached Kraft Linerboard under S/C ST05 - 016

Dear Mr. Smith,

Thank you for your letter of today with a claim for wet contents of 4MT unbleached kraft linerboard in eight wooden cases.

It is to our firm belief that this unpleasant event happened during sea transit. The Certificate of Quality issued by *CIQ* indicated that the goods were in perfect condition *prior to* departure. Instead of us, your claim for USD1, 600 should be registered against the insurance company. The goods were fully insured under our standard *policy* with the People's Insurance (Property) Company of China.

However, it would be our pleasure to help you *urge* on our side the insurance company to attend to your matter quickly. Their *agent* in Osaka will probably call on you to check the consignment. Please send us promptly more information including a complete *inventory* of the *dampened* cases if you do need us to *facilitate* your claim *at our end*.

Though PICC *enjoys a high prestige*, your claim shall be *submitted* to its Osaka agent as promptly as possible. We would like to *draw your attention to* the time limit *in terms of* settlement. The cover is limited to 60 days upon *discharge* of the insured goods from *seagoing vessel* at the final port of discharge before the insured goods reach the consignee's *warehouse*.

We are sorry about the *inconvenience* caused.

Yours faithfully,
WONDER INTERNATIONAL COMPANY LIMITED

Wonder Li

Wonder Li
Manager of the Sales Department

Notes

① ***on inspection*** 经过检查，经过检验 upon examining, after the act of checking

e. g. 货物到达我方港口，我方立即重新检验了货物。

Re-inspection was made to the goods upon their arrival at our port.

② ***terminal*** *n.* 码头 either end of a transportation line, a terminus

③ ***distort*** *v.* 变形 to alter in shape, to twist

④ ***irretrievably*** *adv.* 无法挽回地，不能复原地 difficult or impossible to recover

⑤ ***proceed*** *v.* 继续下去，进行 to go forward

⑥ ***survey report*** 检验报告，调查报告 an investigation account presented in detail

⑦ ***enclosure*** *n.* 附件 an attachment

⑧ ***initial findings*** 最初的检验结果 sth. that has been found at the beginning

⑨ ***on the strength of*** 凭借，依据 according to, in reliance upon

⑩ ***have no choice but to*** 别无他法，只好，不得不 have to

⑪ ***lodge a claim*** 提出索赔 to raise a demand for something as rightful

因某事向某人提出索赔

to lodge/register/file a claim against sb. for sth.

e. g. 在保险范围内，被保险人或其权益转让人有权就受损货物向保险公司索赔。

The insured or its endorsed person is entitled to lodge a claim against the insurer for the damaged goods under coverage.

⑫ ***settlement*** 解决，清偿 conclusion, agreement, payment

in full settlement of sth. 偿还全部债务

full and final 押头韵修辞法（alliteration），类似的表达有：

bread and butter, by and between, rest and relax, safe and sound, strain and stress

⑬ ***happening*** *n.* 意外发生的事 something that takes place, an occurrence

⑭ ***adversely*** *adv.* 负面地，逆向地 unfavorably, in an opposite way

⑮ ***CIQ*** 中国出入境检验检疫局 China Inspection and Quarantine

⑯ ***prior to*** 在……以前 preceding, before

⑰ ***policy*** *n.* 保险单，保险契约 a written contract or certificate of insurance

⑱ ***urge sb. to do sth.*** *v.* 催促 to press sb. for sth., to push

⑲ ***agent*** *n.* 代理商 one empowered to act for or represent another

⑳ ***inventory*** *n.* 详细目录，货物清单 a detailed list

㉑ ***dampened*** 潮湿的 moisture-bearing, wet

㉒ ***facilitate*** *v.* 使便利 to make easy

㉓ ***at our end*** 我方 on our side

㉔ ***enjoy a high prestige*** 享有极佳的声誉 have a high standing among others

㉕ ***submit*** *v.* 呈交，提交 to present sth. to sb. or an organization

㉖ ***draw sb.'s attention to*** 提请某人注意某事 to direct one's interest to sth.

㉗ ***in terms of*** 在……方面 in the respect of
㉘ ***discharge*** *n.* & *v.* 卸货 unloading cargo from a vessel
㉙ ***seagoing vessel*** 远洋船舶 steamer sailing on the sea
㉚ ***warehouse*** *n.* 仓库 a place in which goods or merchandise are stored, a storehouse
㉛ ***inconvenience*** *n.* 不便 the quality of being not favorable to one's comfort

Exercises

1. Translate the following expressions into English.

检验报告	寄售货物	仓至仓条款
短交	购货合同	发货人

2. Translate the following sentences about claim into English.

1）到货中有破包 20 个，对此我们将向你方提出索赔。(burst, lodge a claim)
2）我们特此向你方提出金额为 1000 美元的索赔。(file a claim against sb. for...)
3）我们以上海检验检疫局的检验报告为依据，向你方提出索赔。(claim...on strength of...)
4）由顺风轮装来的化肥短重 3,000 千克，我们向你方提出索赔。
(lodge a claim against sb. for a short weight of...)
5）这批货估计短重 800 千克，但我们还在等待检验报告。(short weight, estimate, survey report)
6）按照合同规定办事，买方有权退货并提出索赔。(on strength of, file a claim)

3. Translate the following letter into Chinese.

Dear Sirs,

Thank you for your letter of 26 May regarding your order No. 645.

We are sorry to learn that there was a mix-up in your order. We are now sending the consignment to you by air freight. It should be with you within a week.

The necessary documents will be sent under separate cover.

Please hold the goods which were wrongly shipped for collection.

We offer our sincere apologies for the delay. Should you have any further problems, please do not hesitate to contact us immediately.

Yours faithfully,

4. Translate the following letter into English.

先生：

有关上周发运的第 556 号订单的来信收悉。

对于货物在运送途中破损的事宜，本公司感到遗憾。本公司一向特别小心包装货物，然而不当的运输方法亦会引致损坏。

本公司将按照贵公司开列的破损货物清单更换新货，不日将运抵贵处。

已就有关损失向保险公司索偿，烦请保留破损货物供保险公司检查。

不便之处，敬希见谅。

谨上

Business Letter Writing Stylistics 商务函电修辞技巧（II）

2.3 汉语注重尾重，英语注重头重

·尾重句——要是没有结尾的字词，意义就不完整的正式文句。

Despite heavy winds and nearly impenetrable ground fog, the plane landed safely.

→The plane landed safely, despite heavy winds and nearly impenetrable ground fog.

·尾重句（periodic sentence）：主句或谓语在句末的句子。A sentence in which the main clause or its predicate is withheld until the end. It requires us to hold all meanings in mind simultaneously until enlightenment comes at the end. A loose sentence, in which the main clause comes first, makes things easy for the reader, as it does not require the reader to hold in mind everything before the end finally comes.

Despite our dispute on the terms and conditions of the contract, business has been finalized.

→Business has been *concluded* in spite of our dispute on the terms and conditions of the contract.

（1）本公司在广州市东风东路153号设有办事处。

Our company *operates a branch office* at 153, Dongfeng Rd. East, Guangzhou.

（2）双方详细讨论交易合同细节的时候已经到了。

The time has come when two sides come together to discuss in details the terms and conditions of the contract.

（3）请在合同规定的装船期前30天开出相关信用证。

Please open the relative L/C 30 days before the stipulated time of delivery.

（4）收到信用证后30天内我方会发货。

Shipment will be made within 30 days after receipt of your L/C.

（5）货物会在5—7月期间分三个批次均等地装运。

Goods will be delivered in three equal lots during May to July.

（6）该货轮将于1月10日上午8点离开中国南京，预计3月2日抵达美国纽约。

The ship will leave Nanjing, China, at eight o'clock a.m. on the morning of January 10 and is estimated to arrive in New York, USA, on March 2.

2.4 汉语不一定有主语，英语主语则必不可少

（1）承你方订货，实感荣幸，并祝你们一切顺利。

It is certainly a pleasure to have this order from you and we wish you success in everything under the sun.

(2) 由于野蛮装货，弄坏了两箱货。

It was found that due to rough handling at the port of loading, two cartons of goods were severely damaged.

(3) 请给我方寄来样本和价目单。

Would you please send us some samples and your price list?

(4) 希望建立平等、互利、互通有无的业务联系。

It is hoped that we can build up equal trade relations to our mutual benefit on the basis of exchanging needed goods.

It is our hope to establish the business relations of equality, mutual benefit and exchanging needed goods.

(5) 须立即交货。

Immediate delivery would be required.

(6) 期盼早日订货。

We are looking forward to receiving your order as soon as possible.

(7) 盼佳音。

We are looking forward to your favorable reply.

2.5 汉语用有生命词语作主语，英语则爱用无生命物作主语

(1) 我们这个时候要各让一步才能达成交易。

Now is the time to meet each other half way so as to have the business finalized.

(2) 近几年，我公司在东南亚的业务快速发展起来。

The recent years has witnessed a quick development of our company in the region of Southeast Asia.

(3) 由于直达船稀少，我们将分三批装运。

Shipment will be made in three equal lots due to the fact that direct steamers from our port to your port are few and far between.

(4) 我们很抱歉无法在半个月内发货。

It is regrettable that we are not in a position to dispatch the goods within half a month.

It is regrettable that goods cannot be shipped within half a month.

(5) 我方对你方目录中的最新产品感兴趣。

The latest product described in your catalogue is of interest to us.

(6) 我们希望通过折中把这笔交易做成。

It is our hope that we might conclude the business by meeting each other half way.

It is hoped that this transaction will be concluded by meeting each other half way.

(7) 本公司去年出口额达 1,000 万美元，成为了本行业的领先企业。

The total export of US $10,000,000 last year has earned the company a leading position in this line.

(8) 本公司开发了一个新型号，扩大了市场份额。

The newly-developed product saw us getting a bigger market share.

(9) 你方延误开证，会给我们带来不便。

Any delay in the establishment of L/C will involve us in inconvenience.

(10) 我们已经在价格上作了减让。

Efforts have been made to get the price down to this level.

(11) 我方提请你方尽早就上述货物开立以我方为受益人的信用证。

It is understood that a letter of credit in our favor covering the above-mentioned goods will be established promptly.

3. 函电写作达至正式语体的技巧

3.1 使用物称作主语可以增强文章的正式程度

(1) It was found that through an oversight, two cases of the goods were short shipped to you.

(2) It is certainly a pleasure to have this order from you and we wish you the best of success in your sales promotion of the goods.

3.2 将主动语态转换成被动语态，可使行文显得更正式，让人更加信服

(1) Every single one of our products is made from 100% natural ingredients.

(2) You can be assured that shipment will be made before the end of this month.

3.3 名词化结构用在比较正式的函电中，使叙述更加客观

(1) My suggestion is a reduction of 5%.

(2) Our business network is undergoing extension.

(3) Please give us your recommendation of a reliable item.

Drill (II) 实训操作

训练要求：

1. 根据所给的合同、信用证与补充资料写出双方所往来的函电（共13个），如下图所示。
2. 根据所给的合同、信用证与补充资料制作出卖方履行合同所必备的9份单据，如下图所示。
3. 往来的空白信笺和空白单据请见电子文本附件：

函电1—2：建立业务关系	单据1：商业发票
函电3—4：询盘、发盘	单据2：装箱单
函电5—6：还盘、再还盘	单据3：普惠制原产地证
函电7—8：下订单、寄送合同	单据4：报检单
函电9—10：催开信用证、信用证开出信	单据5：保险单
函电11—12：要求改证、催促装运	单据6：报关单
函电13：装运通知书	单据7：海运提单
	单据8：受益人证明
	单据9：汇票

卖方公司：

The Seller：GUANGDONG TEAPOT TRADING COMPANY

Address：JINMAO BUILDING 35－39，HUANSHI ROAD 7，

GUANGZHOU，CHINA

买方公司：

The Buyer：SMITHS BROTHERS VANCOUVER

Address：76 MALL STREET，VANCOUVER，CANADA

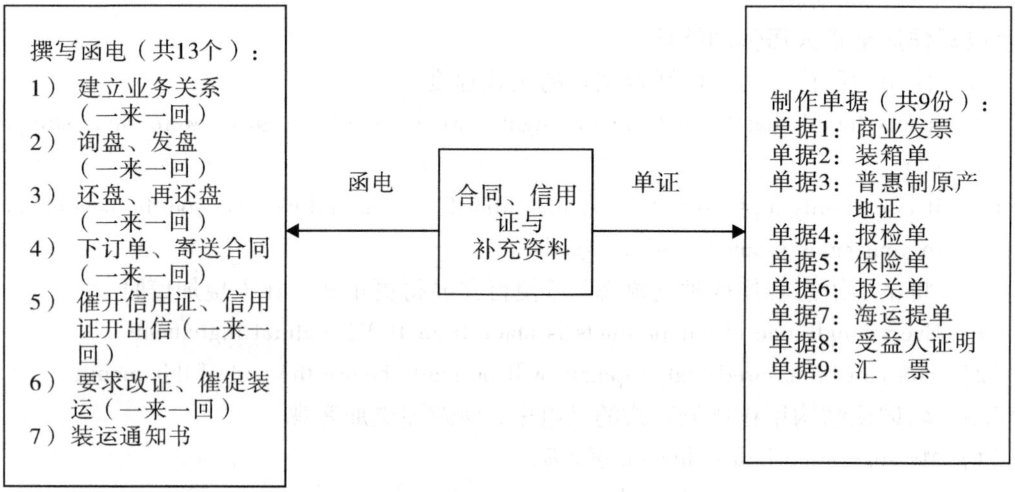

销 售 确 认 书

SALES CONFIRMATION

合同号码 S/C No. ：90815KM 200

签约日期 Date：20××－1－05

签约地点 Signed At：GUANGZHOU

卖方 The Seller：GUANGDONG TEAPOT TRADING COMPANY

地址 Address：JINMAO BUILDING 35－39，HUANSHI ROAD 7，

GUANGZHOU，CHINA

买方 The Buyer：SMITHS BROTHERS VANCOUVER

地址 Address：76 MALL STREET，VANCOUVER，CANADA

买卖双方同意成交下列商品订立条款如下：

The sellers and Buyers have agreed to close the following transactions：

1. 商品名称 COMMODITY	2. 数量 QTY	3. 单位 UNIT	4. 单价 PRICE	5. 总值 AMOUNT
PURPLE CLAY TEAPOT	20000	PCS	USD1.40	USD28,000.00
CERAMIC TEAPOT	12000	PCS	USD1.00	USD12,000.00
CIF VANCOUVER USD40,000.00				

With 5% more or less both in amount and quantity at the sellers option.
（数量及总值有 5 %的增减，由卖方决定）
6. 包装
Packing：EACH PC IS WRAPPED IN ONE BOX
100 BOXES ARE PACKED IN EACH CARTON
TOTAL：320 CARTONS
7. 装运期限
Time of shipment：IN JULY 20 × ×
8. 装运口岸和目的港
Loading Port and Destination Port：GUANGZHOU, CHINA TO VANCOUVER, CANADA
9. 分批装运和转船
Partial Shipment and Transshipment：ALLOWED
10. 支付条款
Terms of Payment：BY IRREVOCABLE LETTER OF CREDIT PAYABLE BY DRAFT AT SIGHT. THE RELEVANT L/C SHOULD BE OPENED AND REACH THE SELLER 30 DAYS BEFORE THE MONTH OF SHIPMENT, AND VALID FOR NEGOTIATION IN GUANGZHOU, CHINA TILL THE 15TH DAY AFTER THE LATEST DATE OF SHIPMENT.
11. 保险条款
Insurance：TO BE COVERED BY THE SELLER FOR 110% OF TOTAL INVOICE VALUE AGAINST W. A. AND SRCC SUBJECT TO THE OCEAN MARINE CARGO CLAUSES OF THE PEOPLE'S INSURANCE (PROPERTY) COMPANY OF CHINA, DATED 1/1/1981.
12. 运输标记
Shipping Mark：AS PER SELLER'S OPTION
THE SELLERS THE BUYERS

Some useful information：
Invoice No.：09C8K420897 Invoice Date：JUL. 1, 20 × × Packing List No.：66954PK32
G. W.：22. 6KGS/CTN N. W.：20. 4KGS/CTN M.：15. 44M^3
H. S. Code：6912001000

Issuing Bank：BANK OF VANCOUVER		
Sequence of Total：	*27	1/1
Form of Doc. Credit	*40 A	IRREVOCABLE
Doc. Credit Number	*20	BOV10382556
Date of Issue	31 C	× ×0523
Expiry	*31 D	DATE × ×0815 PLACE CHINA
Applicant	*50	SMITHS BROTHERS VANCOUVER 76 MALL STREET, VANCOUVER, CANADA
Beneficiary	*59	GUANGDONG TEAPOT TRADING COMPANY JINMAO BUILDING 35－39, HUANSHI ROAD 7,

		GUANGZHOU CHINA
Amount	*32B	CURRENCY USD AMOUNT 40,000.00
Pos. / Neg. Tol.	39A	05 / 05
Available with/by	*41A	ANY BANK BY NEGOTIATION
Drafts at…	42 C	SIGHT FOR FULL INVOICE OF GOODS
Drawee	42 A	ISSUING BANK
Partial Shipments	43 P	ALLOWED
Transshipment	43 T	ALLOWED
Loading in Charge	44 A	ANY PORT IN CHINA
For Transport to…	44 B	VANCOUVER, CANADA
Latest Date of Ship.	44 C	××0731
Descript. Of Goods	45 A :	

CIF VANCOUVER, CANADA

1) 20,000 PCS OF PURPLE CLAY TEAPOT AT USD1.40/PC
AS PER CONTRACT NO: 90815KM 200

2) 12,000 PCS OF CERAMIC TEAPOT AT USD1.00/PC
AS PER CONTRACT NO: 90815KM 200

Documents Required 46A :

+ SIGNED COMMERCIAL INVOICE IN TRIPLICATE CONSIGNED TO SMITHS BROTHERS VANCOUVER, CANADA
+ PACKING LIST IN TRIPLICATE SHOWING NET WEIGHT, GROSS WEIGHT AND MEASUREMENT PER PACKAGE.
+ FULL SET OF CLEAN ON BOARD OCEAN BILLS OF LADING MADE OUT TO ORDER, BLANK ENDORSED, MARKED FREIGHT PREPAID AND NOTIFY APPLICANT WITH FULL ADDRESS.
+ INSURANCE POLICY OR CERTIFICATE BLANK ENDORSED FOR FULL 110 PERCENT INVOICE VALUE COVERING W. A. AND SRCC INCLUDING W/W CLAUSE AS PER OMCC OF PICC DATED 1/1/1981. CLAIMS, IF ANY, WILL BE PAYABLE AT DESTINATION IN CURRENCY OF DRAFT.
+ GSP CERTIFICATE OF ORIGIN FORM A
+ BENEFICIARY'S CERTIFICATE CERTIFYING THAT ONE SET OF SHIPPING DOCUMENTS HAS BEEN FAXED TO APPLICANT WITHIN 1 DAY AFTER SHIPMENT.
+ SHIPPING ADVICE BY BENEFICIARY TO APPLICANT ON OR BEFORE B/L ON BOARD DATE CONTAINING ADVICE OF ESTIMATED TIME OF DEPARTURE, ESTIMATED TIME OF ARRIVAL, B/L NO., ETC.

Details of Charges 71B : ALL CHARGES OUTSIDE COUNTRY OF ISSUE FOR ACCOUNT OF BENEFICIARY/EXPORTER

Module 3

Business Correspondence and Documents under L/C & D/P + CIF

Learning Objectives

Following are the goals for this module. Read them and consider your personal goals.

1. To learn writing business emails in casual and informal style.
2. To know the transaction flow under L/C & D/P + CIF.
3. To know the application for L/C and the notification of L/C.
4. To know the booking of shipping space before issuance of B/L.
5. To know the application of Generalized System of Preferences Certificate of Origin Form A.
6. To know the verification of Foreign Currencies' Flow.
7. To consolidate the understanding and making of documents.

Case Study of Transaction under L/C & D/P + CIF

A business of cotton towels had been concluded between a Chinese company, called Shanghai Lanxing Co., Ltd. and a Canadian company, named West Agent Company in Toronto. They exchanged business letters before they finally reached an agreement. Most prominent in this transaction is the requirement of payment, i. e. half by L/C, and another half by D/P. Two bills of exchange are needed for each payment method. A full set of documents follows the draft under D/P, while credit is a clean L/C without any thing following, a difference from documentary L/C, which calls for documents attached. In addition to strengthening correspondence-writing and documents making, students can follow the detailed routes of applying for credit, booking shipping space, application of insurance coverage, application of GSP Certificate of Origin Form A, and the verification of Foreign Currencies' Flow. Drill and exercises in certain respects are also available.

D/P is one of the payment methods. It is the abbreviation of documents against payment. D/P is a term of payment arrangement in which an exporter entrusts the ownership documents of the consignment of goods to his/her bank, which then presents them to an importer only after the bank has received payment for the goods. Essentially, the bank holds hostage the ownership of documents, which the importer needs to take possession of the merchandise, until the bank, and, by extension, the exporter, are paid. A risk for the exporter is the possibility that the importer will refuse to pay, and, while he/she will not be able to take possession of the merchandise. The terms of this agreement are set between the importer and exporter at the time of the sale. Under D/P, the exporter is to ship the goods ordered and deliver the relevant shipping documents to the buyer abroad through the remitting bank and the collection bank with instructions not to release the documents to the buyer until the full payment is effected.

Noteworthy of this case is the use of both documentary D/P and clean L/C. Documentary D/P calls for actual payment against transfer of shipping documents. Clean L/C calls for actual payment against nothing but the draft.

I. Exchanging Business Letters or Emails*

1. **Outgoing Email** (1)

July 20

Dear Sir or Madam,

We learned from the internet that you import various kinds of Chinese Silk Scarves.

We specialize in exporting Chinese Silk Scarves. Our items are excellent in quality and fashionable in design. Large amount of business has been concluded with our American customers. Besides, there is one more attractive advantage of our silk products that is our very competitive price because of our cheap cost of labor here in China.

Enclosed are our latest catalogue and price-list. It is to our great interest if you could have substantial business connections with us.

We are looking forward to a productive trade relation with you.

2. **Incoming Email** (1)

July 21

YR 20th EMAIL RECEIVED, INTERESTED IN SPECIFICATIONS 10" ×10", 20" ×20" AND 30" × 30". PLS OFFER MOST FAVOURABLE PRICE CIF TORONTO, OCT. SHIPMENT. SMPLS APPRECIATED.

3. **Outgoing Email** (2)

July 22

RECEIVED YR EMAIL 21ST, CHINESE SILK SCARVES, QUOTE AS FOLLOWS:

CIF TORONTO

10" ×10"	USD2 per DOZ
20" ×20"	USD3 per DOZ
30" ×30"	USD5 per DOZ

SAMPLES TO BE SENT BY COURIER.

OCT. SHIPMENT, SUBJECT TO OUR FINAL CONFIRMATION.

T/T PAYMENT BEFORE SHIPMENT REQUIRED.

4. **Incoming Email** (2)

July 25

RE: CHINESE SILK SCARVES

TKS FR UR OFFER AS WELL AS SMPLS OF THE SUBJECT GDS. ON EXAMG, UNIT PRICE TOO HIGH. MUST REDUCE $ 0.5, OTHERWISE TRANSACTION HOPELESS.

10" ×10"	QUANTITY 20,000 DOZ
20" ×20"	QUANTITY 10,000 DOZ
30" ×30"	QUANTITY 25,000 DOZ

D/P PAYMENT. PROMPT CONFIRMATION APPRECIATED.

5. **Outgoing Email** (3)

July 26

RE: CHINESE SILK SCARVES

YR COUNTER-OFFER LEAVES US WITH NO PROFIT.

SPECIAL OFFER AND QUANTITIES SUPPLIABLE AS FOLLOWS:

CIF TORONTO

10" ×10"	USD1.3 per DOZ	10,000 DOZ
20" ×20"	USD2.5 per DOZ	5,000 DOZ
30" ×30"	USD4.7 per DOZ	15,000 DOZ

AS A COMPROMISE, PAYMENT 50% BY SIGHT AND IRREVOCABLE CLEAN L/C AND ANOTHER 50% BY D/P REQUIRED.

DUE TO KEEN DEMAND, PLS SEND ACCEPTANCE ASAP.

6. **Incoming Email** (3)

July 27

RE: CHINESE SILK SCARVES

WE ACCEPT YR EMAIL 26th QUOTING

CIF TORONTO

10" ×10"	USD1.3 per DOZ	10,000 DOZ
20" ×20"	USD2.5 per DOZ	5,000 DOZ
30" ×30"	USD4.7 per DOZ	15,000 DOZ

50% BY SIGHT AND IRREVOCABLE CLEAN L/C AND ANOTHER 50% BY D/P ACCEPTABLE

PLS AIRMAIL S/C ENABLING TO OPEN L/C

7. **Outgoing Email** (4)

July 29

RE：CHINESE SILK SCARVES
OUR S/C NO. SHDS03027 AIRMAILED. PLS COUNTERSIGN AND RETURN ONE COPY. PLS INSTRUCT BANK TO OPEN L/C SO AS TO ARRANGE SHIPMENT.

上海蓝星有限公司

SHANGHAI LANXING CO. , LTD.

1286 HUAIHAI ROAD, SHANGHAI, CHINA
Fax：86-21-6855 × × × × Tel：86-21-6855 × × × × Zip Code：200023

销售合同
SALES CONTRACT

卖方	SHANGHAI LANXING CO. , LTD.	编号 NO.：	SHDS03027
SELLER：	1286 HUAIHAI ROAD, SHANGHAI, CHINA	日期 DATE：	JULY 29,20 × ×
		地点 SIGNED IN：	SHANGHAI

买方 WEST AGENT COMPANY
BUYER： #362 JALAN STREET, TORONTO, CANADA

买卖双方同意以下条款达成交易：
This contract is made by and agreed between the BUYER and SELLER , in accordance with the terms and conditions stipulated below.

1. 品名及规格 **Commodity & Specification**	2. 数量 **Quantity**	3. 单价及价格条款 **Unit Price & Trade Terms**	4. 金额 **Amount（USD）**
CHINESE SILK SCARVES		**CIF TORONTO**	
10" ×10"	10,000 DOZ	USD1. 3 per DOZ	13,000. 00
20" ×20"	5,000 DOZ	USD2. 5 per DOZ	12,500. 00
30" ×30"	15,000 DOZ	USD4. 7 per DOZ	70,500. 00
Total:	**30,000 DOZ**		**USD96,000. 00**

With 5% more or less of shipment allowed at the sellers' option

SHIPING MARK W. A. C
TORONTO
C/NO. 1—300

Total Value SAY US DOLLARS NINETY SIX THOUSAND ONLY

1. PACKED IN ONE CARTON OF 100 DOZ EACH, TOTALING 300 CARTONS.
2. LOADING PORT AND DESTINATION：FROM SHANGHAI TO TORONTO
3. TIME OF SHIPMENT：NOT LATER THAN SEP. 1,20 × ×
4. PARTIAL SHIPMENT：NOT ALLOWED
5. TRANSSHIPMENT：NOT ALLOWED
6. INSURANCE：FOR AT LEAST 110 PCT OF INVOICE VALUE COVERING W. P. A. AND WAR RISKS OF PICC INCLUDING WAREHOUSE TO WAREHOUSE CLAUSE UP TO FINAL DESTINATION AT TORONTO. IF ADDITIONAL INSURANCE AMOUNT OR COVERAGE IS REQUIRED, THE BUYER MUST HAVE THE CONSENT OF THE SELLER BEFORE SHIPMENT AND THE ADDITIONAL PREMIUM IS TO BE BORNE BY THE BUYER.

7. TERMS OF PAYMENT: THE BUYER SHALL OPEN THROUGH A BANK ACCEPTABLE TO THE SELLERS AN IRREVOCABLE SIGHT L/C TO REACH THE SELLER 30 DAYS BEFORE THE MONTH OF SHIPMENT, STIPULATING THAT 50% OF THE INVOICE VALUE AGAINST CLEAN DRAFT AT SIGHT WHILE THE REMAINING 50% ON D/P AT SIGHT ON COLLECTION BASIS. THE FULL SET OF THE SHIPPING DOCUMENTS OF 100% INVOICE VALUE SHALL ACCOMPANY THE COLLECTION ITEM AND SHALL ONLY BE RELEASED AFTER FULL PAYMENT OF THE INVOICE VALUE.

8. DOCUMENTS REQUIRED:

* COMMERCIAL INVOICE 1 SIGNED ORIGINAL AND 5 COPIES

* PACKING LIST IN 2 COPIES

* FULL SET OF CLEAN ON BOARD BILL OF LADING, MADE OUT TO ORDER, MARKED "FREIGHT PREPAID" AND NOTIFY THE L/C APPLICANT

* GSP CERTIFICATE OF ORIGIN FORM A, CERTIFYING GOODS OF ORIGIN IN CHINA, ISSUED BY THE ADMINISTRATION OF EXIT AND ENTRY INSPECTION AND QUARANTINE.

* INSURANCE POLICY/CERTIFICATE COVERING W. P. A. AND WAR RISKS OF PICC INCLUDING WARWHOUSE TO WAREHOUSE CLAUSE UP TO FINAL DESTINATION AT TORONTO, FOR AT LEAST 110 PCT OF CIF-VALUE.

* SHIPPING ADVICES MUST BE SENT TO APPLICANT WITHIN 2 DAYS AFTER SHIPMENT ADVISING NUMBER OF PACKAGES, GROSS & NET WEIGHT, VESSEL NAME, BILL OF LADING NO. AND DATE, CONTRACT NO., VALUE.

* BENEFICIARY'S CERTIFICATE CERTIFYING THAT ORIGINAL C/O FORM A, COPY OF COMMERCIAL INVOICE, DETAILED PACKING LISTS AND A COPY OF BILL OF LADING WILL BE SENT DIRECT TO EXPORTER'S BANK FOR COLLECTION ON THE BASIS OF D/P WITHIN 5 DAYS AFTER SHIPMENT.

9. QUALITY/QUANTITY DISCREPANCY: IN CASE OF QUALITY OR QUANTITY DISCREPANCY, CLAIM SHOULD BE FILED BY THE BUYER WITHIN 30 DAYS AFTER THE ARRIVAL OF THE GOODS AT PORT OF DESTINATION. IT IS UNDERSTOOD THAT THE SELLER SHOULD BEAR NO LIABILITY FOR ANY DISCREPANCY DUE TO CAUSES FOR WHICH THE INSURANCE COMPANY OR SHIPPING COMPANY ARE LIABLE.

10. THE SELLER SHALL NOT BE HELD LIABLE FOR FAILURE OR DELAY IN DELIVERY DUE TO FORCE MAJEURE.

The Buyer	The Seller
WEST AGENT COMPANY	SHANGHAI LANXING CO., LTD.
Tony Stone	××× (签名)

Notes

1. ***scarf pl. scarves*** 围巾，头巾 a long piece of cloth worn about the head, neck, or shoulders
2. ***specialize in*** 专营 to pursue a special field of business, to concentrate on, to focus on, to center on
3. ***substantial*** adj. 实质性的，相当大的 actual, considerable
4. ***productive*** adj. 建设性的 yielding favorable results, constructive
5. **Informal abbreviations in Email:**

YR/UR	→YOUR	PLS	→PLEASE
SMPLS	→SAMPLES	TKS	→THANKS
FR	→FOR	GDS	→GOODS
EXAMG	→EXAMINING	ASAP	→AS SOON AS POSSIBLE

6. **Formal abbreviations:**

CIF →Cost, Insurance and Freight 成本、保险费加运费

FOB →Free on Board 装运港船上交货
CFR →Cost and Freight 成本加运费
T/T →Telegraphic Transfer 电汇
D/P →Documents against Payment 付款交单
D/A →Documents against Acceptance 承兑交单
L/C →Letter of Credit 信用证

7. **Link verbs such as "be" are largely omitted.**

YR EMAIL RECEIVED →Your Email has been received.
SAMPLS APPRCIATED →Samples would be appreciated.
→ It would be appreciated if you could send us samples.
PAYMENT REQUIRED →Payment is required.
PRICE TOO HIGH →Price is too high.
OTHERWISE TRANSACTION HOPELESS → Otherwise transaction will be hopeless.
PROMPT CONFIRMATION APPRCIATED → Prompt confirmation is appreciated.
→ It would be appreciated if you could send us your prompt confirmation.
50% BY L/C AND ANOTHER 50% BY D/P ACCEPTABLE
→ 50% payment by L/C and another 50% payment by D/P are acceptable.
OUR S/C AIRMAILED →Our S/C has been airmailed to you.

8. **Subject words are mostly omitted.**

(WE ARE) INTERESTED IN...
(WE) RECEIVED YR EMAIL

Exercises

Fill in the following subsequent emails by quoting and compromising so as to reach the consensus of the contract given below. （见表 3 – 1 销售确认书）

1. **Incoming Email** (1)

Sep. 2,20 × ×

CHINA NATIONAL NATIVE PRODUCES AND ANIMAL BY-PRODUCTS IMP. & EXP. CO.
GUAVGXI ANIMAL BRANCH
18 XINGHU ROAD, NANNING, GUANGXI, CHINA

Re: Down Filled Jacket

Dear Sir,

We learn from your advertising website that you are selling the above-mentioned goods, for which we are now in the market. We are an Italian company dealing in importing Chinese clothing. Chinese Down Filled Jackets are selling well here in San Marco, Italy.

It would be appreciated if you could give us reasonable quotations. We should be grateful as well if you could send us pictures of the goods taken from different angles showing the general features and materials in and out.

We are looking forward to receiving your offer and pictures.

Yours faithfully,
DIADORA S. P. A.
20 VIA MAZZINI, 310310 CAERANO,
SAN MARCO, ITALY

2. **Outgoing Email** (1)

Requirement: Write to answer the above email based on the followings:

1. Make an offer: Down Filled Jacket Model: 20072 at EUR28. 5/PC CIF Venice
Down Filled Jacket Model: 37408 at EUR30/PC CIF Venice
2. Send pictures of the products as enclosure and tell more about the products.
3. Shipment on November.
4. Require payment by T/T before shipment

Sep 3,20 × ×

Dear Sir:

3. **Incoming Email** (2)

Sep. 5,20 × ×

YOUR PRICES SEP. 3 ACCEPTED. AS TO PAYMENT, WE PREFER D/P. PLEASE SEND CONFIRMATION.

REGARDS.

4. **Outgoing Email** (2)

Requirement: Write to answer the above email based on the followings:

1. Decline D/P payment
2. As a compromise, suggest 70% by clean L/C and 30% by documentary D/P.
3. Request acceptance as soon as possible.

Sep. 6,20 × ×

5. **Incoming Email** (3)

Sep. 9,20 × ×

THANK YOU FOR YOUR EMAIL SEP 6. BOTH THE PRICES AND PAYMENT TERMS ARE FINALLY ACCEPTED. WE ORDER 1110 PCS OF MODEL 20072 AND ANOTHER 1110 PCS OF MODEL 37408. AS TO PACKING, WE PREFER CTNS CONTAINING 10 PCS EACH. PLEASE SEND CONTRACT.

BEST RGDS.

6. **Outgoing Email** (3)

Requirement: Write to answer the above email based on the followings:

1. S/C NO. DFJ001 has already been sent by courier.

2. Ask to countersign the contract and return one copy for file.

3. Ask to apply to the bank for opening clean L/C for 70% as down payment, i. e. EUR45,454. 50.

Sep. 10,20 × ×

表 3－1 销售确认书

<table>
<tr><td colspan="6">SALES CONFIRMATION</td></tr>
<tr><td>BUYER:</td><td colspan="3">DIADORA S. P. A.
20 VIA MAZZINI, 310310 CAERANO,
SAN MARCO, ITALY</td><td colspan="2" rowspan="2">S/C NO. : DFJ001

DATE: SEP. 10,20 × ×

SIGNED AT: NANNING, CHINA</td></tr>
<tr><td>SELLER:</td><td colspan="3">CHINA NATIONAL NATIVE PRODUCES AND ANIMAL BY-PRODUCTS IMP. & EXP. CO. GUANGXI ANIMAL BRANCH
18 XINGHU ROAD, NANNING, GUANGXI, CHINA
中国土畜产进出口公司广西畜产分公司</td></tr>
<tr><td colspan="6">This contract is made by the seller, whereby the buyer agrees to buy and the seller agrees to sell the under－mentioned commodity according to the terms and conditions stipulated below:</td></tr>
<tr><td colspan="2">Description Of Goods</td><td>Quantity</td><td>Unit</td><td>Unit Price</td><td>Amount</td></tr>
<tr><td colspan="2">
DOWN FILLED JACKET MODEL: 20072
DOWN FILLED JACKET MODEL: 37408</td><td>
1110
1110</td><td>
PC
PC</td><td>CIF VENICE
EUR 28. 50
EUR 30. 00</td><td>
EUR31,635
EUR33,300</td></tr>
<tr><td colspan="2">Total:</td><td>2220</td><td>PC</td><td></td><td>EUR64,935</td></tr>
<tr><td>Say Total:</td><td colspan="5">SAY EUROS SIXTY FOUR THOUSAND NINE HUNDRED AND THIRTY FIVE ONLY</td></tr>
<tr><td>Payment:</td><td>L/C & D/P</td><td colspan="4">70% by irrevocable clean L/C at sight, which should be opened and reach the seller before Oct. 30,20 × ×.
The rest 30% by documentary D/P on collection basis after shipment.</td></tr>
<tr><td>Packing:</td><td colspan="5">10 PCS/CTN, TOTAL: 222CARTONS</td></tr>
<tr><td>Port of Shipment:</td><td colspan="5">Nanning, China</td></tr>
<tr><td>Port of Destination:</td><td colspan="5">Venice, Italy</td></tr>
<tr><td>Shipment:</td><td colspan="5">All the goods will be shipped on or before Nov. 30,20 × × subject to clean L/C for 70% payment reaching the seller before Oct. 30, 20 × ×. Partial shipment not allowed. Transshipment at Hong Kong allowed.</td></tr>
<tr><td>Shipping Mark:</td><td colspan="5">DOWN FILLED JACKET
ITALY
C/NO. 1－222
MADE IN CHINA</td></tr>
<tr><td>Quality:</td><td colspan="5">As per sample submitted by seller</td></tr>
<tr><td>Insurance:</td><td colspan="5">The seller shall arrange marine insurance covering ICC (A) plus institute War Risks for 110% of CIF value and provide of claim, if any, payable in Venice, Italy in EUR currency.</td></tr>
<tr><td rowspan="2">Documents required:</td><td colspan="5">Full set of shipping documents must accompany the draft on collection basis:</td></tr>
<tr><td colspan="3">1. Signed Commercial Invoice
2. Packing List
3. Full set of clean on board B/L made out to order, marked "Freight Prepaid" and notify applicant
4. Certificate of Origin of China</td><td colspan="2">5. Insurance Policy
6. Shipping advice sent to the importer within 2 days after shipment.
7. Beneficiary's certificate certifying that shipping advice will be sent to the importer within 2 days after shipment.</td></tr>
<tr><td>Remarks:</td><td colspan="5">To validate, both sides are requested to sign on the two copies, one of which will be kept by each.</td></tr>
<tr><td></td><td>BUYER</td><td colspan="4">SELLER</td></tr>
<tr><td colspan="2">DIADORA S. P. A.
× × ×</td><td colspan="4">CHINA NATIONAL NATIVE PRODUCE AND ANIMAL
BY-PRODUCTS IMP. AND EXP. CO.
GUANGXI ANIMAL BRANCH
× × ×</td></tr>
<tr><td colspan="2">(Manager Signature)</td><td colspan="4">(Manager Signature)</td></tr>
</table>

II. Notification of L/C and L/C Application*

中国银行 上海市分行
Bank of China, Shanghai Branch

信用证通知书
Notification of Documentary Credit

日期：20××-08-02

NDC125879402

TO（致）： SHANGHAI LANXING CO., LTD. 1286 HUAIHAI ROAD, SHANGHAI, CHINA	WHEN CORRESPONDING PLEASE QUOTE OUR REF NO.
ISSUING BANK（开证行） CITIBANK, TORONTO	TRANSMITTED TO US THROU（转递行） REF NO.

L/C NO.（信用证号） LTR0505457	DATED（开证日期） 050801	AMOUNT（金额） USD 48,000.00	EXPIRY PLACE（有效地） China（中国）
EXPIRTY DATE(有效期) ××0930	TENOR（期限） SIGHT	CHARGE（未付费用） RMB0.00	CHARGE BY（费用承担人） BENE
RECEIVED VIA（来证方式） SWIFT	AVAILABLE（是否生效） VALID	TEST/SIGN（印押是否相符） YES	COFIRM（我行是否保兑） NO

DEAR SIRS（敬启者），
WE HAVE PLEASURE IN ADVISING YOU THAT WE HAVE RECEIVED FROM THE A/M BANK A（N）**LETTER OF CREDIT**, CONTENTS OF WHICH ARE AS PER ATTACHED SHEET（S）.
THIS ADVICE AND THE ATTACHED SHEET（S）MUST ACCOMPANY THE RELATIVE DOCUMENTS WHEN PRESENTED FOR NEGOTIATION.
兹通知贵公司，我行收自上述银行信用证一份，现随附通知。贵司交单时，请将本通知书及信用证一并提示。

REMARK 备注：
PLEASE NOTE THAT THIS ADVICE DOES NOT CONSTITUTE OUR CONFIRMATION OF THE ABOVE L/C NOR DOES IT CONVEY ANY ENGAGEMENT OR OBLIGATION ON OUR PART.
本通知书不构成我行对此信用证的保兑，也不构成我行对此信用证的任何责任和义务。
THIS L/C CONSISTS OF SHEET（S）, INCLUDING THE COVERING LETTER AND THE ATTACHEMENT（S）.
本信用证连同面函及附件共 张纸。
IF YOU FIND ANY TERMS AND CONDITIONS IN THE L/C WHICH YOU ARE UNABLE TO COMPLY WITH AND/OR ANY ERROR（S）, IT IS SUGGESTED THAT YOU CONTACT APPLICANT DIRECTLY FOR NECESSARY AMENDMENT（S）SO AS TO AVOID ANY DIFFICULTIES WHICH MAY ARISE WHEN DOCUMENTS ARE PRESENTED.
如信用证中有无法办到的条款及/或错误，请直接与开证申请人联系，进行必要的修改，以排除交单时可能发生的问题。
THIS L/C IS ADVISED SUBJECT TO ICC UCP PUBLICATION NO. 600.
本信用证之通知系遵循国际商会跟单信用证统一惯例第600号出版物办理。
对此证如有任何问题及疑惑，请与结算业务部审证科联络，电话：86-021-5562××××

YOURS FAITHFULLY,
FOR BANK OF CHINA, SHANGHAI BRANCH

ISSUE OF CLEAN LETTER OF CREDIT

ISSUING BANK	CITIBANK, TORONTO
CLEAN CREDIT NUMBER	LTR0505457
DATE OF ISSUE	××0801
EXPIRY	DATE ××0930 PLACE IN COUNTRY OF BENEFICIARY
APPLICANT	WEST AGENT COMPANY #362 JALAN STREET, TORONTO, CANADA
BENEFICIARY	SHANGHAI LANXING CO., LTD. 1286 HUAIHAI ROAD, SHANGHAI, CHINA
AMOUNT	CURRENCY USD AMOUNT 48,000.00
POS. /NEG. TOL. (%)	5/5
AVAILABLE WITH/BY	ANY BANK IN ADVISING COUNTRY BY NEGOTIATION
DRAFT AT…	DRAFTS AT SIGHT
PARTIAL SHIPMENTS	NOT ALLOWED
TRANSSHIPMENT	NOT ALLOWED
LOADING IN CHARGE	SHANGHAI
FOR TRANSPORT TO	TORONTO
SHIPMENT PERIOD	AT THE LATEST SEP. 1,20××
DESCRIPT. OF GOODS	CHINESE SILK SCARVES CIF TORONTO 10"×10" USD1.3 per DOZ 10,000 DOZ 20"×20" USD2.5 per DOZ 5,000 DOZ 30"×30" USD4.7 per DOZ 15,000 DOZ
CHARGES	ALL BANKING CHARGES OUTSIDE CANADA ARE FOR ACCOUNT OF BENEFICARY

IRREVOCABLE CLEAN CREDIT APPLICATION

TO: CITIBANK, TORONTO — Date: × ×0725

☐Issue by airmail ☐With brief advice by tele-transmission
☐Issue by express delivery
☒Issue by tele – transmission (which shall be the operative instrument)

Credit No. LTR0505457

Date and place of expiry SEP. 30,20 × × IN CHINA

Applicant
WEST AGENT COMPANY
#362 JALAN STREET, TORONTO, CANADA

Beneficiary (Full name and address)
SHANGHAI LANXING CO., LTD.
1286 HUAIHAI ROAD, SHANGHAI, CHINA

Advising Bank

Amount
USD 48,000.00
SAY U. S. DOLLARS FOURTY EIGHT THOUSAND ONLY

Partial shipments ☐allowed ☒not allowed

Transshipment ☐allowed ☒not allowed

Loading on board/dispatch/taking in charge at/from SHANGHAI
not later than SEP. 1,20 × ×
For transportation to: TORONTO, CANADA
☐FOB ☐CFR ☒CIF
☐or other terms

Credit available with ANY BANK
By
☐sight payment ☐acceptance ☒negotiation
☐deferred payment at
against the documents detailed herein
☒and beneficiary's draft (s) for 50% of invoice value at **** sight
drawn on ISSUING BANK

Documents required: (marked with X)

1. ( ) Signed commercial invoice in ____ copies indicating L/C No. and Contract No.
2. ( ) Full set of clean on board Bills of Lading made out to order and blank endorsed, marked "freight [ ] to collect / [ ] prepaid [ ] showing freight amount" notifying ____
   ( ) Airway bills/cargo receipt/copy of railway bills issued by ____ showing "freight [ ] to collect/ [ ] prepaid [ ] indicating freight amount" and consigned to ____
3. ( ) Insurance Policy/Certificate in ____ copies for ____ % of the invoice value showing claims payable in ____ currency of the draft, blank endorsed, covering All Risks, War Risks and ____.
4. ( ) Packing List/Weight Memo in ____ copies indicating quantity, gross and weights of each package.
5. ( ) Certificate of Quantity/Weight in ____ copies issued by ____.
6. ( ) Certificate of Quality in ____ copies issued by [ ] manufacturer/ [ ] public recognized surveyor ____.
7. ( ) Certificate of Origin in ____ copies.
8. ( ) Beneficiary's certified copy of fax / telex dispatched to the applicant within ____ days after shipment advising L/C No., name of vessel, date of shipment, name, quantity, weight and value of goods.

Other documents, if any

Description of goods:
CHINESE SILK SCARVES
10" ×10"
20" ×20"
30" ×30"

Additional instructions:

1. (X) All banking charges outside the opening bank are for beneficiary's account.
2. ( ) Documents must be presented within ____ days after date of issuance of the transport documents but within the validity of this credit.
3. ( ) Third party as shipper is not acceptable, Short Form/Blank back B/L is not acceptable.
4. ( ) Both quantity and credit amount ____ % more or less are allowed.
5. ( ) All documents must be sent to issuing bank by courier/speed post in one lot.
   ( ) Other terms, if any

Notes

1. The opening of an L/C can be divided into three stages: application, issuance and notification.

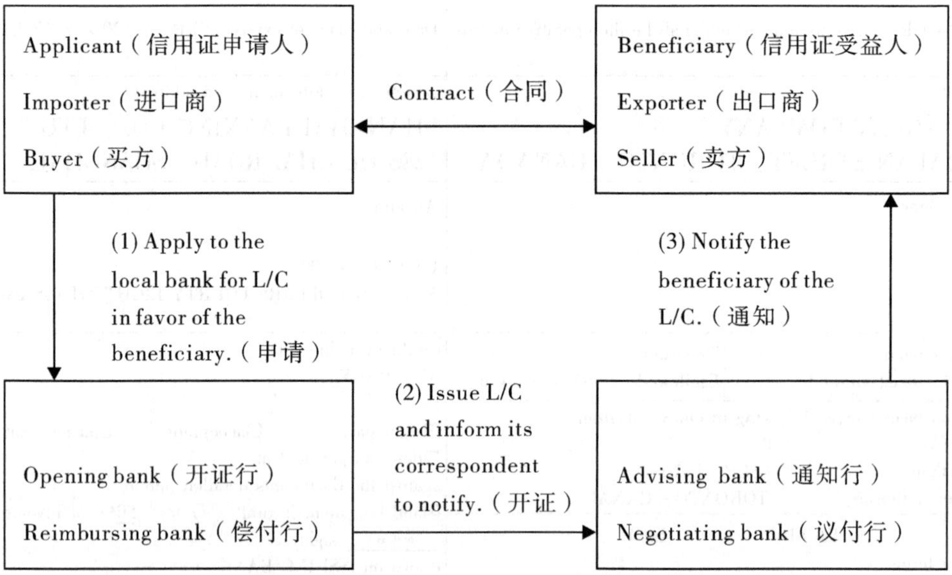

（1）The importer makes application for a letter of credit with his bank and signs the opening bank's agreement form. The opening bank approves the application and issues the actual letter of credit document.

（2）The opening bank forwards the letter of credit to the advising bank.

（3）The advising bank delivers the letter of credit to the beneficiary.

2. ***Issued by tele - transmission*** 电开信用证

3. ***negotiation*** n. 议付 the act or process of conferring to reach settlement in matters of business

After shipping the goods to the importer, the beneficiary prepares documents, if necessary, draws a draft and presents them to his bank. The beneficiary's bank negotiates the documents and pays funds to the beneficiary in accordance with the letter of credit. 出口商向买方发货后，备妥信用证规定的单据，送交当地银行议付。议付行确认单据后，按照信用证规定将垫款给受益人。

4. ***draw*** v. 提领，支取 to use or call upon a fund, to withdraw money

sth drawn on sb 以某人为付款人的，向某人支取的，要求某人付款的

a draft drawn on the issuing bank 向开证行支取款项的汇票，以开证行为付款人的汇票

5. ***against*** prep. 以……抵付；凭……换取 in return for, in compensation for, in exchange for

e. g. 光票信用证只需凭汇票付款，不需其他单据。

A clean L/C is payable against draft without other documents.

6. ***for sb' s account*** 费用由某人承担 borne by sb, paid by sb

Exercises

Correct the discrepancies in the following L/C according to the contract signed between Diadora S. P. A. and China National Native Produces and Animal By-Products Imp. and Exp. Co.. (见表 3－1 销售确认书)

: TO 0944 26 BKCHCNBJANNG01851
: FM: 1566 25VRBPIT2VAXXX32463
VRBPIT2VXXX
+BANK POLOLARE DI CAERANO
+CAERANO
: 20 DOC. CREDIT NUMBER: DLC566443132
: 31C: DATE OF ISSUE: OCT. 5,20××
: 31D: EXPIRY: DATE: DEC. 15,20××
PLACE: CHINA
: 50: APPLICANT: DIADORA S. P. A.
20 VIA MAZZINI,
310310 CAERANO, SAN MARCO, ITALY
: 59: BENEFICIARY: CHINA NATIONAL NATIVE PRODUCES AND
ANIMAL BY-PRODUCTS IMP. AND EXP. CO.
GUANGXI ANIMAL BRANCH
18 XINGHU ROAD,
NANNING, GUANGXI, CHINA
: 32B: AMOUNT: USD32, 467. 50
: 41D: AVAILABLE WITH/BY : ANY BANK
BY NEGOTIATION
: 42C: DRAFTS AT… : AT SIGHT
: 42D: DRAWEE : ISSUING BANK
: 43P: PARTIAL SHIPMENTS : NOT ALLOWED
: 47T: TRANSSHIPMENT : NOT ALLOWED
: 44A: LOADING IN CHARGE : CHINA PORT
: 44B: FOR TRANSPORT TO : VENICE, ITALY
: 44C: LATEST DATE OF SHIPMENT. : NOV. 03,20××
……
: 45B: SHIPMENT OF GOODS:
1110PCS DOWN FILLED JACKET MODEL: 20072 AT USD 28. 50/PC
1110PCS DOWN FILLED JACKET MODEL: 37408 AT USD 30. 00/PC
CIF VENICE, ITALY

III. Making Commercial Invoice

上海蓝星有限公司

SHANGHAI LANXING CO., LTD.

1286 HUAIHAI ROAD, SHANGHAI, CHINA

Fax: 86－21－6855×××× Tel: 86－21－6855×××× Zip Code: 200023

COMMERCIAL INVOICE

To: WEST AGENT COMPANY
#362 JALAN STREET, TORONTO, CANADA

Invoice No.: WAC-SL001
Invoice Date: AUG. 10, 20××
S/C No.: SHDS03027
S/C Date: JULY 29, 20××

From: SHANGHAI, CHINA **To:** TORONTO, CANADA

Marks and Numbers	Number and kind of package Description of goods	Quantity	Unit Price	Amount
				CIF TORONTO
W. A. C TORONTO C/NO. 1－300	CHINESE SILK SCARVES			
	10"×10"	10,000 DOZ	USD1.3	USD13,000.00
	20"×20"	5,000 DOZ	USD2.5	USD12,500.00
	30"×30"	15,000 DOZ	USD4.7	USD70,500.00

TOTAL: 30,000 **DOZ** **USD**96,000.00

SAY TOTAL: SAY US DOLLARS NINETY SIX THOUSAND ONLY

SHANGHAI LANXING CO., LTD.

×××（签名）

Notes

1. **Commercial Invoice**（商业发票）

The invoice functions mainly as a record of the export transaction for buyers, sellers and customs authorities. Copies of the invoice are used by the exporters, their bank, the paying bank, the receiving agents at the port of discharge, the customs in the exporting country and the importers. The importer needs it to check up whether the goods consigned to him are in compliance with the terms and conditions of the respective contract. The banks need it together with the Bill of Lading and the Insurance Certificate to effect payment. The customs need it to calculate duties, if any. The exporters and importers need it to keep their accounts. In the absence of a draft, the commercial invoice takes its place for drawing money.

2. **Pro Forma Invoice**（形式发票）

Pro forma invoice is issued in advance by the exporter for the importer to apply to their authority for import license. The importer who asks for a pro forma invoice is in fact making an enquiry, and the exporter who sends the pro forma invoice is actually making an offer. If the exporter wants to make a firm offer, he must mention the term of validity in the covering letter when sending the pro forma invoice.

3. **Requirements of invoice**（制发票要求）

There is no standard layout of invoice. However, the contents of invoice must be completed in strict conformity with the terms and conditions of the contract, as well as the terms and conditions of the L/C when payment is made by L/C. Even the slightest unconformity may involve in troubles. All invoices must be filled in correctly and truly under the stipulation of UCP 600.

Exercises

Fill in the following commercial invoice according to the contract signed between Diadora S. P. A. and China National Native Produces and Animal By-Products Imp. and Exp. CO., as well as the corrected L/C.（见表 3 – 1 销售确认书）

COMMERCIAL INVOICE

To: Invoice No.: GXAB20100001

Invoice Date:

S/C No.:

From: To:

L/C No.: Issued by: BANK POLOLARE DI CAERANO, CAERANO

Marks & Nos.	Description of Goods	Quantity	Unit Price	Amount

TOTAL:

SAY TOTAL:

IV. Making Packing List

上海蓝星有限公司

SHANGHAI LANXINGCO., LTD.

1286 HUAIHAI ROAD, SHANGHAI, CHINA

Fax: 86 − 21 − 6855 × × × × Tel: 86 − 21 − 6855 × × × × Zip Code: 200023

PACKING LIST

To: WEST AGENT COMPANY
#362 JALAN STREET, TORONTO, CANADA

Invoice No.: WAC-SL001
Invoice Date: AUG. 10, 20 × ×
S/C No.: SHDS03027
S/C Date: JULY 29, 20 × ×

From: SHANGHAI, CHINA **To:** TORONTO, CANADA

Marks and Numbers	Number and kind of package Description of goods	Quantity	Package	G. W	N. W	Meas.
	CHINESE SILK SCARVES			@2.5KGS/CTN	@2.0KGS/CTN	@0.02CBM/CTN
W. A. C	10" × 10"	10,000 DZ	100 CTNS	250KGS	200KGS	2CBMS
TORONTO	20" × 20"	5,000 DZ	50 CTNS	125KGS	100KGS	1CBM
C/No. 1-300	30" × 30"	15,000 DZ	150 CTNS	375KGS	300KGS	3CBMS
	PACKED IN ONE CARTON OF 100 DOZ EACH					
TOTAL:		30,000DZS	300CTNS	750KGS	600KGS	6CBMS

SAY TOTAL: SAY THREE HUNDRED CARTONS ONLY

SHANGHAI LANXING CO., LTD.

× × × (签名)

Notes

1. **Packing List**（装箱单）

Packing list is an independent document. It confirms the name of commodity, quantity, marks and numbers of carton, weight and measurement of the goods and other packing details. However, it doesn't need to indicate the quality and value of the goods.

2. **Weight Memo**（重量单）

As requested by the buyer, Packing List can bear another name called Weight memo, which is a document made out by the seller in foreign trade to indicate the gross weight, net weight of each package. It is used to make up the deficiency of an invoice. It is also used to facilitate the customs formalities and the general check of the goods by the consignee on their arrival at the destination.

3. **Measurement List**（尺码单）

While Weight Memo may focus on the gross weight and net weight, Measurement List, another form of packing document, may serve to concentrate on the length, the width and the height of each package, as well as the total volume of the goods. It serves to make up the deficiency of an invoice. It is also used to facilitate the customs formalities and the general check of the goods by the consignee on their arrival at the destination.

4. **Layout of the List**（装箱单据格式）

Generally speaking, there is no fixed layout of Packing List, Weight Memo, or Measurement List. Different exporters have various ways of filling in the list, but the difference in the contents is little. The contents of them show mostly no difference. On the other hand, Packing List, Weight Memo and Measurement List usually come out in a combined form.

Exercises

Fill in the following packing list according to the contract signed between Diadora S. P. A. and China National Native Produces and Animal By-Products Imp. and Exp. CO. , as well as the corrected L/C. （见表 3 - 1 销售确认书）

PACKING LIST

To: ______________ Invoice No. : ______________

Invoice Date: ______________

Marks and Numbers	Number and Kind of Packages Description of Goods	Weight (KGS)		Measurement (M^3)
		Net	Gross	
		20KGS/CTN	22KGS/CTN	1 × 0.6 × 1.2M/CTN

TOTAL: ______________

SAY TOTAL: ______________

V. Making Ordering for Shipping Space*

出口货物订舱委托书

中国外运上海公司
SINOTRANS SHANGHAI COMPANY

出口货物订舱委托书　　日期 20××年 8 月 11 日

① 发货人 **SHANGHAI LANXING CO., LTD.** 1286 **HUAIHAI ROAD, SHANGHAI, CHINA**	④ 信用证号码 **LTR**0505457	
	⑤ 开证银行 **CITIBANK, TORONTO**	
	⑥ 合同号码 **SHDS**03027	⑦ 成交金额 **USD**96,000.00
	⑧ 装运口岸 **SHANGHAI**	⑨ 目的港 **TORONTO**
② 收货人 **TO ORDER**	⑩ 转船运输 **NOT ALLOWED**	⑪ 分批装运 **NOT ALLOWED**
	⑫ 信用证有效期 20××-09-30	⑬ 装船期限 20××-09-01
	⑭ 运费 **PREPAID**	⑮ 成交条件 **CIF**
	⑯ 公司联系人×××	⑰ 电话/传真 021-6855××××
③ 通知人 **WEST AGENT COMPANY** # 362 **JALAN STREET, TORONTO, CANADA**	⑱ 公司开户行　中国银行上海分行	⑲ 银行帐号　25936514858
	⑳ 特别要求	

㉑ 标记唛码	㉒ 货号规格	㉓ 包装件数	㉔ 毛重	㉕ 净重	㉖ 数量	㉗ 单价	㉘ 总价
W. A. C **TORONTO** **C/No.** 1-300	**CHINESE** **SILK** **SCARVES**	300 **CARTONS**	750**KGS**	600**KGS**	30,000**DZ**	**USD**3.2	**USD**96,000.00

㉙ 总件数	㉚ 总毛重	㉛ 总净重	㉜ 总尺码	㉝ 总金额
300 **CARTONS**	750**KGS**	600**KGS**	6**CBMS**	**USD**96, 000. 00

㉞ 备注

集装箱货物托运单（Booking Note for Export Cargo）

中国外运上海公司

出口货物托运单

提单编号 SH556231849 | 托运日期 AUG. 11,20×× | 托运单位编号

合约编号 SHDS03027

船 名 DONGHAI V336 | 船 期 SEP. 1,20×× | 运往地点 多伦多

托运人 上海蓝星有限公司（上海××路 1286 号）

收货人 TO ORDER

通知 WEST AGENT COMPANY #362 JALAN STREET, TORONTO, CANADA

标记及号码	件数	货名	重量		尺码
			净重	毛重	
W. A. C TORONTO C/No. 1－300	300 CTNS	CHINESE SILK SCARVES	600 KGS	750 KGS	6 CBMS

合计：SAY THREE HUNDRED CARTONS ONLY 共重：SEVEN HUNDRED AND FIFTY KILOGRAMS ONLY

特约事项	

可否转船	是			（托运人盖章）	
可否分批	是	需要提单正本 3 份		副本 份	
货物堆存地点	上海	装船期限	SEP. 1,20××	结汇期限	
运费缴付方式	预付		运费账单开送	上海蓝星有限公司	
信用证号码	LTR0505457		货价	CIF USD96,000,00	
运往香港船名			实际装船日期		

运费吨： 运费率： 运费金额：USD 1000

装货单（Shipping Order）

<table>
<tr><td colspan="3">Shipper（发货人）
SHANGHAI LANXING CO. , LTD.
1286 HUAIHAI ROAD, SHANGHAI, CHINA</td><td colspan="3" rowspan="4">委托号：WAC-SL001
Forwarding agents:
Bill of Lading No. SH556231849

装货单
Shipping Order

Received by the Carrier the Total number of containers or other Packages or units stated below to be transported subject to the terms and conditions of the Carrier's regular form of B/L (for Combined Transport or Port to Port Shipment) which shall be deemed to be incorporated herein.</td></tr>
<tr><td colspan="3">Consignee（收货人）
TO ORDER</td></tr>
<tr><td colspan="3">Notify Party（通知人）
WEST AGENT COMPANY
#362 JALAN STREET, TORONTO, CANADA</td></tr>
<tr><td colspan="3">Pre-carriage by（前程运输）　Place of Receipt（收货地点）</td></tr>
<tr><td colspan="2">Ocean Vessel（船名）
DONGHAI</td><td>Voyage No.（航次）
V336</td><td colspan="2">Port of loading（装货港）
SHANGHAI</td><td>Date（日期）</td></tr>
<tr><td colspan="2">Port of Discharge（卸货港）
TORONTO</td><td>Place of Delivery（交货地点）
TORONTO</td><td colspan="3">Final Destination for the Merchant's Reference（目的地）</td></tr>
<tr><td>Container No.
（集装箱号）
SINU3622
753 (20')</td><td>Seal No.（封号）
Marks & No.（标记与号码）
W. A. C
TORONTO
C/No. 1－300</td><td>No. of Containers or Packages（箱数与件数）
300CTNS</td><td>Kind of Packages
Description of Goods
（包装种类与货名）
CHINESE SILK
SCARVES</td><td>Gross Weight（KGS）
（毛重）
750KGS</td><td>Measurement（M^3）
（尺码 M^3）
6 M^3</td></tr>
<tr><td colspan="6">Total number of containers or packages (in words) SAY THREE HUNDRED CARTONS ONLY
集装箱或件数合计（大写）</td></tr>
<tr><td colspan="6">Container No.（集装箱号）　Seal No.（封号）　Packages（件数）　Container No.（集装箱号）　Seal No.（封号）　Packages（件数）</td></tr>
<tr><td colspan="6">Received（实收）　By Terminal Clerk/Tally clerk（场站员/理货员签字）</td></tr>
<tr><td rowspan="2">Freight & Charges</td><td colspan="2">Prepaid at
（预付地点）</td><td>Freight payable at
（到付地点）</td><td colspan="2">Place of Issue（签发地电）SHANGHAI　Booking Approved by（订舱确认）</td></tr>
<tr><td colspan="2">Total Prepaid
（预付总额）</td><td>No. of Original B/L
（正本提单分数）3</td><td colspan="2">货值金额
CIF USD96,000.00</td></tr>
<tr><td colspan="2">Service Type on Receiving
×CY　CFS□　DOOR□</td><td>Service Type on Delivery
×CY　□CFS　DOOR□</td><td colspan="2">Reefer Temperature Required
（冷藏温度）</td><td>F　C</td></tr>
<tr><td>Type of Goods
（货物种类）</td><td colspan="2">× Ordinary　Reefer□　Dangerous□　Auto□
Liquid□　Live Animal□　Bulk□</td><td>危险品</td><td colspan="2">Class: Property
IMDG Code Page UN No.</td></tr>
<tr><td colspan="4">发货人或代理地址：1286 HUAIHAI ROAD, SHANGHAI, CHINA</td><td>联系人：×××（签名）</td><td>电话：*******</td></tr>
<tr><td>可否转船　否</td><td>可否分批　否</td><td>装期　SEP. 1,20××</td><td rowspan="3">备注</td><td colspan="2" rowspan="3">装箱场站名称</td></tr>
<tr><td colspan="2">有效期　SEP. 1,20××</td><td>制单日期 AUG. 12,20××</td></tr>
<tr><td colspan="3">海运费由　支付
如预付运费托收承付，请填准银行账号</td></tr>
</table>

Notes

出口托运订舱装船及报关流程

（1）出口商填制货物出口订舱委托书（Application for Export Goods），并随附商业发票、装箱单及其他必要单证，委托货运代理代为订舱，有时还委托其代理报关。

（2）货代接受委托后缮制集装箱货物托运单（Booking Note for Export Cargo），随同商业发票、装箱单及其他必要单证向船运公司办理订舱。

（3）船运公司根据托运单内容，结合舱位等条件考虑，如果接受订舱则在托运单上注明与提单一致的编号，并填上拟装货物的船名和航次，表示确认订舱，然后将与托运人有关的装货单（Shipping Order，S/O）、配舱回单等退还给托运人。

（4）托运人持船运公司签署的S/O，填制出口报关单，连同商业发票、装箱单及海关要求的其他单证报关。

（5）海关根据有关程序进行查验，如同意出口，则在S/O上加盖放行章，并将S/O退还给托运人。

（6）托运人持海关盖章的S/O要求船长装货。

（7）装货后，由船上的大副签署大副收据（Mate's Receipt，M/R），交给托运人。

（8）托运人持M/R向船公司缴纳运费。

（9）船运公司凭M/R签发正本已装船提单给托运人。

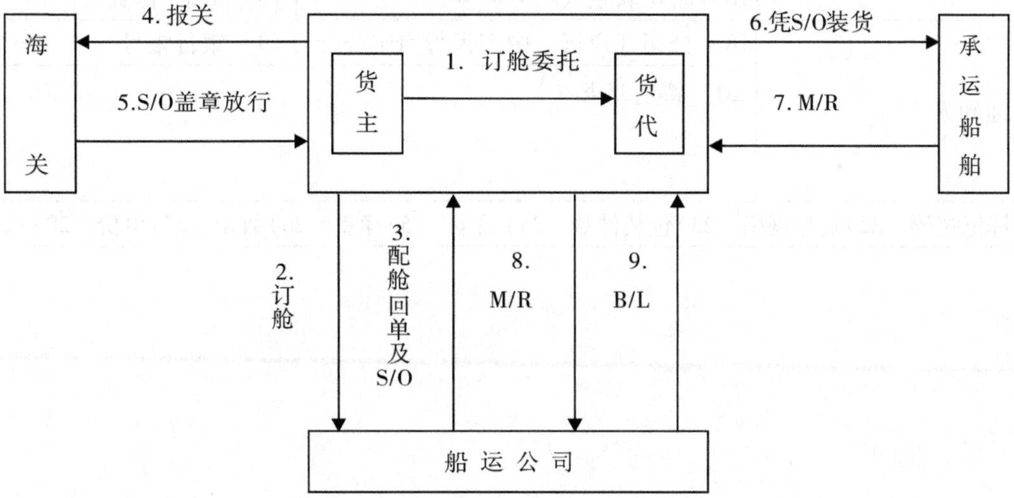

Exercises

Fill in the following booking form of shipment according to the contract signed between Diadora S. P. A. and China National Native Products and Animal By-Products Imp. and Exp. CO, as well as the corrected L/C.（见表 3－1 销售确认书）

中国外运上海公司

SINOTRANS SHANGHAI COMPANY

出 口 货 物 订 舱 委 托 书　　　　日期　　年　月　日

1）发货人	4）信用证号码	
	5）开证银行	
	6）合同号码	7）成交金额
	8）装运口岸	9）目的港
2）收货人	10）转船运输	11）分批装运
	12）信用证有效期	13）装船期限
	14）运费　PREPAID	15）成交条件
	16）公司联系人　＊＊＊	16）电话/传真 -----------
3）通知人	18）公司开户行　中国银行南宁分行	19）银行帐号 -----------
	20）特别要求	

21)标记唛码	22)货号规格	23)包装件数	24)毛重	25)净重	26)数量	27)单价	28)总价

29）总件数　30）总毛重　31）总净重　32）总尺码　33）总金额

34）备注

VI. Making Application for Insurance*

中保财产保险有限公司上海分公司

The People's Insurance (Property) Company of China Ltd.

Shanghai Branch

出口货物运输保险投保单

<table>
<tr><td>发票号码</td><td>WAC-SL001</td><td>投保条款和险别</td></tr>
<tr><td rowspan="2">被保险人</td><td>客户抬头
SHANGHAI LANXING CO., LTD.
1286 HUAIHAI ROAD, SHANGHAI, CHINA</td><td rowspan="13">(✓) PICC CLAUSE
( ) ICC CLAUSE
( ) ALL RISKS
(✓) W. P. A. /W. A.
( ) F. P. A.
(✓) WAR RISKS
( ) S. R. C. C.
( ) STRIKE
( ) ICC CLAUSE A
( ) ICC CLAUSE B
( ) ICC CLAUSE C
( ) AIR TPT ALL RISKS
( ) AIR TPT RISKS
( ) O/L TPT ALL RISKS
( ) O/L TPT RISKS
( ) TRANSSHIPMENT RISKS
( ) W TO W
( ) T. P. N. D.
( ) F. R. E. C.
( ) R. F. W. D.
( ) RISKS OF BREAKAGE
( )</td></tr>
<tr><td>过户
WEST AGENT COMPANY
#362 JALAN STREET, TORONTO, CANADA</td></tr>
<tr><td rowspan="3">保险金额</td><td>USD (105,600.00)</td></tr>
<tr><td>HKD ( )</td></tr>
<tr><td>( ) ( )</td></tr>
<tr><td>启运港</td><td>SHANGHAI</td></tr>
<tr><td>目的港</td><td>TORONTO</td></tr>
<tr><td>转内陆</td><td></td></tr>
<tr><td>开航日期</td><td>20××.9.1</td></tr>
<tr><td>船名航次</td><td>DONGHAI V336</td></tr>
<tr><td>赔款地点</td><td>CANADA</td></tr>
<tr><td>赔付币别</td><td>USD</td></tr>
<tr><td>正本份数</td><td>1份正本，1份副本</td></tr>
<tr><td>其他特别条款</td><td colspan="2">COVERING W. P. A. AND WAR RISKS INCLUDING W/W CLAUSE AS PER AND SUBJECT TO THE RELEVANT OCEAN MARINE CARGO CLAUSES OF THE PEOPLE'S INSURANCE (PROPERTY) COMPANY OF CHINA DATED 1/1, 1981</td></tr>
<tr><td colspan="3">以下由保险公司填写</td></tr>
</table>

保单号码		费率	
签单日期		保费	

投保日期： 20××年8月20日　　　　投保人签章：

中保财产保险有限公司

The People's Insurance (Property) Company of China Ltd.

Head Office: BEIJING

Established in 1949

海洋货物运输保险单
MARINE CARGO INSURANCE POLICY

发票号码
Invoice No. WAC-SL001

保险单号次
Policy No. MCIP05SH00126

被保险人:

Insured: SHANGHAI LANXING CO., LTD.
1286 HUAIHAI ROAD, SHANGHAI, CHINA

中国人民保险公司（以下简称本公司）根据被保险人的要求，及其所缴付的保险费，按照本保险单承保险别和背面所载条款与下列特别条款承保下述货物运输保险，特签发本保单。

This Policy of Insurance witnesses that The People's Insurance Company of China (hereinafter called "The Company") at the request of the "Insured" and in consideration of the agreed premium paid to the Company by the Insured undertakes to Insure the under-mentioned goods in transportation subject to the conditions of this Policy as per the Clauses printed overleaf and other special clauses attached hereon.

标记及号码 Marks & Nos.	包装数量 Quantity	保险货物项目 Description of Goods	保险金额 Amount Insured
W. A. C TORONTO C/No. 1-300	300 CARTONS	CHINESE SILK SCARVES	USD 105,600

总保险金额
Total Amount Insured: SAY U. S. DOLLARS ONE HUNDRED AND FIVE THOUSAND SIX HUNDRED ONLY

保费 Premium	费率 Rate	装载运输工具 Per conveyance S. S.
AS ARRANGED		DONGHAI V336

开航日期
Slg. on or abt SEP. 1, 20××

起运港
From SHANGHAI, CHINA

目的港
To TORONTO, CANADA

承保险别
Conditions

COVERING W. P. A. AND WAR RISKS INCLUDING W/W CLAUSE AS PER AND SUBJECT TO THE RELEVANT OCEAN MARINE CARGO CLAUSES OF THE PEOPLE'S INSURANCE (PROPERTY) COMPANY OF CHINA DATED 1/1, 1981

所保货物，如发生本保单项下可能引起索赔的损失或损坏，应立即通知本公司下述代理人勘察。如有索赔，应向本公司提交保险单正本（本保险单共有　　份正本）及有关部门文件。如一份正本已用于索赔，其余正本则自动失效。

In the event of loss or damage which may result in a claim under this Policy, immediate notice applying for Survey must be given to the Company's Agent as mentioned hereunder. Claims, if any, one of the Original Policy which has been issued in ____ Original (s) together with other relevant documents shall be surrendered to the Company. If one of the Original Policy has been accomplished, the others to be void.

赔款偿付地点
Claim payable at
TORONTO, CANADA IN USD

中保财产保险有限公司
THE PEOPLE'S INSURANCE (PROPERTY) COMPANY OF CHINA LTD.

日期
Date AUG. 25, 20××

地址
Address SHANGHAI

(Endorsement overleaf)

Notes

1. PICC CLAUSES (CIC CLAUSES 中国保险条款)

According to *People's Insurance Company of China Ocean Marine Cargo Clauses* (《中国人民保险公司海洋运输货物保险条款》), the insurance is mainly classified into two groups: Basic Insurance Coverage and Additional Insurance Coverage. The applicant can purchase Basic Insurance Coverage individually. However, before purchasing an Additional Insurance Coverage, he has to purchase a Basic Insurance Coverage.

(1) Basic Insurance Coverage (基本险) is further classified into three conditions:

Free from Particular Average (F. P. A. 平安险);

With Particular Average (W. P. A. or W. A. 水渍险);

All Risks (一切险).

The All Risks cover, in addition to the scope of W. P. A., extraneous risks, such as Shortage Risk, Intermixture and Contamination Risk, Leakage Risk, Clash and Breakage Risk, Taint of Odor Risk, Sweating and Heating Risk, Hook Damage Risk, Rust Risk, Breakage of Packing Risk, etc. In case of F. P. A. or W. P. A., one or several kinds of these extraneous risks may be covered in addition.

(2) General Additional Risks (一般附加险) complement the basic risks.

Theft, Pilferage and Non-delivery	偷窃、提货不着险 (TPND)
Rain and/or Fresh Water Damage	淡水雨淋险 (R. F. W. D)
Shortage Risk	短量险
Intermixture and Contamination Risk	混杂玷污险
Leakage Risk	渗漏险
Clash and Breakage Risk	碰撞、破碎险
Taint of Odor Risk	串味险
Sweating and Heating Risk	受潮受热险
Hook Damage Risk	钩损险
Breakage of Packing Risk	包装破损险
Rust Risk	锈损险

(3) Special Additional Risks (特殊附加险) differ from general additional risks in that the former covers loss or damage caused by some special extraneous reasons such as politics, law, regulations and war. Like general additional risks, however, special additional risks can not be used to insure goods alone either.

War Risk	战争险
Strike Risk	罢工险
On Deck Risk	舱面险
Import Duty Risk	进口关税险
Rejection Risk	拒收险

Aflatoxin Risk	黄曲霉素险
Failure to Delivery Risk	交货不到险

Fire Risk Extension Clause for Storage of Cargo at destination Hong Kong, including Kowloon and Macao

出口货物到香港（包括九龙在内）或澳门存仓火险责任扩展条款（F. R. E. C.）

2. **ICC CLAUSES**（伦敦保险协会海运货物保险条款）

The revised London Insurance Institute Cargo Clauses in 1982 include six kinds:

(1) Institute Cargo Clause A.	协会货物条款（A）
(2) Institute Cargo Clause B	协会货物条款（B）
(3) Institute Cargo Clause C	协会货物条款（C）
(4) Institute War Clause-Cargo	协会战争条款（货物）
(5) Institute Strike Clause-Cargo	协会罢工条款（货物）
(6) Malicious Damage Clause	恶意损害险条款

3. **Terms of other common risks**

Strike, Riots and Civil Commotion	罢工、暴动、民变险（S. R. C. C.）
Overland Transportation Risks	陆运险（O/L TPT RISKS）
Overland Transportation All Risks	陆运综合险（O/L TPT ALL RISKS）
Air Transportation Risks	航空运输险（AIR TPT RISKS）
Air Transportation All Risks	航空运输综合险（AIR TPT ALL RISKS）
Air Transportation War Risks	航空运输战争险（AIR TPT WAR RISKS）
Parcel Post Risks	邮包险
Parcel Post All Risks	邮包综合险
Parcel Post War Risks	邮包战争险
Warehouse to Warehouse Clause	仓至仓条款（W to W）
Transshipment Risks	转运险

Exercises

Fill in the following insurance policy according to the contract signed between Diadora S. P. A. and China National Native Products and Animal By-Products Imp. and Exp. CO, as well as the corrected L/C. （见表 3－1 销售确认书）

中保财产保险有限公司

The People's Insurance（Property）Company of China Ltd.

Head Office：BEIJING

Established in 1949

海洋货物运输保险单

MARINE CARGO INSURANCE POLICY

发票号码
Invoice No.：

保险单号次
Policy No.： GXPICC2200110033

被保险人：
Insured：

中国人民保险公司（以下简称本公司）根据被保险人的要求，及其所缴付的保险费，按照本保险单承保险别和背面所载条款与下列特别条款承保下述货物运输保险，特签发本保单.

This Policy of Insurance witnesses that The People's Insurance Company of China（hereinafter called "The Company"）at the request of the "Insured" and in consideration of the agreed premium paid to the Company by the Insured undertakes to Insure the under-mentioned goods in transportation subject to the conditions of this Policy as per the Clauses printed overleaf and other special clauses attached hereon.

标记及号码 Marks & Nos.	包装数量 Quantity	保险货物项目 Description of Goods	保险金额 Amount Insured

总保险金额
Total Amount Insured：

保费 Premium	费率 Rate	装载运输工具 Per conveyance S. S.
As Arranged		DONGFENG V668 / MARCO P777

开航日期 Slg. on or abt	起运港 From ________	目的港 To ________

承保险别
Conditions

所保货物，如发生本保单项下可能引起索赔的损失或损坏，应立即通知本公司下述代理人勘察。如有索赔，应向本公司提交保险单正本（本保险单共有　　份正本）及有关部门文件。如一份正本已用于索赔，其余正本则自动失效。

In the event of loss or damage which may result in a claim under this Policy, immediate notice applying for Survey must be given to the Company's Agent as mentioned hereunder. Claims, if any, one of the Original Policy which has been issued in ___ Original (s) together with other relevant documents shall be surrendered to the Company. If one of the Original Policy has been accomplished, the others to be void.

赔款偿付地点
Claim payable at

中保财产保险有限公司

THE PEOPLE'S INSURANCE（PROPERTY）COMPANY OF CHINA LTD.

日期
Date

地址
Address

VII. Applying for GSP Certificate of Origin Form A*

普惠制产地证明书申请书

FORM A No. 58032564941

申请人郑重声明：

本人是被正式授权代表出口单位办理和签署本申请的。

本申请书及普惠制产地证书所列内容正确无误，如发现弄虚作假，冒充证书所列货物，擅改证书，自愿接受签证机关的处罚及负法律责任。现将有关情况申报如下：

商品名称：丝绸围巾　　H. S. 税目号（十位数码）：6214100010

发票号：WAC-SL001　　商品 FOB 总值（以美元计）：USD *******

最终目的地国家/地区：加拿大　　预定自中国出口日期：20××年 9 月 1 日

包装数量：300 纸箱　　毛重或其他数量：30,000 打

拟出运日期：20××.9.1

贸易方式（划“√”）				企业性质（划“√”）			
一般贸易	来料加工	零　售	展　卖	中　资	中外合资	中外合作	外商独资
√				√			

原产地标准：

本项商品系在中国生产，完全符合给惠国给惠方案规定，其原产地情况符合以下第 1 条：

1. “P”（完全中国产，不含有任何进口成分）；
2. “W”其进口国税目号为______，进口原材料占制成品出厂价的______%。
3. “F”（对加拿大出口产品，其进口成分不超过产品出厂价值的 40%）。
4. “Y”（对俄罗斯、乌克兰、白俄罗斯、捷克及斯洛伐克出口产品，其进口成分不超过产品离岸价的 50%）

现提交中国出口商业发票副本一份，普惠制产地证明书格式 A（FORM A）一正二副以及其他附件　　份，请予审核签证。

生产单位：*******

生产单位联系人及电话：*******

进口商特殊要求或申请人备注：

申请单位：（盖章）

上海蓝星有限公司

申请人：（签名）×××

电话：*******

日期：20××年 8 月 20 日

领证人：（签名）

电话：

日期：20××年×月×日

ORIGINAL

<table>
<tr><td colspan="3">1. Goods consigned from (Exporter's business name, address, country)
SHANGHAI LANXING CO., LTD.
1286 HUAIHAI ROAD, SHANGHAI, CHINA</td><td colspan="3" rowspan="2">Reference No. 58032564941
GENERALIZED SYSTEM OF PREFERENCES
CERTIFICATE OF ORIGIN
(Combined declaration and certificate)
FORM A
Issued in THE PEOPLE'S REPUBLIC OF CHINA
(country)
See Notes overleaf</td></tr>
<tr><td colspan="3">2. Goods consigned to (Consignee's name, address, country)
WEST AGENT COMPANY
#362 JALAN STREET, TORONTO, CANADA</td></tr>
<tr><td colspan="3">3. Means of transport and route (as far as known)
SHIPMENT FROM SHANGHAI, CHINA TO TORONTO, CANADA BY VESSEL ON SEP. 1, 20 × ×</td><td colspan="3">4. For official use</td></tr>
<tr><td>5. Item number</td><td>6. Marks and numbers of packages</td><td>7. Number and kind of packages; description of goods</td><td>8. Origin criterion (see Notes overleaf)</td><td>9. Gross weight or other quantity</td><td>10. Number and date of invoices</td></tr>
<tr><td>1</td><td>W. A. C
TORONTO
C/No. 1-300</td><td>THREE HUNDRED CARTONS OF CHINESE SILK SCARVES
***************************</td><td>"P"</td><td>30,000DOZ</td><td>WAC-SL001
AUG. 10, 20 × ×</td></tr>
<tr><td colspan="3">11. Certification
It is hereby certified, on the basis of control carried out, that the declaration by the exporter is correct.

上海出入境检验检疫局
SHANGHAI ADMINISTRATION OF EXIT AND ENTRY INSPECTION AND QUARANTINE

SHANGHAI AUG. 25, 20 × × × × × (签名)

Place and date, signature and stamp of certifying authority</td><td colspan="3">12. Declaration by the exporter
The undersigned hereby declares that the above details and statements are correct, that all the goods were
produced in CHINA
(country)
and that they comply with the origin requirements specified for those goods in the Generalized System of Preferences for goods exported to
CANADA

SHANGHAI LANXING CO., LTD
SHANGHAI AUG. 20, 20 × × × × × (签名)

Place and date, signature and stamp of authorized signatory</td></tr>
</table>

Notes

1. **原产地证书的种类**

(1) 一般原产地证书（Certificate of Origin of the People's Republic of China，C/O）

(2) 普惠制原产地证（Generalized System of Preference Certificate of Origin，Form A）

(3) 欧盟纺织品产地证（European Union Certificate of Origin）

(4) 对美国出口的纺织品原产地声明书（Declaration of Country Origin）

2. **出口单据与出具机构**

单据或证书	出具机构
一般原产地证书 普惠制原产地证 检验证书 出入境货物通关单	国家出入境检验检疫局
一般原产地证书	贸易促进委员会
出口收汇核销单	外汇管理局
出口货物报关单	海关
输欧纺织品产地证	商务部
对美国出口的纺织品原产地声明书	出口商
出口退税申请单	国家税务局

Exercises

Fill in the following certificate of origin according to the contract signed between Diadora S. P. A. and China National Native Products and Animal By-Products Imp. and Exp. CO., as well as the corrected L/C.（见表 3 – 1 销售确认书）

ORIGINAL

<table>
<tr><td colspan="2">①Exporter</td><td colspan="3" rowspan="2">Certificate No.: COGX6987544

CERTIFICATE OF ORIGIN
OF
THE PEOPLE'S REPUBLIC OF CHINA</td></tr>
<tr><td colspan="2">②Consignee</td></tr>
<tr><td colspan="2">③Means of transport and route
FROM NANNING, CHINA TO VENICE, ITALY WITH TRANSSHIPMENT AT HONG KONG BY DONGFENG V668 / MARCO P777</td><td colspan="3" rowspan="2">⑤For certifying authority use only</td></tr>
<tr><td colspan="2">④Country / region of destination</td></tr>
<tr><td>⑥Marks and numbers</td><td>⑦Number and kind of packages; description of goods</td><td>⑧H. S. Code</td><td>⑨Quantity</td><td>⑩Number and date of invoices</td></tr>
<tr><td></td><td></td><td>6201931000</td><td></td><td></td></tr>
<tr><td colspan="2">⑪Declaration by the exporter
The undersigned hereby declares that the above details and statements are correct, that all the goods were produced in China and that they comply with the Rules of Origin of the People's Republic of China.</td><td colspan="3">⑫Certification
It is hereby certified that the declaration by the exporter is correct.</td></tr>
<tr><td colspan="2">Place and date, signature and stamp of authorized signatory</td><td colspan="3">Place and date, signature and stamp of certifying authority</td></tr>
</table>

VIII. Making Export Commodity Inspection Application

中华人民共和国出入境检验检疫
出境货物报检单

报检单位（加盖公章）：上海蓝星有限公司　　　　*编　　号________

报检单位登记号：……　联系人：×××　电话：021－6855××××

报检日期：20××年8月20日

发货人	（中文）上海蓝星有限公司 （外文）SHANGHAI LANXING CO.，LTD.				
收货人	（中文） （外文）WEST AGENT COMPANY				
货物名称（中/外文）	H. S. 编码	产地	数/重量	货物总值	包装种类及数量
丝绸围巾 CHINESE SILK SCARVES	6214100010	上海	30000打	USD96,000	300纸箱

运输工具名称号码	东海 V336	贸易方式	一般贸易	货物存放地点	上海
合同号	SHDS03027	信用证号	LTR0505457	用途	其他
发货日期	SEP. 1,20××	输往国家（地区）	加拿大	许可证/审批号	------------
启运地	上海	到达口岸	多伦多	生产单位注册号	------------
集装箱规格、数量及号码	1×20'（SINU3622753）				

合同、信用证订立的检验检疫条款或特殊要求	标记及号码	随附单据（划"√"或补填）	
	W. A. C TORONTO C/No. 1－300	☑合同 ☑信用证 ☑发票 ☐换证凭单 ☑装箱单 ☐厂检单	☐包装性能结果单 ☐许可/审批文件 ☐ ☐ ☐

需要证单名称（划"✓"或补填）		*检验检疫费	
✓品质证书　1 正____副 ☐重量证书　____正____副 ☐数量证书　____正____副 ☐兽医卫生证书　____正____副 ☐健康证书　____正____副 ☐卫生证书　____正____副 ☐动物卫生证书　____正____副	☐植物检疫证书　____正____副 ☐熏蒸/消毒证书　____正____副 ☐出境货物换证凭单 ✓出境通关单 ☐ ☐	总金额（人民币元）	
		计费人	
		收费人	

报检人郑重声明：	领取证单	
1. 本人被授权报检。 2. 上列填写内容正确属实，货物无伪造或冒用他人的厂名、标志、认证标志，并承担货物质量责任。	日期	
签名：×××	签名	

注：有"＊"号栏由出入境检验检疫机关填写　　　◆国家出入境检验检疫局制

Notes

1. Issuance of Inspection Certificate 检验单的签发

Inspection certificate can be issued, according to the stipulations in S/C or L/C, by CIQ, China Inspection and Quarantine or other surveyors based on the application of the exporter. The inspection certificate and the application should be clean and correct, made out carefully and can not be modified willfully. The specification, quality and quantity should comply with the requirements of the relevant contract or L/C.

2. CIF 出口业务环节单据时间安排

CIF 出口业务环节单据	履约出单时间举例
签订合同	若 20××年 6 月 6 日签订合同
落实信用证	装运前落实信用证，以信用证规定交单期、有效期是 12 月 15 日为例
备货	若备妥货物的时间为 10 月 8 日
制发票和装箱单	10 月 10 日—10 月 31 日
租船订舱	做好发票和装箱单后，10 月 31 日前确定装船日，如船期为 11 月 20 日
保险单	11 月 20 日前
申领产地证	11 月 20 日前 3 天申办一般原产地证书，前 5 天申办普惠制原产地证
报检单	11 月 20 日前 5 天报检
报关单	11 月 20 日前 3 天报关
海运提单	11 月 20 日
装船通知	11 月 21 日前
汇票	12 月 11 日前（提单日后 21 天之内，信用证到期日之前）

Exercises

Fill in the following commodity inspection application according to the contract signed between Diadora S. P. A. and China National Native Products and Animal By-Products Imp. and Exp. CO., as well as the corrected L/C.（见表 3－1 销售确认书）

出境货物报检单

报检单位（加盖公章）： *编　号________

报检单位登记号：　联系人：×××　电话：******　报检日期：　年　月　日

发货人	（中文） （外文）					
收货人	（中文） （外文）					
货物名称（中/外文）	H. S. 编码	产地	数/重量	货物总值	包装种类及数量	
运输工具名称号码		贸易方式	一般贸易	货物存放地点		
合同号		信用证号			用途	其他
发货日期		输往国家（地区）		许可证/审批号	------------	
启运地		到达口岸		生产单位注册号	------------	
集装箱规格、数量及号码	1×20'（SINU6954874）					

合同、信用证订立的检验检疫条款或特殊要求	标 记 及 号 码	随附单据（划"√"或补填）	
		☑合同 ☑信用证 ☑发票 ☐换证凭单 ☑装箱单 ☐厂检单	☐包装性能结果单 ☐许可/审批文件 ☐ ☐ ☐

需要证单名称（划"✓"或补填）				*检验检疫费	
☑品质证书 ☐重量证书 ☐数量证书 ☐兽医卫生证书 ☐健康证书 ☐卫生证书 ☐动物卫生证书	1 正 1 副 __正__副 __正__副 __正__副 __正__副 __正__副 __正__副	☐植物检疫证书 ☐熏蒸/消毒证书 ☐出境货物换证凭单 ☑出境通关单 ☐ ☐	__正__副 __正__副	总金额（人民币元）	
				计费人	
				收费人	

报检人郑重声明：	领 取 证 单	
1. 本人被授权报检。 2. 上列填写内容正确属实，货物无伪造或冒用他人的厂名、标志、认证标志，并承担货物质量责任。 签名：______	日期	
	签名	

IX. Making the Customs Declaration

中华人民共和国海关出口货物报关单

预录入编号： 海关编号：（由海关填写）

出口口岸	备案号	出口日期	申报日期
上海海关（2200）		20××-9-1	20××-8-23

经营单位	运输方式	运输工具名称	提运单号
上海蓝星有限公司（2453263212）	江海运输	东海 V336	CHNSP9021855845

发货单位	贸易方式	征免性质	结汇方式
上海蓝星有限公司（2453263212）	一般贸易	一般征税	信用证、付款交单

许可证号	运抵国（地区）	指运港	境内货源地
	加拿大	多伦多	上海

批准文号	成交方式	运费	保费	杂费
	CIF	502/1100/3	502/956/3	

合同协议号	件数	包装种类	毛重（公斤）	净重（公斤）
SHDS03027	300	纸箱	825 KGS	660 KGS

集装箱号	随附单据	生产厂家
1×20'（SINU3622753）	B	上海丝绸×厂

标记唛码及备注 随附单证号：出口货物通关单（4126423554）
W. A. C
TORONTO
C/No. 1-300

项号	商品编号	商品名称、规格型号	数量及单位	最终目的国（地区）	单价	总价	币制	征免
1	6214100010	丝绸围巾 CHINESE SILK SCARVES	30,000 打	加拿大	3.2	96,000	美元	照章

税费征收情况

合计总价：

录入员 录入单位 *** 上海××报关行	兹声明以上申报无讹并承担法律责任	海关审单批注及放行日期(签章)
报关员 ***	申报单位：上海××报关行 （3569121412）	审单 审价
单位地址：上海××路 153 号		征税 统计
邮编：200000 电话：021-2358×××× 填制日期 20××-8-23		查验 放行

Notes

1. **Customs Examination** 海关查验

The exporter must apply to the customs for declaration of the commodity before shipment. The examination is held by China Customs at all levels. The customs officer will release the Customs Declaration and let go the goods if they are up to the requirements of the authorities. Customs Declarations are classified into types of different colors: white for general trade; pink for processing trade; light yellow for export tax refund; light blue for foreign invested enterprise; light green for processing or compensation trade. However the contents of these documents are similar.

2. **出口报关单缮制技巧**

出处及推断	缮制的内容
商业发票	5 合同协议号；8 经营单位；9 发货单位；21 境内货源地；23 成交方式；37 商品名称、规格型号；38 数量及单位；39 最终目的国；40 单价；41 总价；42 币制
海运提单、装箱单	3 出口口岸；11 运输方式；12 运输工具名称；13 航次号；14 提/运单号；19 运抵国（地区）；20 指运港；27 件数；28 包装种类；29 毛重；30 净重；31 集装箱号；34 标志唛码及备注
已知信息	4 备案号；6 出口日期；7 申报日期；9 发货单位；10 申报单位；18 许可证号；21 境内货源地；22 批准文号；32 随附单据；33 生产厂家
逻辑推断	15 贸易方式；16 征免性质；17 征税比例；24 运费；25 保费；26 杂费；30 商品编码；43 征免

Exercises

Fill in the following customs declaration according to the contract signed between Diadora S. P. A. and China National Native Products and Animal By-Products Imp. and Exp. CO., as well as the corrected L/C.（见表 3－1 销售确认书）

出口口岸	备案号	出口日期	申报日期	
经营单位	运输方式	运输工具名称	提运单号	
发货单位	贸易方式	征免性质	结汇方式	
许可证号	运抵国（地区）	指运港	境内货源地	
批准文号	成交方式	运费	保费	杂费
合同协议号	件数	包装种类	毛重（千克）	净重（千克）
集装箱号	随附单据	生产厂家		
标记唛码及备注	随附单证号：			

项号	商品编号	商品名称、规格型号	数量及单位	最终目的国（地区）	单价	总价	币制	征免

税费征收情况 合计总价：

录入员 录入单位 报关员	兹声明以上申报无讹并承担法律责任 申报单位：	海关审单批注及放行日期(签章) 审单 审价
单位地址：		征税 统计
邮编： 电话：	填制日期	查验 放行

X. Making Shipping Advice*

上海蓝星有限公司

SHANGHAI LANXING CO. , LTD

1286 HUAIHAI ROAD, SHANGHAI, CHINA

Fax: 86－21－6855×××× Tel: 86－21－6855×××× Zip Code: 200023

SHIPPING ADVICE

TO: WEST AGENT COMPANY
#362 JALAN STREET, TORONTO, CANADA

ISSUE DATE: SEP. 1,20××
Invoice Date: AUG. 10,20××
S/C No.: SHDS03027
S/C Date: JULY 29,20××

Dear Sir or Madam,

We are Pleased to advice you that the following-mentioned goods have been shipped out. Full details were shown as follows:

Invoice Number:	WAC×SL001
Bill of Lading Number:	SH556231849
Ocean Vessel:	DONGHAI V336
Port of Loading:	SHANGHAI PORT
Date of shipment:	SEP. 1,20××
Port of Destination:	TORONTO
Estimated Date of Arrival:	OCT. 10,20××
Containers/Seals Number:	SINU3622753
Description of Goods:	**CHINESE SILK SCARVES** 10″ ×10″ 20″ ×20″ 30″ ×30″
Shipping Marks:	W. A. C TORONTO C/No. 1－300
Quantity:	300 CARTONS
Gross Weight:	750KGS
Measurement:	6CBMS
Total Value:	USD96,000.00

Thank you for your patronage. We look forward to the pleasure of receiving your valuable repeat orders.

Sincerely yours,

SHANGHAI LANXING CO. , LTD.

××× (签名)

Notes

1. **Under CIF**, the seller, shortly after the goods are placed on board the vessel, should at the agreed time, notify the buyer of the contract No., the name and weight of the goods, the invoice amount, the vessel's name and the date of shipment so that the buyer can make necessary arrangements for taking delivery of the goods.

一般情况下装船通知书是通知进口商准备接收货物。

2. **Under FOB**, the seller shall send a notice to the buyer before the agreed shipment date (usually 30 — 45 days before the shipment date) so that the buyer can arrange the relevant vessel for taking the delivery. The buyer, after receiving the relevant notice from the seller, should at the agreed time, notify the seller of the name of the vessel and the estimated arrival date of the vessel. And the seller, after the goods are placed on board the vessel, should at the agreed time, notify the buyer of the contract No., the name and weight of the goods, the invoice amount, the vessel's name and the date of shipment so that the buyer can make necessary arrangements for purchasing the relevant insurance and taking delivery of the goods.

Under CFR, shortly after the booking for cargo ship is confirmed and the shipping order is received from the shipping company, the seller should at the agreed time, notify the buyer of the vessel's name and the date of shipment as well as the contract No., the name and weight of the goods and the invoice amount so that the buyer can make necessary arrangements for taking delivery of the goods, and most importantly for insuring the goods.

CFR 或 FOB 情况下，更为重要的是让进口商及时办理保险。

3. **There is no fixed format** of Shipping Advice. Exporters can make it according to their own practice, but the contents should comply with the stipulations in the L/C.

装船通知书格式由各出口商自定。

Exercises

Fill in the following shipping advice according to the contract signed between Diadora S. P. A. and China National Native Products and Animal By-Products Imp. and Exp. CO, as well as the corrected L/C.（见表 3－1 销售确认书）

SHIPPING ADVICE

FAX: **INVOICE No.:** ____________

TELEX: **L/C No.:** ____________

TEL: **S/C No.:** ____________

MESSRS:

DEAR SIRS,

WE HEREBY INFORM YOU THAT THE GOODS UNDER THE ABOVE MENTIONED CREDIT HAVE BEEN SHIPPED. THE DETAILS OF THE SHIPMENT ARE STATED BELOW.

COMMODITY: ____________

NUMBER OF PACKAGES: ____________

TOTAL G. W: ____________

OCEAN VESSEL: ____________

DATE OF DEPARTURE: NOV. 30, 20 × ×

B/L No.: ____________

PORT OF LOADING: ____________

DESTINATION: ____________

SHIPPING MARKS: ____________

XI. Bill of Lading*

<table>
<tr><td colspan="2">Shipper
SHANGHAI LANXING CO., LTD.
1286 HUAIHAI ROAD, SHANGHAI, CHINA</td><td colspan="3" rowspan="6">B/L No. SH556231849

中国外运上海公司
SINOTRANS SHANGHAI COMPANY
OCEAN BILL OF LADING
SHIPPED on board in apparent good order and condition (unless otherwise indicated) the goods or packages specified herein and to be discharged at the mentioned port of discharge or as near there to as the vessel may safely get and be always afloat.
The weight, measure, marks and numbers, quality, contents and value, being particularly furnished by the Shipper, are not checked by the Carrier on loading.
The Shipper, Consignee and the Holder of this Bill of Lading hereby expressly accept and agree to all printed, written or stamped provisions, exceptions and conditions of this Bill of Lading, including those on the back hereof.
IN WITNESS where of the number of original Bills of Lading stated below have been signed, one of which being accomplished, the other (s) to be void.</td></tr>
<tr><td colspan="2">Consignee or order
TO ORDER</td></tr>
<tr><td colspan="2">Notify address
WEST AGENT COMPANY
#362 JALAN STREET, TORONTO, CANADA</td></tr>
<tr><td>Pre-carriage by</td><td>Port of lading
SHANGHAI</td></tr>
<tr><td>Vessel
DONGHAI V336</td><td>Port of transshipment</td></tr>
<tr><td>Port of discharge
TORONTO</td><td>Final destination
TORONTO</td></tr>
<tr><td>Container seal No. or marks and Nos.</td><td colspan="2">Number and kind of packages Description of goods</td><td>Gross weight (kgs)</td><td>Measurement (m^3)</td></tr>
<tr><td>W. A. C
TORONTO
C/No. 1 - 300
SINU3622753 (20')</td><td colspan="2">300 CARTONS OF
CHINESE SILK SCARVES</td><td>750KGS

ON BOARD</td><td>$6m^3$</td></tr>
<tr><td colspan="3">Freight and charges
FREIGHT PREPAID</td><td colspan="2">REGARDING TRANSSHIPMENT INFORMATION PLEASE CONTACT</td></tr>
</table>

<table>
<tr><td rowspan="2">Ex. rate</td><td>Prepaid at</td><td>Freight payable at</td><td>Place and date of issue
SHANGHAI SEP. 1, 20 × ×</td></tr>
<tr><td>Total Prepaid</td><td>Number of original Bs/L
THREE</td><td>Signed for or on behalf of the Master
× × × as Agent</td></tr>
</table>

(SINOTRANS STANDARD FORM 5) _ SUBJECT TO THE TERMS AND CONDITIONS ON BACK 98C No.

Notes

1. **Use and contents of Bill of Lading**（提单用途与内容）

The bill of lading is the central documents of a sea export transaction. A bill of lading doesn't only contain a full description of the consignment-numbers and weights and marks of packages-but a lot of other information as well. It quotes the name of the shipper and the carrying vessel, the ports of shipment and destination, the freight rate, the name of consignee (unless the B/L is "to order"), and the date of shipment, which is very important from a contractual point of view. It may also contain other terms and conditions. Some bills of lading are marked "freight paid", when a shipper is selling under CIF or CFR, others may allow transshipment, which means that the cargo may be transferred from one ship to another at some intermediate port.

It is often important to a shipper that his bill of lading should be "clean" rather than "dirty", that is, the shipping company should not have made any qualification about the quantity or condition of the cargo actually shipped. L/C calls for clean bills, just as it may insist on "on board".

2. **Classification of Bill of Lading**（提单的种类）

(1) On board B/L and received for shipment B/L 已装船提单和备运提单
(2) Clean B/L and unclean B/L 清洁提单和不清洁提单
(3) Straight B/L, Order B/L and Blank B/L 记名提单、指示提单和不记名提单
(4) Direct B/L, Transshipment B/L and Through B/L 直达提单、转船提单和联运提单
(5) Long Form B/L and Short Form B/L 全式提单和略式提单
(6) Freight Prepaid B/L and Freight to Collect B/L 运费预付提单和运费到付提单
(7) Liner B/L and Charter Party B/L 班轮提单和租船提单
(8) Container B/L, On Deck B/L, Stale B/L, Groupage B/L, House B/L, antedated B/L and Advanced B/L 集装箱提单、舱面提单、过期提单、成组提单、货代提单、倒签提单和预借提单

3. **Number of originals**（正本提单份数）

A B/L is usually made out in sets of three or four original. The shipper may ask for several extra copies. One copy of the B/L is kept for the ship. The other copies are sent to the exporters or directly to their bank for payment. Then the B/L and other shipping documents are presented by the buyers to the shipping company when the ship arrives. The shipping company can then compare the B/L with the copy on the ship. In this way the importers can show their right to the goods and obtain them from the ship.

Exercises

Fill in the following bill of lading according to the contract signed between Diadora S. P. A. and China National Native Products and Animal By-Products Imp. and Exp. CO. , as well as the corrected L/C.（见表 3-1 销售确认书）

Shipper (Insert Name, Address and Phone)	B/L No.: GXCOSCO66445124
Consignee (Insert Name, Address and Phone)	中远集装箱运输有限公司 COSCO CONTAINER LINES TLX: 33057 COSCO CN FAX: +86 (020) 6545 × × × × ORIGINAL Port-to-Port or Combined Transport BILL OF LADING
Notify Party (Insert Name, Address and Phone) (It is agreed that no responsibility shall attach to the Carrier or his agents for failure to notify)	RECEIVED in external apparent good order and condition except as other-wise noted. The total number of packages or unites stuffed in the container, the description of the goods and the weights shown in this Bill of Lading are furnished by the Merchants, and which the carrier has no reasonable means Of checking and is not a part of this Bill of Lading contract. The carrier has Issued the number of Bills of Lading stated below, all of this tenor and date, One of the original Bills of Lading must be surrendered and endorsed or signed against the delivery of the shipment and whereupon any other orig-inal Bills of Lading shall be void. The Merchants agree to be bound by the terms And conditions of this Bill of Lading as if each had personally signed this Bill of Lading. SEE clause 4 on the back of this Bill of Lading (Terms continued on the back Hereof, please read carefully). * Applicable Only When Document Used as a Combined Transport Bill of Lading.

Combined Transport * Pre-carriage by	Combined Transport * Place of Receipt
Ocean Vessel Voy. No.	Port of Loading
Port of Discharge	Combined Transport * Place of Delivery

Container/Seal No.	Marks & Nos.	No. of Containers or Packages	Description of Goods (If Dangerous Goods, See Clause 20)	Gross Weight(kgs)	Measurement (m^3)

Total Number of containers and/or packages (in words)

Freight & Charges As Arranged	Revenue Tons	Rate	Per	Prepaid	Collect

Ex. Rate:	Prepaid at	Payable at	Place and date of issue Nanning Nov. 30, 20 × ×
	Total Prepaid	No. of Original B (s) /L 3	Signed for the Carrier, **COSCO CONTAINER LINES**

LADEN ON BOARD THE VESSEL
DATE BY COSCO CONTAINER LINES

XII. Making Beneficiary's Certificate*

上海蓝星有限公司

SHANGHAI LANXING CO. , LTD.

1286 HUAIHAI ROAD, SHANGHAI, CHINA

Fax: 86 - 21 - 6855 × × × × Tel: 86 - 21 - 6855 × × × × Zip Code: 200023

BENEFICIARY'S CERTIFICATE

To: WEST AGENT COMPANY
#362 JALAN STREET, TORONTO, CANADA

Invoice No. : WAC-SL001
Date: SEP. 5, 20 × ×

WE CERTIFY HEREBY THAT ORIGINAL CERTIFICATE OF ORIGIN FORM A, COPY OF COMMERCIAL INVOICE, DETAILED PACKING LISTS AND A COPY OF BILL OF LADING HAVE BEEN SENT DIRECT TO BANK OF CHINA, SHANGHAI BRANCH FOR COLLECTION ON THE BASIS OF D/P WITHIN 5 DAYS AFTER SHIPMENT.

SHANGHAI LANXING CO. , LTD.
(经办人签名)

Notes

1. **Example Terms of Beneficiary's Certificate in L/C**（信用证中有关受益人证明书条款举例）

BENEFICIARY TO CERTIFY ONE SET OF NON-NEGOTIABLE DOCUMENETS TO APPLICANT IMMEDIATELY BY DHL AND BENEFICIARY'S CERTIFICATE TO THIS EFFECT MUST ACCOMPANY THE DOCUMENTS.

ORIGINAL BENEFICIARY'S SIGNED LETTER/CERTIFICATE TOGETHER WITH THE COURIERS RECEIPT CERTIFYING THAT THE FULL SET OF ORIGINAL DOCUMENTS HAVE BEEN SENT TO ABC COMPANY BY SPEED POST AFTER SHIPMENT.

2. **Examples of Certification**（证明字句举例）

WE HEREBY CERTIFY THAT ONE SET OF NON-NEGOTIABLE DOCUMENTS HAVE BEEN SENT BY AIRMAIL TO APPLICANT WITHIN 2 DAYS AFTER SHIPMENT AND A CONFIRMATION TO THIS EFFECT HAS ACCOMPANIED THE DOCUMENTS.

WE HEREBY CERTIFY THAT ONE SET OF SHIPPING DOCUMENTS HAS BEEN FAXED TO APPLICANT WITHIN 1 DAY AFTER SHIPMENT.

3. 受益人证明书完全按信用证和合同要求填写，但在缮制时要注意时态、人称的变化，不应照搬照抄

WILL SEND ——→HAVE BEEN SENT
MUST ACCOMPANY ——→HAS ACCOMPANIED
THE BENEFICIARY ——→WE

Exercises

Fill in the following beneficiary's certificate according to the contract signed between Diadora S. P. A. and China National Native Products and Animal By-Products Imp. and Exp. Co. , as well as the corrected L/C.（见表 3－1 销售确认书）

BENEFICIARY'S CERTIFICATE

DATE：________

INVOICE NO. ：____________________ CONTRACT NO. ：____________________

L/C NO. ：________________________

TO：__________________________

WE HEREBY ____

____

____

____

____

____

VIII. Making Bill of Exchange*

BILL OF EXCHANGE					
凭 Drawn Under	CITIBANK, TORONTO		不可撤销信用证 Irrevocable L/C No.	LTR0505457	
日期 Date	××0801	支取 Payable With Interest	@ % 按 息 付款		
号码 No.	WAC-SL001	汇票金额 Exchange for	USD48,000.00	上海 Shanghai	SHANGHAI, CHINA SEP. 5, 20××
	见票 at	----	日后（本汇票之副本未付）付交 Sight of this FIRST of Exchange (Second of Exchange		
Being unpaid) Pay to the order of	BANK OF CHINA, SHANGHAI BRANCH				
金额 the sum of	SAY U.S. DOLLARS FOURTY EIGHT THOUSAND ONLY				
此致 To	CITIBANK, TORANTO		SHANGHAI LANXING CO., LTD. 1286 HUAIHAI ROAD, SHANGHAI, CHINA ×××（经办人签名）		

BILL OF EXCHANGE					
凭 Drawn Under	330 CTNS CHINESE SILK SCARVES FROM SHANGHAI TO TORONTO S/C NO.: SHDS03027 FOR COLLECTION		不可撤销信用证 Irrevocable L/C No.	----	
日期 Date	JULY 29, 20××	支取 Payable With Interest	@ % 按 息 付款		
号码 No.	WAC-SL001	汇票金额 Exchange for	USD48,000.00	上海 Shanghai	SHANGHAI, CHINA SEP. 5, 20××
	见票 at	----	日后（本汇票之副本未付）付交 Sight of this FIRST of Exchange (Second of Exchange		
Being unpaid) Pay to the order of	SHANGHAI LANXING CO., LTD 1286 HUAIHAI ROAD, SHANGHAI, CHINA				
金额 the sum of	SAY U.S. DOLLARS FOURTY EIGHT THOUSAND ONLY				
此致 To	WEST AGENT COMPANY #362 JALAN STREET, TORONTO, CANADA		SHANGHAI LANXING CO., LTD. 1286 HUAIHAI ROAD, SHANGHAI, CHINA ×××（经办人签名）		

Notes

1. **Three parties to a draft**（汇票当事人）

Drawer（出票人） is the person who writes the order and gives directions to the person to make a specific payment of money. He is the exporter in international trade.

Drawee（受票人、付款人）is usually the opening bank under letter of credit or the importer on collection basis. He is the person to whom the order is addressed and who is to pay the money. Therefore, he is also the payer requested by the draft.

Payee（收款人）is the person to whom the payment is ordered to be made. The payee is usually the exporter's appointed bank in foreign trade. If a bill with such instruction "Pay to the order of sb.", it means to pay the payee or anyone to whom he in turn directs payment to be made. In this way, such bill is transferable, passing from the former payee on to a new payee by endorsement.

2. **Documents' transfer under L/C**（信用证项下的单据流转）

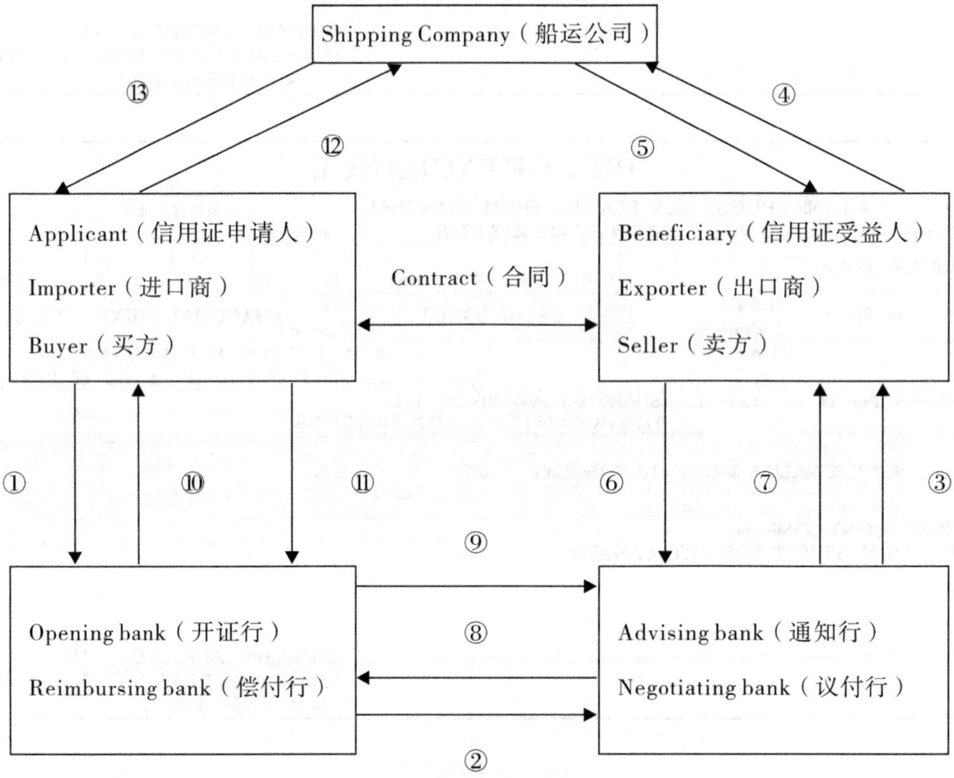

①The importer makes application to his local bank for an L/C.

②The opening bank forwards the L/C to the advising bank.

③The advising bank delivers the L/C to the beneficiary.

④Having examined the L/C, the beneficiary ships the goods to the buyer.

⑤The beneficiary receives the B/L from the shipping company in exchange for the goods shipped on board.

⑥The beneficiary prepares documents with the B/L, draws a draft and presents them to his bank for negotiation.

⑦The beneficiary's bank negotiates the documents and pays funds to the beneficiary in accordance with the L/C.

⑧The negotiating bank forwards the documents to the opening bank for reimbursement.

⑨The opening bank receives the documents and checks them. If the documents are in order and comply with the L/C, the opening bank credits the negotiating bank's account.

⑩The opening bank notifies the importer to make payment for documents.

⑪After making payment, the importer receives the documents and get ready to take delivery of the goods.

⑫The importer presents the documents, B/L in particular, to the shipping company to collect the goods.

⑬After verifying the documents presented, the shipping company releases the goods to the importer.

3. Documents' transfer under D/P（付款交单项下的单据流转）

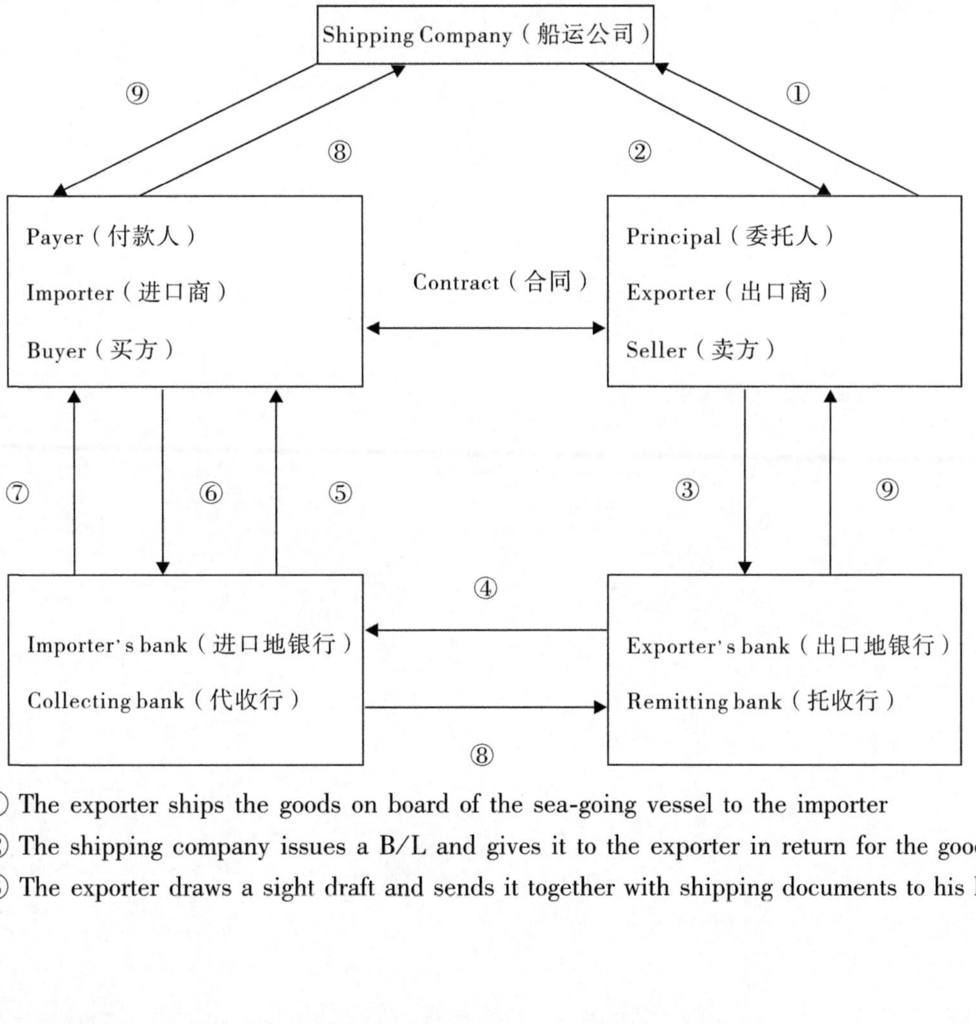

① The exporter ships the goods on board of the sea-going vessel to the importer

② The shipping company issues a B/L and gives it to the exporter in return for the goods.

③ The exporter draws a sight draft and sends it together with shipping documents to his bank for collecting a documentary bill on his behalf, thus getting the name of principal.

④ The remitting bank sends the documentary bill to a correspondent bank overseas for collecting money.

⑤ The collecting bank presents the bill and documents to the importer for payment.

⑥ The importer makes payment.

⑦ The collecting bank hands over the documents in exchange for the money paid by the importer.

⑧ The importer presents the documents to the shipping company. The collecting bank transfers the payment to the exporter's bank by crediting the account of the remitting bank.

⑨ The shipping company releases the goods to the importer. The remitting bank makes payment to the exporter.

Exercises

Fill in the following two drafts according to the contract signed between Diadora S. P. A. and China National Native Products and Animal By-Products Imp. and Exp. CO., as well as the corrected L/C.（见表 3－1 销售确认书）

BILL OF EXCHANGE

凭 Drawn Under		不可撤销信用证 Irrevocable L/C No.	
日期 Date		支取 Payable With Interest @ % 按 息 付款	
号码 No.		汇票金额 Exchange for	南宁 Nanning
	见票 at	日后（本汇票之副本未付）付交 Sight of this FIRST of Exchange (Second of Exchange	
Being unpaid) Pay to The Order of			
金额 The Sum of			
此致 To			

BILL OF EXCHANGE

凭 Drawn Under		不可撤销信用证 Irrevocable L/C No.	
日期 Date		支取 Payable With Interest @ % 按 息 付款	
号码 No.		汇票金额 Exchange for	南宁 Nanning
	见票 at	日后（本汇票之副本未付）付交 Sight of This FIRST of Exchange (Second of Exchange	
Being Unpaid) Pay to The Order of			
金额 The Sum of			
此致 To			

XIV. Applying for Verification of Foreign Currencies*

出口收汇核销单 存根 （沪）编号：SH39882320
出口单位： 上海蓝星有限公司①
单位编码：629651574
出口币种总价： USD96,000.00②
收汇方式：L/C & D/P③
预计收款日期： 20××年9月15日④
报关日期： 20××年8月23日⑤
备注：⑥
此单报关有效期截止到

（出口单位盖章）

出口收汇核销单 监制章 （沪）编号：SH39882320				
出口单位： 上海蓝星有限公司①				
单位编码：629651574				
银行签注栏	类别	币种金额	日期	盖章
		⑩		
海关签注栏：⑨				
外汇局签注栏⑪ 年 月 日（盖章）				

（出口单位盖章）

出口收汇核销单 监制章 （沪）编号：SH39882320		
出口单位： 上海蓝星有限公司		
单位编码：629651574		
货物名称	数量	币种总价
丝绸围巾⑦	30,000打	USD96,000.00
报关单编号：⑧		
外汇局签注栏 年 月 日（盖章）		

未经核销此联不得撕开

出口收汇核销单送审登记表

出口单位：上海蓝星有限公司　　　　送审日期：20××年9月7日

核销单编号(1)	发票编号(2)	商品大类(3)	国别地区(4)	贸易方式(5)	结算方式(6)	报关日期(7)	货款		收汇核销金额	
							币别(8)	报关金额(9)	FOB金额(10)	收汇核销金额(11)
SH39882320	WAC-SL001	纺织品	加拿大	一般	L/C&D/P	20××.8.23	USD	96,000.00	94,070.72	96,000.00

第一联 外汇局留存

出口单位填表人　×××（签名）　　　　外汇局审核人

Notes

1. **出口收汇核销规定**

　　我国自外汇管理部门对境内出口企业的一切出口收汇实行跟踪管理和监督收汇以来，出口企业无论是在货物报关、向银行交单收汇，还是向外汇管理部门办理核销，都必须使用出口收汇核销单。出口收汇核销单是我国特有的国际商务单据，是实现我国货物进出境管理和外汇管制的有效单据，也是外贸企业出口退税、获得国家补贴的必要单据。

2. **出口收汇核销程序**

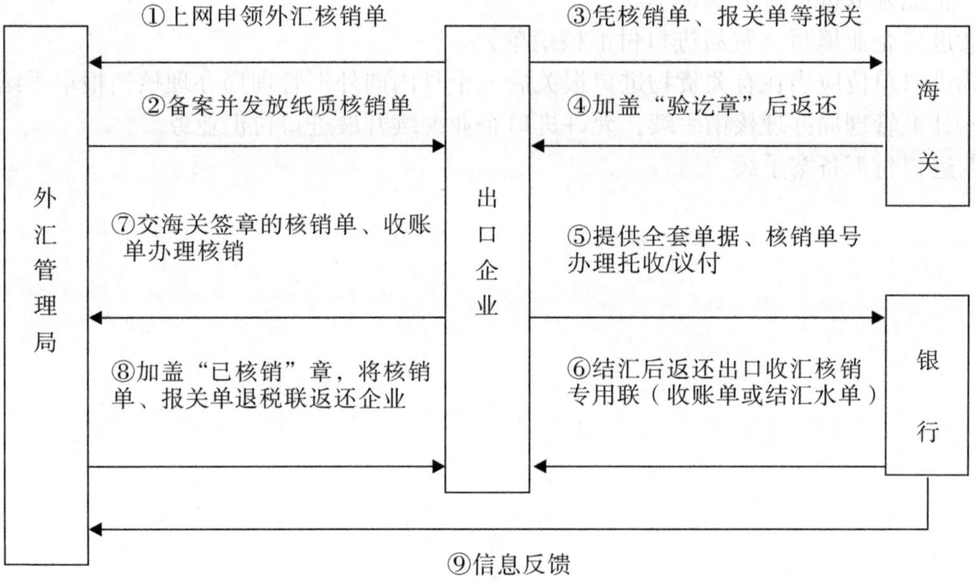

3. **出口收汇核销表内容**

　　① 出口单位、单位编码。
　　② 出口币种总价。
　　③ 收汇方式。
　　④ 预计收款日期。
　　⑤ 报关日期。
　　⑥ 报关单位备注。
　　⑦ 货物名称、数量、币种总价。
　　⑧ 报关单编号。
　　⑨ ~ ⑪项分别由海关、银行、外汇管理局签注，企业无需填写。

4. **出口收汇核销单送审登记表内容**

　　①核销单编号。
　　②发票编号。
　　③商品大类。
　　④国别地区。

⑤贸易方式。

⑥结算方式。

⑦报关日期。

⑧币别。

⑨报关金额。

⑩FOB 金额。

⑪收汇核销金额。

5. 进口付汇核销程序

①企业领取进口付汇核销单。

②进口企业填写《贸易进口付汇核销单》。

③进口单位应当在有关货物进口报关后一个月内向外汇管理局办理核销报审手续。

④外汇管理局办理核销手续，允许进口企业继续开展进口付汇业务。

⑤进口付汇备案手续。

Exercises

Fill in the following two forms of foreign currencies verification according to the contract signed between Diadora S. P. A. and China National Native Products and Animal By-Products Imp. and Exp. CO., as well as the corrected L/C. （见表 3 - 1 销售确认书）

出口收汇核销单 存根 （沪）编号：GX558823209
出口单位：
单位编码：574629651
出口币种总价：
收汇方式：
预计收款日期：
报关日期：
备注：
此单报关有效期截止到

（出口单位盖章）

出口收汇核销单 监制章 （沪）编号：GX558823209				
出口单位：				
单位编码：574629651				
银行签注栏	类别	币种金额	日期	盖章
海关签注栏：				
外汇局签注栏 年 月 日（盖章）				

（出口单位盖章）

出口收汇核销单 监制章 （沪）编号：GX558823209		
出口单位：		
单位编码：574629651		
货物名称	数量	币种总价
报关单编号：		
外汇局签注栏 年 月 日（盖章）		

未经核销此联不得撕开

出口收汇核销单送审登记表

出口单位： 送审日期： 年 月 日

核销单编号	发票编号	商品大类	国别地区	贸易方式	结算方式	报关日期	货款		收汇核销金额	
							币别	报关金额	FOB 金额	收汇核销金额

第一联 外汇局留存

出口单位填表人 外汇局审核人

Business Letter Writing Stylistics 商务函电修辞技巧（III）

4. **函电邮件达至非正式语体的技巧**

4.1 动词的语体比起名词化结构不那么正式；短语动词比起单个动词不那么正式

• The timely arrival of your shipment is being expected. (formal)

→We are expecting your shipment to arrive on time. (less formal)

→We are looking forward to your shipment to arrive on time. (much less formal)

• We will reply to you as soon as we finish investigating the case. (formal)

→We will give you an answer as soon as we finish looking into the matter.

• The prompt establishment of an L/C is appreciated. (formal)

→We would appreciate it if you could open an L/C promptly.

4.2 使用主动语态

• You are requested to deliver the goods at the stipulated time. (formal)

→Please dispatch the goods at the stipulated time. (informal)

• As the date of shipment is approaching, you are requested to expedite the establishment of the L/C. (formal)

→…, please rush the establishment of the L/C.

• Your interest in our commodities is appreciated.

→We appreciate your interest in our commodities.

4.3 比起复合句，简单句、省略句、疑问句非正式色彩更浓

• The firm, whose bank is the Industrial Bank of Japan Limited, Osaka, is Jae and Sons Papers Company, distributor of kraft lineboard in Osaka. (formal)

→The firm is Jae and Sons Papers Company, distributor of kraft lineboard in Osaka. Their bank is the Industrial Bank of Japan Limited, Osaka. (informal)

• I can not find the catalogue for the newly launched products. I would be grateful to you if you fax me about it. (formal)

→Can't find the catalogue for the newly launched products. Could you fax me it? Thanks! (informal)

4.4 使用非虚拟语气的句子

• We should be obliged to you if you would change the price and let us have a favorable reply. (formal)

→Please change the price and let us have a favorable reply.

4.5 使用非倒装句

• Had I known the material price would rise, I would have told you earlier. (formal)

→If I had known the material price would rise, I would have told you earlier. (informal)

• Enclosed please find the S/C No. 123. (formal)

→Please find the enclosed S/C No. 123. (informal)

• Enclosed is the Sales Confirmation in duplicate. (formal)

→The Sales Confirmation in duplicate is enclosed. (informal)

4.6 使用缓和语气

- Unfortunately this is our rock – bottom price, we can't make any further reduction.
- It seems to me that we are giving up too much in this case.
- I'm afraid that I could not agree with you for such a big discount. In this way, it would leave us with no profit.
- I'm really sorry that our products can hardly satisfy your requirement.

4.7 使用私人随便语气（老客户间开头或结尾的叙旧或友情）

Dear Mr. Black,

It was a pleasure to meet you while I was at the trade fair in Guangzhou last month. It was interesting to hear about your idea on computer security.

I am afraid we have a small problem with your dispatch of computer paper for our last order. We asked for white computer paper. Unfortunately, when we opened the box, we found that there was only green paper. I would be grateful if you could send us the right order.

I am looking forward to seeing you at the computer exhibition in London next month.

Yours sincerely,

Drill（III）实训操作

训练要求：

1. 根据所给的合同、信用证写出双方所往来的函电（共13个），如下图所示。
2. 根据所给的合同、信用证制作出卖方履行合同所必备的9份单据（没有提供的信息免填），如下图所示。
3. 往来的空白信笺和空白单据请见电子文本附件。

函电1—2：建立业务关系
函电3—4：询盘、发盘
函电5—6：还盘、再还盘
函电7—8：下订单、寄送合同
函电9—10：催开信用证、信用证开出信
函电11—12：要求改证、催促装运
函电13：装运通知书

单据1：商业发票
单据2：装箱单
单据3：一般原产地证书
单据4：报检单
单据5：保险单
单据6：报关单
单据7：海运提单
单据8：受益人证明
单据9：汇票

卖方公司：

The Seller：NANTONG BLANKET TRADING COMPANY

Address：TRADING MANSION，ZHONGSHAN ROAD
NANTONG，JIANGSU，CHINA

买方公司：

The Buyer：LAWRENCE TRADING CO.，LTD.

Address：1206 FINANCIAL BUILDING，MAHATTEN，NEW YORK，U. S. A.

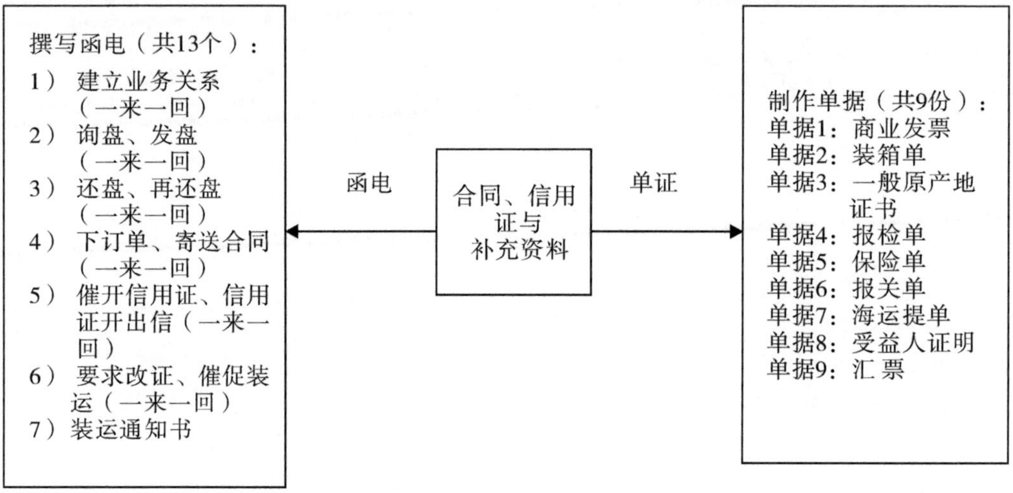

南通毛毯贸易公司
NANTONG BLANKET TRADING COMPANY

TRADING MANSION, ZHONGSHAN ROAD, NANTONG, JIANGSU, CHINA

SALES CONTRACT

TO: LAWRENCE TRADING CO., LTD.
1206 FINANCIAL BUILDING, MAHATTEN, NEW YORK, U. S. A.

Dear Sirs,

We hereby confirm having sold to you the following commodity on terms and conditions as specified below:

1. Commodity & Specification (品名及规格)	2. Quantity (数量)	3. Unit Price & Trade Terms (单价及价格条款)	4. Amount (USD) (金额)
		CIF NEW YORK	
COTTON BLANKET (RED)	1000PCS	USD6. 5/PC	USD6,500
COTTON BLANKET (YELLOW)	1500PCS	USD6/PC	USD9,000
Total:	2500PCS		USD15, 500. 00

LOADING PORT: NANTONG, CHINA
DESTINATION: NEW YORK, USA
TIME OF SHIPMENT: LASTEST DATE OF SHIPMENT MAR. 16, 20××
PARTIAL SHIPMENT: PROHIBITED
TRANSSHIPMENT: PROHIBITED
PAYMENT: 50% BY CLEAN L/C AT SIGHT; ANOTHER 50% BY D/P AT SIGHT
INSURANCE: TO BE COVERED BY THE SELLER FOR 110 PERCENT OF THE INVOICE VALUE COVERING ALL RISKS AND WAR RISK.
DOCUMENTS REQUIRED:

Full set of shipping documents must accompany the draft on collection basis:

1. Signed Commercial Invoice
2. Packing List
3. Full set of clean on board B/L made out to order, marked "Freight Prepaid" and notify applicant
4. Certificate of origin of China
5. Insurance Policy
6. Shipping advice sent to the importer within 2 days after shipment.
7. Beneficiary's certificate certifying that shipping advice will be sent to the importer within 2 days after shipment.

THE BUYER: THE SELLER:
LAWRENCE TRADING CO., LTD. NANTONG BLANKET TRADING COMPANY

ISSUING BANK	BANK OF AMERICA
CLEAN CREDIT NUMBER	BOA2010669955
DATE OF ISSUE	20×× 0112
EXPIRY	DATE 20×× 0317 PLACE IN COUNTRY OF BENEFICIARY
APPLICANT	LAWRENCE TRADING CO., LTD. 1206 FINANCIAL BUILDING, MAHATTEN, NEW YORK, U.S.A.
BENEFICIARY	NANTONG BLANKET TRADING COMPANY TRADING MANSION, ZHONGSHAN ROAD, NANTONG, JIANGSU, CHINA
AMOUNT	CURRENCY USD AMOUNT 7,750.00
POS. /NEG. TOL. (%)	5/5
AVAILABLE WITH/BY	ANY BANK IN ADVISING COUNTRY BY NEGOTIATION
DRAFT AT…	DRAFTS AT SIGHT
PARTIAL SHIPMENTS	NOT ALLOWED
TRANSSHIPMENT	NOT ALLOWED
LOADING IN CHARGE	NANTONG
FOR TRANSPORT TO	NEW YORK
SHIPMENT PERIOD	AT THE LATEST MAR. 16, 20××
DESCRIPT. OF GOODS	COTTON BLANKET
	CIF NEW YORK COTTON BLANKET (RED) 1000PCS USD 6.5/PC COTTON BLANKET (YELLOW) 1500PCS USD 6/PC
CHARGES	ALL BANKING CHARGES OUTSIDE USA ARE FOR ACCOUNT OF BENEFICARY

Some useful information:

S/C No.: NT-LT001 S/C Date: Jan. 4, 20××

Invoice No.: NBTC5562134 Invoice Date: Jan. 24, 20××

Packing List No.: PK327898 H.S. Code: 6301300000（机制棉毯）

Packing: One piece wrapped in plastic, one piece in a box, ten pieces to a carton

G.W.: 31KGS/CTN N.W.: 30KGS/CTN Measurement: 1×0.6×0.5M/CTN

S.S.: HUANGHAI 330 B/L No.: CHNS022778954 B/L Date: Mar. 16, 20××

Freight Fee: USD2560 Insurance Policy No.: NT52134666

报检单位编号：022541236 报检单编号：CIQ56412376 海关编号：6598758498

境内货源地：南通 生产厂家：南通毛毯贸易公司

随附单据：出口货物通关单（7841263585）

代理报关公司：南通迅达报关行（3321456444）（地址：南通人民路28号）

单据附录

1．实迹汇票

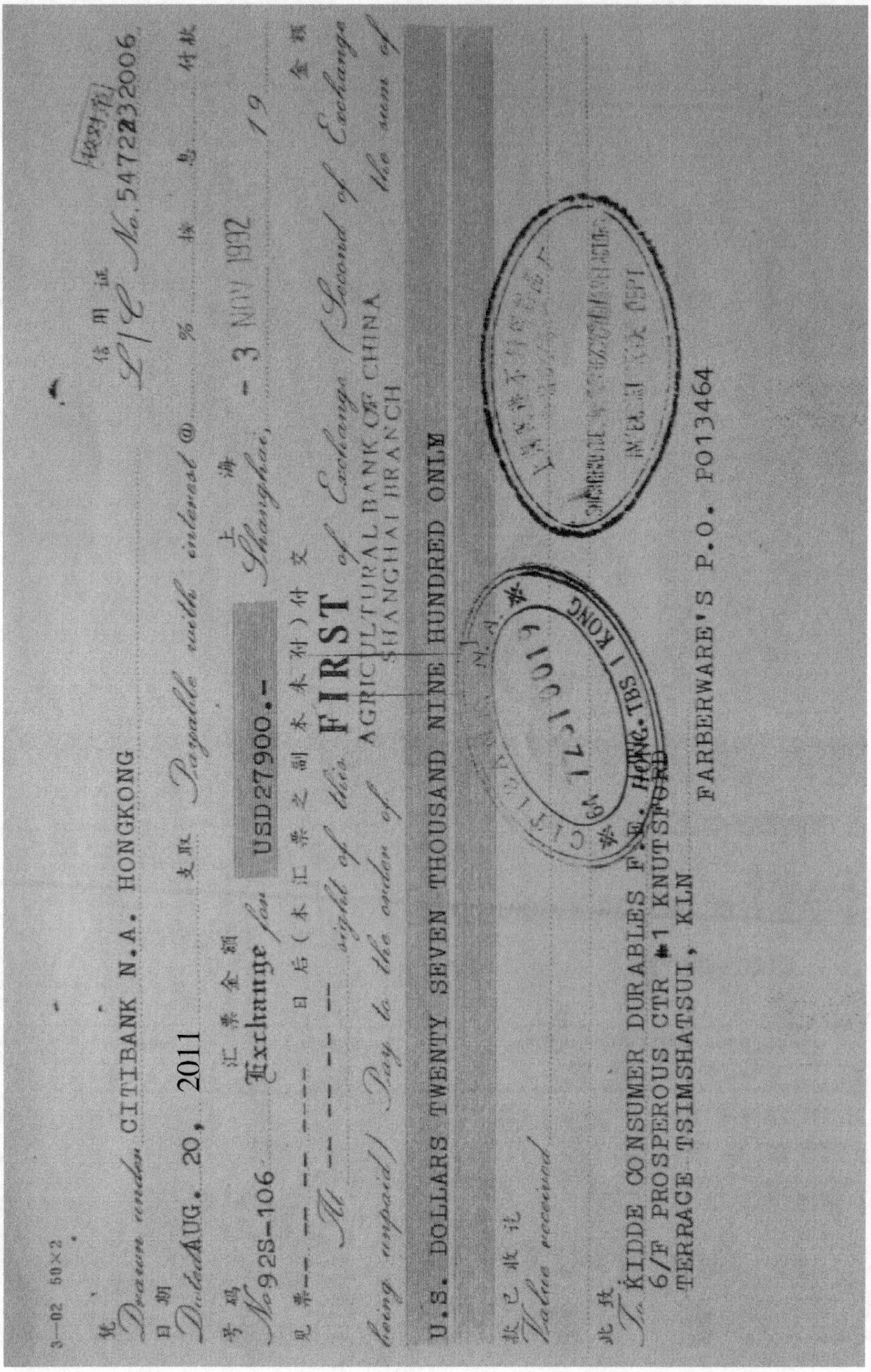
3—02 50×2
凭 Drawn under CITIBANK N.A. HONGKONG
信用证 L/C No. 5472232006
日期 Dated AUG. 20, 2011
支取 Payable with interest @ % 按 息 付款
号码 No. 92S-106
汇票金额 Exchange for USD27900.-
上海 Shanghai, - 3 NOV 1992 19
见票 At -- -- -- -- 日后（本汇票之副本未付）付交 sight of this FIRST of Exchange (Second of Exchange being unpaid) Pay to the order of
AGRICULTURAL BANK OF CHINA SHANGHAI BRANCH
金额 the sum of
U.S. DOLLARS TWENTY SEVEN THOUSAND NINE HUNDRED ONLY
款已收讫 Value received
此致 To KIDDE CONSUMER DURABLES F.E. HONG KONG
6/F PROSPEROUS CTR #1 KNUTSFORD
TERRACE TSIMSHATSUI, KLN
FARBERWARE'S P.O. PO13464

2. 实迹发票

上海跃进不锈钢制品厂进出口贸易部
SHANGHAI YUE JIN STAINLESS STEEL WARE FACTORY
IMPORT & EXPORT TRADE DEPARTMENT
NO. 717, JU LU ROAD, SHANGHAI CHINA.

FAX: 2475073
TEL: 2475175
2474442
TELEX: 33933 HSH CN

发 票
INVOICE

第 NO. 92S-106 号
日期 Date SEP. 28, 2011
开证行 Drawn under CITIBANK N.A. H.K.
信用证第 L/C No. 5472232006 号

致 TO: KIDDE CONSUMER DURABLE F.E. LTD.

下列商品自上海运至
Under mentioned goods from Shanghai to NEW YORK

唛头号码 Marks & Numbers	数量与品名 Quantities and Descriptions	单价 Unit Price	金额 Amount
ARBERWARE INC. HANSON COMPANY 500 BASSETT AVENUE RONX NY 10461-2395 .S.A.	KITCHENWARE TOTAL 5580 PIECES KITCHENWARE P/N 762 FARBERWARE'S P.O. 13464	FOB SHANGHAI USD5.00	USD27900.-
		TOTAL:	USD27900.-

兹证明上列商品确系中华人民共和国出产或制造
This is to certify that the above mentioned commodities were produced or manufactured in The People's Republic of China.

上海跃进不锈钢制品厂进出口贸易部
SHANGHAI YUE JIN STAINLESS STEEL WARE FACTORY IMPORT & EXPORT TRADE DEPARTMENT

3．实迹装箱单

上海跃进不锈钢制品厂进出口贸易部
SHANGHAI YUE JIN STAINLESS STEEL WARE FACTORY
IMPORT & EXPORT TRADE DEPARTMENT
NO. 717, JU LU ROAD, SHANGHAI CHINA.

FAX:2475073
TEL:2475175
2474442
TELEX:33933 HSH CN

装　箱　单（重量单）
PACKING LIST (Weight Memo)

发票号码
INVOICE No.92S-106
日　期
DATE: SEP. 28, 2011

TO: KIDDE CONSUMER DURABLE F.E. LTD.

MARKS	DESCRIPTION	SPECIFICATION	PACKING
FARBERWARE INC. A HANSON COMPANY 150 BASSETT AVENUE BRONX NY10461-2395 U. S. A.	KITCHENWARE 762	6PCS/CTN	5580PCS/930CTNS

TOTAL: 930 CTNS

FARBERWARE'S
P.O. P013464

G.W. 6510kgs
N.W. 4650kgs
MEAS. 59.52M^3

上海跃进不锈钢制品厂进出口贸易部
SHANGHAI YUE JIN STAINLESS STEEL WARE
FACTORY IMPORT & EXPORT TRADE DEPARTMENT

4. 实迹受益人证明书

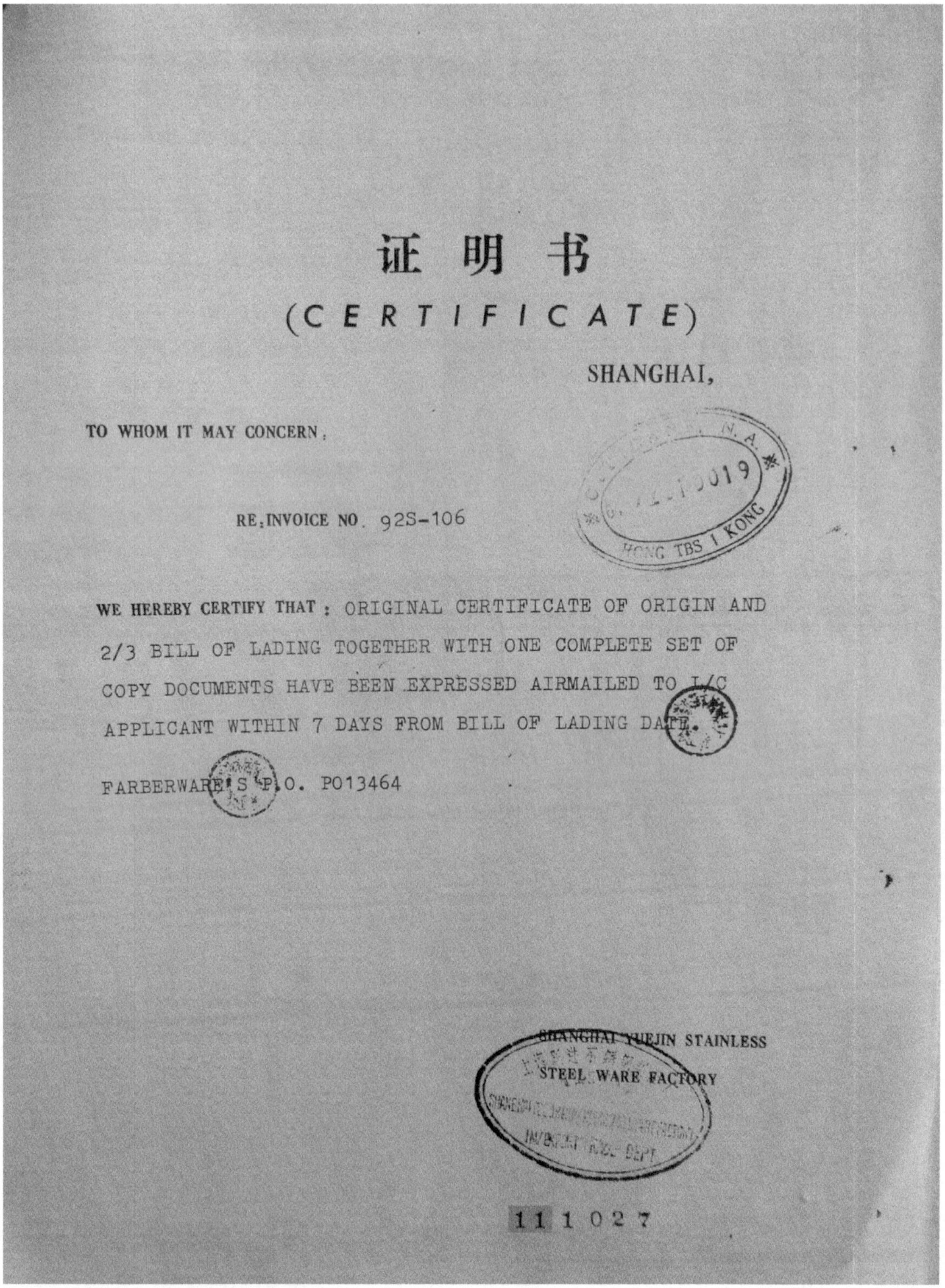

证 明 书
(CERTIFICATE)

SHANGHAI,

TO WHOM IT MAY CONCERN:

RE: INVOICE NO. 92S-106

WE HEREBY CERTIFY THAT: ORIGINAL CERTIFICATE OF ORIGIN AND 2/3 BILL OF LADING TOGETHER WITH ONE COMPLETE SET OF COPY DOCUMENTS HAVE BEEN EXPRESSED AIRMAILED TO L/C APPLICANT WITHIN 7 DAYS FROM BILL OF LADING DATE.

FARBERWARE'S P.O. PO13464

SHANGHAI YUEJIN STAINLESS
STEEL WARE FACTORY

111027

5．实迹海运提单

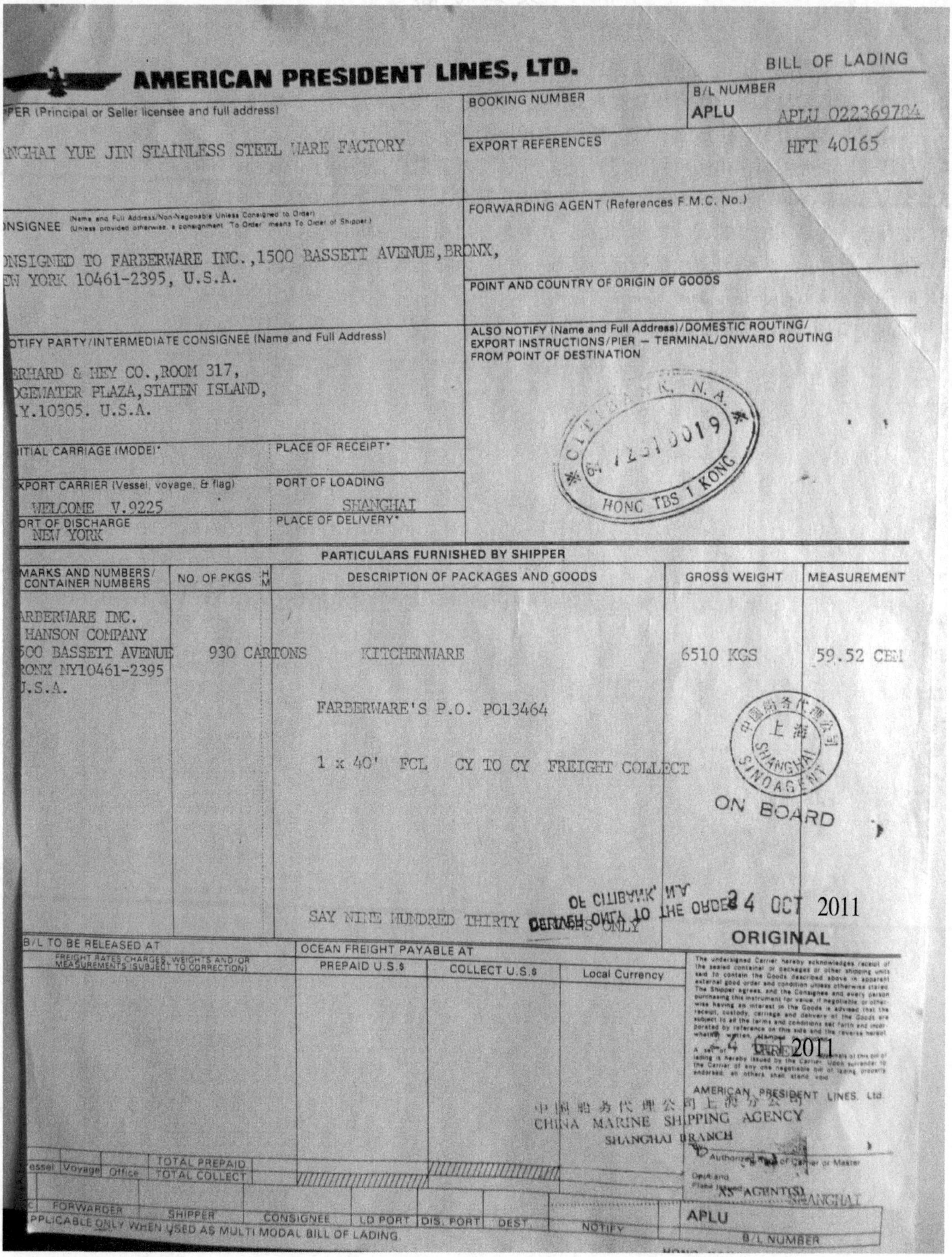

AMERICAN PRESIDENT LINES, LTD.

BILL OF LADING

PPER (Principal or Seller licensee and full address)
NGHAI YUE JIN STAINLESS STEEL WARE FACTORY

BOOKING NUMBER

B/L NUMBER
APLU APLU 022369784

EXPORT REFERENCES
HFT 40165

NSIGNEE (Name and Full Address/Non-Negotiable Unless Consigned to Order) (Unless provided otherwise, a consignment "To Order" means To Order of Shipper.)
NSIGNED TO FARBERWARE INC.,1500 BASSETT AVENUE,BRONX,
EW YORK 10461-2395, U.S.A.

FORWARDING AGENT (References F.M.C. No.)

POINT AND COUNTRY OF ORIGIN OF GOODS

OTIFY PARTY/INTERMEDIATE CONSIGNEE (Name and Full Address)
ERHARD & HEY CO.,ROOM 317,
DGEWATER PLAZA,STATEN ISLAND,
.Y.10305. U.S.A.

ALSO NOTIFY (Name and Full Address)/DOMESTIC ROUTING/
EXPORT INSTRUCTIONS/PIER — TERMINAL/ONWARD ROUTING
FROM POINT OF DESTINATION

CITIBANK, N.A.
HONG KONG TBS 1
64 7231 0019

ITIAL CARRIAGE (MODE)* | PLACE OF RECEIPT*

XPORT CARRIER (Vessel, voyage, & flag) | PORT OF LOADING
WELCOME V.9225 | SHANGHAI

ORT OF DISCHARGE | PLACE OF DELIVERY*
NEW YORK

PARTICULARS FURNISHED BY SHIPPER

MARKS AND NUMBERS/ CONTAINER NUMBERS	NO. OF PKGS	H M	DESCRIPTION OF PACKAGES AND GOODS	GROSS WEIGHT	MEASUREMENT
ARBERWARE INC. HANSON COMPANY 500 BASSETT AVENUE RONX NY10461-2395 U.S.A.	930 CARTONS		KITCHENWARE FARBERWARE'S P.O. PO13464 1 x 40' FCL CY TO CY FREIGHT COLLECT SAY NINE HUNDRED THIRTY CARTONS ONLY	6510 KGS	59.52 CBM

中国外轮代理公司 上海 SHANGHAI SINOAGENT

ON BOARD

24 OCT 2011

DELIVER ONLY TO THE ORDER OF CITIBANK, N.A.

ORIGINAL

B/L TO BE RELEASED AT

FREIGHT RATES,CHARGES, WEIGHTS AND/OR MEASUREMENTS (SUBJECT TO CORRECTION)

OCEAN FREIGHT PAYABLE AT

PREPAID U.S.$	COLLECT U.S.$	Local Currency

The undersigned Carrier hereby acknowledges receipt of the sealed container or packages or other shipping units said to contain the Goods described above in apparent external good order and condition unless otherwise stated. The Shipper agrees, and the Consignee and every person purchasing this instrument for value, if negotiable, or otherwise having an interest in the Goods is advised that the receipt, custody, carriage and delivery of the Goods are subject to all the terms and conditions set forth and incorporated by reference on this side and the reverse hereof, whether written, stamped ...

24 OCT 2011

... lading is hereby issued by the Carrier. Upon surrender to the Carrier of any one negotiable bill of lading properly endorsed, all others shall stand void.

AMERICAN PRESIDENT LINES, Ltd.

中国外轮代理公司上海分公司
CHINA MARINE SHIPPING AGENCY
SHANGHAI BRANCH

Authorized Signature of Carrier or Master

Dated and Place Issued
AS AGENT(S)
SHANGHAI

Vessel | Voyage | Office | TOTAL PREPAID | TOTAL COLLECT

FORWARDER | SHIPPER | CONSIGNEE | LD PORT | DIS. PORT | DEST. | NOTIFY

APPLICABLE ONLY WHEN USED AS MULTI MODAL BILL OF LADING

APLU
B/L NUMBER

参考文献

1. 刘杰英. 世纪商务英语函电与单证（第二版）[M]. 大连：大连理工大学出版社，2007.
2. 姜宏. 国际贸易实务与综合模拟实训 [M]. 北京：清华大学出版社，2008.
3. 易露霞. 国际贸易实务双语教程 [M]. 北京：清华大学出版社，2006.
4. 杜清萍. 商务英语函电实训指导 [M]. 广州：广东省语言音像电子出版社，2009.
5. 李大志. 商务英语言语修辞艺术 [M]. 北京：国防工业出版社，2007.
6. 徐有志. 英语文体学教程 [M]. 北京：高等教育出版社，2005.
7. 张雪鹏，马祯. 精编外贸单证理论与实务 [M]. 天津：天津大学出版社，2010.
8. http://www.thefreedictionary.com/.
9. http://127.0.0.0/Simtrade 外贸实训平台.